W.B. YEATS

VISIONS AND REVISIONS

Irish *Writers* in their Time

Series Editor: Stan Smith

This innovative series meets the urgent need for comprehensive new accounts of Irish writing across the centuries which combine readability with critical authority and information with insight. Each volume addresses the whole range of a writer's work in the various genres, setting its vision of the world in biographical context and situating it within the cultural, intellectual and political currents of the age, in Ireland and the wider world. This series will prove indispensable for students and specialists alike.

1. Patrick Kavanagh
(Editor: STAN SMITH)

2. Elizabeth Bowen
(Editor: EIBHEAR WALSHE)

3. John Banville
(JOHN KENNY)

4. Jonathan Swift
(BREAN HAMMOND)

5. James Joyce
(Editor: SEAN LATHAM)

6. W.B. Yeats
(Editor: EDWARD LARRISSY)

W.B. Yeats

Editor

EDWARD LARRISSY

Queen's University, Belfast

First published in 2010 by Irish *Academic Press*

2 Brookside,	920 NE 58th Avenue, Suite 300
Dundrum Road,	Portland, Oregon,
Dublin 14, Ireland	97213-3786, USA

This edition © 2010 Irish Academic Press
Chapters © Indvidual Contributors

www.iap.ie

British Library Cataloguing-in-Publication Data
An entry can be found on request

978 0 7165 3104 3 (cloth)
978 0 7165 3105 0 (paper)

Library of Congress Cataloging-in-Publication Data
An entry can be found on request

Printed by Good News Digital Books, Ongar, Essex

*The author gratefully acknowledges Simon & Schuster, and the estate of Michael B. Yeats, for permission to
quote from 'Remorse for Intemperate Speech'*

Contents

List of Contributors   vii

Acknowledgements   x

W.B. Yeats: A Chronology   xi

1. Yeats in the Light of Recent Criticism   1
   Edward Larrissy

2. W.B. Yeats: Biographical Reflections   14
   Terence Brown

3. Early Yeats: 'The Essences of Things'   31
   Michael O'Neill

4. Middle Yeats: In the Seven Woods (1903) to Responsibilities (1914)   48
   Vicki Mahaffey and Joseph Valente

5. The Wild Swans at Coole (1919) and Michael Robartes and the Dancer
   (1921): Gender, History and the Esoteric   66
   Edward Larrissy

6. Later Poetry   75
   Stephen Regan

7. W.B. Yeats as Dramatist   93
   Michael McAteer

8. Yeats's Thought   109
   David Dwan

9. Yeats and Women, or, Yeats and Woman: 127
   An Introduction, and Some Conclusions
   Anne Margaret Daniel

10. Yeats's Influence   159
      Steven Matthews

Select Bibliography   176

Index   183

Contributors

Terence Brown is Professor Emeritus in Trinity College, Dublin where he formerly held a personal Chair of Anglo-Irish Literature. He is also a member of the Royal Irish Academy and of Academia Europaea. He has published books on Louis MacNeice, on Northern Irish Poetry, and on the Social and Cultural History of Ireland. He has lectured on Irish subjects in many parts of the world. His *The Life of W.B.Yeats: A Critical Biography* was published in 1999.

Anne Margaret Daniel is currently the associate director of the Yeats International Summer School in Sligo. She has taught Irish literature and culture at the New School University in Manhattan since 2001, and her recent publications include a tribute to Liam Clancy for the *Irish Echo*.

David Dwan is a lecturer at Queen's University Belfast. He has published several articles on modernism, critical theory and Irish intellectual history. His book, *The Great Community: Culture and Nationalism in Ireland*, was published by Field Day in 2008.

Edward Larrissy is Professor of Poetry at Queen's University, Belfast, where he is affiliated to the Seamus Heaney Centre for Poetry. He was a lecturer at the Yeats International Summer School in Sligo in 2007 and 2009. He is the author of, among other things, *Yeats the Poet: The Measures of Difference* (Harvester Wheatsheaf, 1994), and the editor of *W.B. Yeats: The Major Works* (Oxford World's Classics, 2001), and of *The First Yeats: Poems by W.B. Yeats 1889–1899* (Fyfield Books, 2010).

Vicki Mahaffey is currently the Clayton and Thelma Kirkpatrick Professor of English at the University of Illinois. She is the author of *Reauthorizing Joyce* (Cambridge University Press, 1995); *States of Desire: Wilde, Yeats, Joyce and the Irish Experiment* (Oxford University Press, 1998); and *Modernist Literature: Challenging Fictions* (Blackwell, 2007). Her edition of collaborative essays on Joyce's *Dubliners: Collaborative Dubliners: Joyce in Dialogue*, is forthcoming. She is currently finishing a book-length manuscript on *The Joyce of Everyday Life*.

Michael McAteer teaches at the School of English, Queen's University, Belfast. He is the author of *Standish O'Grady, AE, Yeats: History, Culture, Politics* (Irish Academic Press, 2002) and *Yeats and European Drama*, forthcoming with Cambridge University Press. He has published a wide range of journal essays and book chapters on Irish writers, including Yeats, AE, Lady Gregory, Samuel Beckett, Sean O'Casey, Ciaran Carson, as well as essays on Irish criticism.

Steven Matthews is Professor of English at Oxford Brookes University, and Assistant Dean for Research in the School of Arts and Humanities. He is author of *Irish Poetry: Politics, History, Negotiation. The Evolving Debate, 1969 to the Present* (Macmillan, 1997); *Yeats as Precursor* (Macmillan, 2000); and *Les Murray* (Manchester University Press Contemporary World Writers Series, 2001). He has edited the Contexts series of monographs addressing the major periods of English Literature in the light of recent ideas about historicism, for Arnold, to which he has contributed the volume on *Modernism* (2004). He is also currently editor of the Sourcebooks series for Palgrave, and his volume on *Modernism* appeared in June 2008. He is completing a study of influence and the Renaissance in T.S. Eliot's poetry for Oxford University Press.

Michael O'Neill is Professor of English and a director of the Institute of Advanced Study at Durham University. His recent publications include *The All-Sustaining Air: Romantic Legacies and Renewals in British, American, and Irish Poetry since 1900* (Oxford University Press, 2007) and *Wheel* (Arc, 2008), a collection of poems. He is also the editor of *The Poems of W.B. Yeats: A Sourcebook* (Routledge, 2004) and of *The Cambridge History of English Poetry* (Cambridge University Press, 2010).

Stephen Regan is Professor of English and Head of the Department of English Studies at Durham University. His publications include *Irish Writing: An Anthology of Irish Writing 1789–1939* (2004), *The Eagleton Reader* (1998) and *The Politics of Pleasure: Aesthetics and Cultural Theory* (1992). He has also published two books on the poetry of Philip Larkin. He is editor, with Richard Allen, of *Irelands of the Mind: Memory and Identity in Modern Irish Culture* (2008).

Joseph Valente is Professor of English and Director of Irish Studies at the University of Illinois. He is the author of *James Joyce and the Problem of Justice: Negotiating Sexual and Colonial Difference* (Cambridge University Press, 1995) and *Dracula's Crypt: Bram Stoker, Irishness and the Question of Blood* (University of Illinois Press, 2002) He is also the editor of *Quare Joyce* (University of Michigan Press, 1998). His most recent book, in which Yeats figures prominently, is entitled *The Myth of Manliness in Irish National Culture, 1880–1922* (forthcoming).

Acknowledgements

I wish to acknowledge the great helpfulness of the staff of Special Collections in the Libraries of Trinity College, Dublin, and Queen's University, Belfast. I am also grateful to colleagues and students at the Yeats International Summer School, Sligo, in 2007 and 2009, and to my students at Queen's.

W.B. Yeats: A Chronology

1865	W.B. Yeats born in Sandymount Ave., Dublin, to John B. Yeats and Susan Pollexfen Yeats.
1867	The Yeats family moves to 23 Fitzroy Road, London.
1872	Susan Yeats returns with WBY and her other children to Sligo.
1874	The Yeats family returns to London.
1877	WBY enrols at Godolphin School, Hammersmith, London.
1881	The Yeats family returns to Dublin to live in Balscadden Cottage, Howth.
1881	WBY goes to Erasmus Smith High School, Dublin.
1883	WBY leaves Erasmus Smith High School.
1884	WBY enrols at Metropolitan School of Art, Dublin.
1885	His first poems published in the *Dublin University Review*.
1885	Founder member of the Dublin Hermetic Society with AE and Charles Johnston. Meets Katharine Tynan.
1886	Leaves the Metropolitan School of Art.
1886	His verse play, *Mosada*, is published privately.
1887	WBY returns to London with his family.
1887	Visits Madame Blavatsky, and joins the Blavatsky Lodge of the Theosophical Society.
1888	The Yeats family moves to Bedford Park.
1888	WBY joins the Esoteric Section of the Theosophical Society.
1889	*The Wanderings of Oisin and Other Poems* published. Begins edition of Blake with Edwin Ellis. Meets Maud Gonne.
1890	WBY initiated into the Hermetic Order of the Golden Dawn.
1891	Proposes to Maud Gonne but is refused.

1892	The Irish Literary Society founded in London, and WBY's *The Countess Kathleen and Various Legends and Lyrics* published.
1893	*The Celtic Twilight* published.
1894	Meets Mrs Olivia Shakespear. Stays with the Gore-Booth family at Lissadell, Co. Sligo.
1895	*Poems* published.
1896 (Feb.)	Takes rooms at Woburn Buildings. Begins affair with Olivia Shakespear.
1896 (Aug.)	Meets Lady Augusta Gregory at Tulira Castle, Galway.
1897	Stays at Coole Park. Planning of Irish Literary Theatre with Lady Gregory, Edward Martyn and the novelist George Moore.
1898	WBY and Maud Gonne contract a mystical marriage.
1899 (Apr.)	*The Wind Among the Reeds* published.
1899 (May)	*The Countess Cathleen* [sic] performed by the Irish Literary Theatre in Dublin.
1900	Death of his mother. He founds a new order of the Golden Dawn after disagreements with Aleister Crowley and MacGregor Mathers.
1902	*Cathleen Ni Houlihan*, with Maud Gonne in the title role, produced by W.G. Fay.
1903 (Feb.)	*In the Seven Woods* and the critical essays in *Ideas of Good and Evil*. Maud Gonne marries John MacBride.
1904	The Abbey Theatre, Dublin, founded with WBY as producer-manager, opening with his *On Baile's Strand*.
1906	*Poems 1895–1905*.
1908	First volumes of W.B. Yeats's *Collected Works* published. Meets Ezra Pound.
1910	WBY receives a Civil List pension of £150 p.a.
1911	Meets his future wife, Georgie Hyde-Lees.
1913	Rents Stone Cottage in Sussex with Ezra Pound.
1915	Hugh Lane, Lady Gregory's nephew, drowned on SS *Lusitania*.
1916 (Mar.)	First volume of his autobiography, *Reveries over Childhood and Youth*, published.
1916 (Apr.)	The play, *At the Hawk's Well*, produced in London.
1916 (Apr.)	Easter Rising in Dublin.

1916 (May)	Execution of leaders of Easter Rising, among them John MacBride.
1916 (July)	WBY visits Maud Gonne in Normandy. She again refuses his offer of marriage.
1917 (Mar.)	WBY buys Ballylee Castle ('Thoor Ballylee'), a Norman tower near Coole in Galway.
1917 (Aug.)	WBY proposes to Maud Gonne's daughter Iseult and is refused.
1917 (Oct.)	Marries Georgie Hyde-Lees. Shortly afterwards she begins to produce the automatic writing on which *A Vision* is based.
1917 (Nov.)	*The Wild Swans at Coole* published.
1918 (Jan.)	Settles in Oxford.
1918 (Jan.)	Death of Lady Gregory's son, Major Robert Gregory, in action as pilot in First World War.
1918 (Sept.)	WBY moves into the renovated Thoor Ballylee.
1918 (Nov.)	End of First World War.
1919 (Feb.)	Birth of daughter Anne in Dublin.
1919 (Oct.)	Beginning of the Irish War of Independence.
1920	Leaves with his wife for US lecture tour.
1921 (July)	Truce between British and the Irish rebel forces.
1921 (Aug.)	Birth of a son, Michael Yeats.
1921 (Oct.)	*Four Plays for Dancers* published.
1921 (Dec.)	Anglo-Irish Treaty signed in London, allowing for partition of Ireland between the 'Irish Free State' and Northern Ireland.
1922 (Jan.)	Civil War in Ireland between pro- and anti-Treaty forces.
1922 (Feb.)	John B. Yeats dies in New York.
1922 (July)	WBY receives honorary degree from Trinity College, Dublin.
1922 (Oct.)	*The Trembling of the Veil*, the second volume of his autobiography, published.
1922 (Dec.)	WBY elected to the Irish Senate.
1923	Awarded the Nobel Prize for Literature.
1926 (Jan.)	First version of *A Vision* published, dated '1925'.
1926 (Feb.)	Sean O'Casey's *The Plough and the Stars* opens at Abbey Theatre. Riots follow, and WBY harangues the rioters from the stage.

1927 (Nov.)	Winters in Algeciras. Ill with congestion of the lungs and influenza.
1928 (Feb.)	*The Tower* published.
1928 (Sept.)	WBY declines to stand for re-election to the Irish Senate.
1929 (Summer)	Last visit Thoor Ballylee.
1932 (May)	Death of Lady Gregory.
1932 (July)	Lives at Rathfarnham, near Dublin.
1932 (Oct.)	Starts on last American lecture tour to raise funds for Irish Academy of Letters.
1933 (July)	Supports fascist Blueshirts in Dublin.
1933 (Sept.)	*The Winding Stair and Other Poems* published.
1934	Has Steinach rejuvenation operation.
1935 (July)	Death of AE.
1936 (Jan.)	WBY's health deteriorates.
1936 (Nov.)	His *Oxford Book of Modern Verse* published.
1938 (Aug.)	First production of *Purgatory* at Abbey Theatre.
1938 (Oct.)	Death of Olivia Shakespear in London.
1939 (Jan.)	WBY dies at Cap Martin in the south of France. Buried nearby at Roquebrune.
1948	WBY's body reinterred at Drumcliff churchyard, Sligo.

CHAPTER ONE

Yeats in the Light of
Recent Criticism

EDWARD LARRISSY

W B. Yeats is a major figure, not just in Irish but in world literature. His works are familiar, a staple of the teaching of poetry, and subject to continuing reflection not only in Ireland, Britain, America and Australia, but in India and anglophone Africa, where his subtle handling of the challenges of reviving a national tradition is seen as compelling and instructive. More narrowly, his influence on modern poetry in English can now be seen as rivalling, if not surpassing, that of his chief competitor for the role of being the key figure, T.S. Eliot. Considering the ascendancy which Yeats exercised over twentieth-century poetry and criticism in English, and continues to exercise over much contemporary poetry, it is perhaps worth beginning an account of recent work on him by simply asking what is being done to understand afresh the way in which he wrote. In fact, there has never been any paucity of work on Yeats and poetic form: important contributions include those by Marjorie Perloff, Adelyn Dougherty and Terry Eagleton.[1] However, a new level of energy seems to have imbued this question in recent years. Peter McDonald's *Serious Poetry: Form and Authority from Yeats to Hill* examines the important fact of Yeats's modelling the overall theme onto the shape and handling of the poem's form. Yeats's concentration on themes of order and disintegration gives him ample scope, and his interest in 'the punning relations between architectural and poetic structures', as represented in poems such as 'Meditations in Time of Civil War', provides a good

1

example.[2] McDonald also argues the persuasive point that the Northern Irish poets have learnt from Yeats to involve their handling of poetic form in their discussion and representation of strife and disorder. Vereen M. Bell, in *Yeats and the Logic of Formalism*, also scrutinizes the link between form and ideas about form. Starting with a strong restatement of the eclecticism of Yeats's intellectual debts, the ambivalence of his sense of identity, and the connected fact of apparent contradictions, he concludes that 'Poetry ... would be the only condition under which the formation and reformation of identities could safely proceed.'[3] Ideas of order and ideas of primitive energy confront each other or seek to negotiate with each other as themes in the poem, and the handling of form enacts the debate. And the fact that the poem is where everything happens itself becomes part of the subject matter. Nicholas Grene's approach, in his *Yeats's Poetic Codes*, has certain broad similarities. We encounter yet again the analogy between form and thought: Yeats's style, language and use of form exhibit a creative tension between the world of forms and the world of experience.[4] This conclusion should not be confused with a restatement of Yeats's Neoplatonic themes and their problems, for it is founded on a multi-faceted approach to style and form, analysing particular stylistic traits, favoured grammatical figures, characteristic Yeatsian lexis and poetic structure. In a comparably multi-faceted approach to the question of form, comprising an assessment of poetic language as well as structure, Helen Vendler has offered a series of formally conscious close readings which contain some fresh and memorable insights.[5]

Strictly speaking, the close reading of a Yeats poem should always advert to its position within a book (whether original collection or subsequent compilation), both in terms of its overall position and in terms of the poems printed on either side of it. Hazard Adams, in *The Book of Yeats's Poems*, has sought to demonstrate what can be learnt from such juxtapositions, which themselves are sometimes informed by Yeats's Blakean sense of the value of contraries. Not only that, but a whole collection may need to be read by comparison and contrast with that which preceded or followed.[6]

The text of the poem also has a history, in journals, and sometimes in anthologies, and Yug Mohit Chaudhry has sought illumination in the unexpected placing of some of Yeats's early poems prior to their first appearances between the covers of one of his collections. In particular, Yeats was publishing 'regularly and simultaneously' in the nationalist journal *United Ireland* and in the imperialist and unionist journals of W.E. Henley, the *Scots* and the *National Observer*.[7]

Perhaps the apparent contradiction should not be surprising, especially in view of recent work on Yeats which is much clearer about where this poet comes from, so to speak. Commentators and critics now pay far more heed to Yeats's middle-class Protestant background and what it implies. No longer does one skim over Yeats's account of the stable-boy at the house in Sligo: 'He had a book of Orange rhymes, and the days when we read them together in the hayloft gave me the pleasure of rhyme for the first time ... When I had begun to dream of my future life, I thought I would like to die fighting the Fenians.'[8] Until recently it was normal to refer to a background such as Yeats's as 'Anglo-Irish'. This usage was intended substantially to refer to the arrival in Ireland from England of many ancestors of the Protestant middle class in the seventeenth century, and to their close links with the English middle and upper classes. It is still not uncommon to encounter references to the 'hyphenated' condition of the Anglo-Irish. Yet this is less and less accepted as the best way of characterizing the origins of someone such as Yeats, for it may seem to elide the complexity of the various origins of Irish people in general. Nowadays, the preferred usage is 'Irish'. However, it might be claimed that something is lost in this change of emphasis, and that the change itself reflects a waning perception of the reality of British imperial power in Ireland, and the way that this, among other things, was bound to inflect the self-understanding of the Protestant middle class. In some ways, the fact of the Yeats family's to-ings and fro-ings between Ireland and London render the idea of a 'hyphenated condition' quite suggestive, one attended by doubts about the security of either terminus of the voyage, a voyage which it is possible to see in terms of *The Wanderings of Oisin*, with its counterposing of pagan Celtic dreams and a type of grey modernity.

As it happened, Yeats's sojourn in Sligo may have offered an analogy in microcosm of this kind of opposition. Terence Brown has emphasized the global, mercantile connections of the port of Sligo, connections which, on his mother's side, his family was prominent in promoting.[9]

Yet this busy modern port was surrounded by a countryside replete with tales of faery. At the same time, there might be other ways of regarding the other world to which the ships of Sligo gave access, for Yeats's brother Jack would refer to it as 'Sindbad's yellow shore' – an orientalist locution which suggests the other world of romance. On the other hand, because of its busy trade, Sligo was known in the period as 'Little Belfast'. While the point is slightly different, it might also be worth noting that a Protestant in Sligo would feel quite at home there. The Oxford *New History of Ireland* gives the Protestant population of Sligo in this period as 75 per cent.[10] The subsequent arrival of the Border has enforced a sense of isolation from its northern neighbours which was not present at the time of Yeats's youth. At that time, this population could feel themselves contiguous with the significant Protestant minorities in south Donegal and south-west Fermanagh, so that Yeats might have experienced his sojourns in Sligo as 'an inhabiting of an uncertain, permeable boundary between Protestant and Catholic Ireland' – not a literal boundary, but a structure of feeling.[11] And, as W.J. McCormack points out, long before the famous words 'Cast a cold eye' were inscribed in Drumcliff, 'a tablet in Tullylish, County Down, commemorated the Reverend William Butler Yeats, rector there from 1836 until his death (in Dublin) in 1862': McCormack asserts that it is a principle of his biography of Yeats 'that these oblique northern traces deserve more attention than they have ever received'.[12] McCormack's attention does not yield much that is quantifiable, but it is suggestive in evoking the industrial revolution of those days in south-east Ulster as an unwelcome setting for the absentee clergyman, and a source of knowledge about industrialization for the Yeats family.[13] Yet on the time-honoured and well-supported principle that Yeats is never one-sided, such a background only provides a part of the picture, and one that has to contend with the indubitable fact of Yeats's nationalism. Edward Said saw Yeats as a 'poet of decolonization'.[14] The greatest difficulty with this is presented by the crudity, in an Irish context, of speaking of 'colonization' without so much qualification as to render the word almost useless: such, at any rate, would be the view of 'revisionist' historians such as Yeats's biographer, R.F. Foster. At the very least, the great date of English (and Anglo-Norman) settlement in Ireland needs to be borne in mind. Even so, there is a post-colonial criticism

which is conscious in a less reductionist way of the problematic relationship of Yeats's class to the affiliations of the majority of Irish people.
David Lloyd, in his influential book *Anomalous States: Irish Writing and the
Post-Colonial Moment* (1993), has a chapter on Yeats called 'The Poetics of
Politics', in which he notes how, in 'Coole Park, 1929', Yeats 'asserts the
value of settlement and tradition, but in a language and imagery which
are deliberately and even hyperbolically detached from any organically
mimetic relationship to their supposed setting'.[15] The reason for this is
that, from 'Easter 1916' onwards, Yeats 'writes out to its logical extremes
the lesson of an act that threatened to displace him both as a poet whose
cultural work becomes redundant and as one of the "colonizers who
refuse"'.[16] This displacement makes itself felt in the language and
imagery of the poems. It must, in justice, be pointed out that Terry
Eagleton had already identified a conflict homologous to that which
Lloyd discovers in an analysis of 'In Memory of Major Robert Gregory':
here, Eagleton notes two conflicting ideas of the aristocrat: that of the
rooted paternalist, and that of the Byronic free spirit.[17] Again, this contradiction arises from a defect in Yeats's confidence in asserting his own
right to a sense of rootedness in Irish tradition.

In *Yeats's Nations: Gender, Class and Irishness*, Marjorie Howes makes a positive virtue of such complexity: 'emphasizing Yeats the dialectician and
self-critic over Yeats the totalizing system-builder, and ... claiming that
Yeats's nations compel their own critiques and reveal their own instabilities'.[18] These instabilities also express themselves in the concepts and
performance of gender in Yeats's poems. After all, Ernest Renan, in his
Poetry of the Celtic Races (1860) had described the Celts as 'an essentially
feminine race', and this notion had been given some support by
Matthew Arnold in his *On the Study of Celtic Literature* (1867), which was an
important influence on Yeats. The fact that such an account of the Celt
could further the imperial ambitions of a 'masculine' British Empire had
already been suggested, prior to Howes's intervention, by David Cairns
and Shaun Richards in their *Writing Ireland: Colonialism, Nationalism and
Culture*.[19] Howes demonstrates, considering both the imagery and the
poetic performance of gender, how Yeats may see his early work as too
'feminine'; or adopt what he sees as a 'masculine' manner; or speak in
the person of a woman (as in 'A Woman Young and Old'). In relation to

the first two points, Howes asserts that 'Yeats's eventual rejection of Celticism as effeminate, blurred and melancholy represents a capitulation to imperial structures of thought rather than a move away from them'.[20] As for the impersonation of a woman, in an original discussion of 'A Woman Young and Old' Howes claims that Yeats wishes to extend his critique of 'postcolonial Catholic Irishness. The series defines femininity and feminine sexuality through precisely those things that the Free State's hegemonic version of nationality depended on excluding from them.'[21]

Howes's analysis, by virtue of its comprehensiveness, builds on and subsumes the insights of previous scholars. Gloria Kline's classic depiction of the mingled abasement and exaltation of Yeats as courtly lover was already a depiction of unstable power relations.[22] At least as important is Elizabeth Cullingford's *Gender and History in Yeats's Love Poetry* (1993), which offers a wide-ranging and detailed analysis of the poetry in the light of a governing conception derived from the realization of Yeats's ambivalent position as male subject.[23] On the one hand, as a Protestant avowedly indebted to the English poetic tradition he could be expected to identify with, and represent, the particular mystique and authority of the male poet. On the other hand, as an Irishman he could identify with the role, insights and creativity of women. This ambivalence has a palpable and enriching effect on his handling of the classic forms and tropes of lyric poetry, and is a key to the relationship of politics and the erotic in his work. Looking at the side of Yeats that identifies with woman, close readings by Ann Saddlemyer and C.L. Innes have shown the depth of Yeats's investment in the adoption of a woman's voice in the Crazy Jane poems.[24] These pithy and irreverent poems – earthy and metaphysical at once – have been much appreciated by modern readers. The same has not always been the case with Yeats's earlier, 'effeminate' style of the 1890s. This has sometimes suffered in the general reaction against late Romanticism. But Anca Vlasopolos turns a cold eye on such critics when she analyses their assumptions about gender and poetic language, noting the revealingly value-laden terms in which they may prefer the 'hardness' of the later Yeats to the supposed 'softness' and 'vagueness' of the earlier.[25]

Yeats may have wished to speak as a woman, but he still harboured some traditional-sounding assumptions about gender definitions. In 'Michael Robartes and the Dancer', which is a dialogue of 'He' and 'She', it is suggested that woman should abjure intellectuality (and especially 'opinion') in favour of the cultivation and enhancement of her own beauty for her lover as in the depiction in 'Easter 1916' of the decline (as Yeats saw it) of Con Markievicz from sweet-voiced aristocrat to rancorous demagogue. The parallel case of Maud Gonne was never far from Yeats's mind. At the same time, in 'Solomon and the Witch', we find a traditional-seeming praise of a specifically feminine kind of wisdom. Yeats's experience of his wife George's mediumship in the period when the matter of *A Vision* was being revealed, led him to develop his understanding of what he saw as the separate, specifically male and female types of wisdom. In the long poem, 'Desert Geometry or the Gift of Harun Al-Raschid', included in the first version of *A Vision* (1925), the learned Kusta ben Luka interprets and codifies the complicated lore offered mediumistically by his young wife, somewhat as Yeats did with George.[26] This makes the male the analytic codifier; but the 'geometry' he codifies is at root the truth of her young, desiring body. Whether this gives priority to male or female wisdom is a moot point; but it certainly makes feminine wisdom essential, and reveals it as more akin to the characteristic mode of the poet than is the analytic mode in which males specialize. This position is consonant with the salient role played by the moon, emblem of femininity, in the imagery and structure of *A Vision*. In this light, *A Vision* can be seen as yet another ordering of Ireland, conceived of as feminine, by the Anglo-Irish magus. It is partly from this kind of consideration that Declan Kiberd, in *Inventing Ireland*, can refer to *A Vision* as 'The Last Aisling'.[27] In Irish, *aisling* means 'vision', and the *aisling* poems of the seventeenth and eighteenth centuries recounted the poet's vision of a *speirbhean* or 'sky-woman', who represented and spoke for Ireland and its values against the 'extirpation of the Saxon occupier and of his levelling administrative methods'.[28] This is an advocacy with which Yeats could identify, choosing to interpret it as an attack on modernity. But however much Yeats might have believed that his wife was writing automatically and mediumistically, contemporary interpreters have been adopting a less mysterious attitude. Ann Saddlemyer has written a biography of Mrs Yeats which is to some extent an account of the sources of her knowledge, of the Yeatses' life together, and of their collaboration on interpreting the spiritual communications.[29] The account of these materials has to be quite circumstantial in a biography: Margaret Mills Harper has gone further in analysing the details of esoteric tradition and symbol which were the subject of their labours, and in clarifying the creative role of Mrs Yeats.[30]

We must not forget his own creative role, of course. The earlier tendency to sideline the esoteric aspect of Yeats has been relegated to history, and replaced with a realization not only of its centrality, but of its being a flowering of his own Protestant inheritance. Here, a seminal text is R.F. Foster's British Academy Lecture, 'Protestant Magic', which glances at the already-familiar fact of Anglo-Irish Gothic, but proceeds to touch on a related phenomenon even more relevant to the study of Yeats, namely the Anglo-Irish interest in occult science and esoteric doctrines, mostly expressed through the inner orders of the pervasive institution of Irish Protestantism, Freemasonry, whose chosen occult path was normally Rosicrucianism.[31] In my own book, *Yeats the Poet: The Measures of Difference* (1994), I develop these points in such a way that Yeats's Rosicrucianism can be seen as his method of discovering the secrets of a Druid magic forbidden to his Catholic compatriots, on the understanding that the lineaments of magic were everywhere the same.[32] Thus, he could feel that his own caste offered a body of ritual and traditional symbolism fit to vie with that offered by Catholicism, but permitting readier access to what he saw as perennial truth. But one may look at Yeats's occultism in a light which throws more emphasis on its innovative potential. In her book *States of Desire* (1999), Vicki Mahaffey, discusses what she calls Yeats's 'Celtic Rosicrucianism', and shows how Yeats was able not only to link Rosicrucianism back to what he understood as Celtic religion and lore, but also to symbols of sexual renewal and fulfilment: symbols which both gave expression to what they represented and at the same time, in transcending a merely natural understanding of desire, embodied the wider connotations of symbols: the political and the institutional.[33] In this light, Yeats's early 'Rosicrucian' poetry is very much a poetry of 'national liberation', as he himself claimed in 'To Ireland in the Coming Times'. In a wider perspective, this harnessing of occultism to a project of political and personal renewal now seems characteristic of Modernism, and not only in Ireland. Leon Surette has offered a ground-breaking account of how Eliot and Pound, as well as Yeats, looked to occult wisdom for clues to the ancient sources that would feed artistic, sexual and social renewal in the modern age.[34] This account fits into a picture of anglophone poetic modernism that has been delineated by Stan Smith in *The Origins of Modernism: Eliot, Pound, Yeats and the Rhetorics of Renewal*.[35]

There is, however, another road by which to trace the connections of Yeats's occultism, and it leads to the East. The nineteenth-century antiquarian Eugene O'Curry, seeking to characterize Druidism, referred to it as 'that form of the Eastern Philosophy or Religion which prevailed in early ages in our own as well as other western nations'.[36] In speaking of the East, he particularly has in mind the Magi.[37] The form of orientalism on which such a belief might draw has been labelled 'Irish Orientalism' in an important book by Joseph Lennon, one that contains an appropriately detailed chapter on Yeats.[38] In my own book, which Lennon discusses, I had emphasized that Yeats inherited that rather capacious nineteenth-century sense of the Orient described by Edward Said, for it was a location that might comprise 'all kinds of things from Morocco to Kyoto – via Byzantium'.[39] At the same time, taking a hint from John Barrell's work on De Quincey, I seek to show how aspects of the Orient may be differentiated according to need. Thus, the Muslim Middle East can be seen as the Other to the West in point of its despotism and capacity for passion, for instance. But it shares with the West a propensity for 'measure' which its absent from the Far East – from what Yeats would call 'Buddha's emptiness'.[40] As far as Yeats was concerned, the Muslim capacity for measure might express itself in a scientific approach to the theory and practice of magic itself. This association makes itself felt in the very title of 'Desert Geometry', and in the dances of the so-called 'Judwali' tribe of Bedouin which were supposed to delineate the diagrams of *A Vision* in the desert sand. Yeats's interest in this supposed characteristic of Islamic societies makes itself felt as early as the 1886 disavowed verse-drama *Mosada*, about a young Moorish woman of Spain, who practises magic but is consigned to death by the Inquisition – an allegory about the danger posed by Irish Catholicism to the Celtic magic he advocated. But it is Yeats's abiding fascination with Indian tradition that Joseph Lennon particularly emphasizes, an interest he shared with George Russell (AE), whose ideas also modified its character.[41] At different times this fascination centred on the figures of the Brahmin, Mohini Chatterjee, who visited the Dublin Theosophical Society in 1886; on the poet Tagore, for the translation of whose *Gitanjali* in 1913 Yeats wrote an introduction; and on Shri Purohit Swami, whom he assisted, among other things, in translating the *Upanishads* in the 1930s. Lennon concludes that Yeats's 'use of Indian themes and philosophy ... continually remained in opposition to both English convention and Empire'.[42] This is a point also noted by Stephen Regan, in a chapter on 'Poetry and Nation: W.B. Yeats', contributed to a volume on literary connections between Britain and India.[43] We are back with Yeats as 'poet of national liberation'.

Such a description raises yet again the wider question of Yeats's politics. Elizabeth Cullingford's *Yeats, Ireland and Fascism* had mounted a cogent and well-supported argument to the effect that the notion of Yeats as friendly to fascism, while it might seek support from certain phrases and actions of the poet, was so one-sided as to be fallacious, and had to contend with much that was clearly liberal, as with his defence in the Irish Senate of the freedom to divorce, and attacks upon censorship legislation.[44] Recently, W.J. McCormack has put the opposing view in a notably stark form, for his *Blood Kindred* presents Yeats as a Nazi sympathizer. If one were only to judge by what some of his friends and acquaintances said, the point would require little argument. It is not quite so easy to lay a finger on Yeats himself, and this is partly because of the notorious contradictions and ambivalences to which we have already referred. David Dwan, in a recent book on culture and nationalism in Ireland, finds a fresh formulation for this difficulty, one which has the advantage of being cast in the terms of political discourse: 'Yeats drew on a counter-revolutionary tradition to condemn the tyrannical features of nationalists armed with democratic principles; if these criticisms had a liberal foundation, this was exceeded and undermined by the poet's anti-democratic animus.'[45] This element of contradiction makes for effects that can seem contradictory, as in his attitude to warfare. Fran Brearton notes this in her book on *The Great War and Irish Poetry*, scrutinizing the relationship between a 'doctrine of conflict' in the spiritual sphere and the vacillating response to actual warfare, which sometimes verged on disgust: Yeats had a continuing difficulty in negotiating the relationship between 'visible and invisible warfare'.[46] Retaining a sense of this kind of complexity makes it easier to understand how Yeats can respond to 'reprobate traditions', such as that represented by Blake, even while advocating aristocracy. By the same token, it is foolish to assume that all those who frankly recognize the 'anti-democratic animus' of Yeats are denigrators of his art, or of his imagination. Many of his readers are clear enough on that score, but presumably are also wise enough not to convert the recognition into a reductionist account even of his politics, let alone his poetry. Such, at any rate, must be part of the explanation for Yeats's extraordinary ascendancy, as craftsman and as thinker in poetry, an ascendancy documented in Steven Matthews' book, *Yeats as Precursor*,[47] upon which he builds in this volume with a particular concentration, as befits this series, on Yeats's influence in Ireland.

NOTES

1. Marjorie Perloff, *Rhyme and Meaning in the Poetry of Yeats* (The Hague: Mouton, 1970); Adelyn Dougherty, *A Study of Rhythmic Structure in the Verse of William Butler Yeats* (The Hague: Mouton, 1973); Terry Eagleton, 'Yeats and Poetic Form', *Crazy John and the Bishop and Other Essays on Irish Culture* (Cork: Cork University Press, 1998), pp.273–95.

2. Peter McDonald, *Serious Poetry: Form and Authority from Yeats to Hill* (Oxford: Oxford University Press, 2002), p.56.

3. Vereen M. Bell, *Yeats and the Logic of Formalism* (Columbia, MO: University of Missouri Press, 2006), pp.3, 145.

4. Nicholas Grene, *Yeats's Poetic Codes* (Oxford: Oxford University Press, 2008).

5. Helen Vendler, *Our Secret Discipline: Yeats and Lyric Form* (Oxford: Oxford University Press, 2007).

6. Hazard Adams, *The Book of Yeats's Poems* (Gainesville, FL: University of Florida Press, 1989).

7. Yug Mohit Chaudhry, *Yeats, The Irish Literary Revival and The Politics Of Print* (Cork: Cork University Press, 2001), p.43.

8. W.B. Yeats, *The Collected Works of W.B. Yeats*, III, *Autobiographies*, ed. William H. O'Donnell and Douglas N. Archibald (New York: Scribners, 1999), p.47.

9. Terence Brown, *The Life of W.B. Yeats: A Critical Biography*, 2nd edn (Oxford: Blackwell, 2001), pp.1–21. David Pierce offers illuminating material about this and other contexts of Yeats's life and work in his *Yeats's Worlds: Ireland, England and the Poetic Imagination* (New Haven, CT: Yale University Press, 1995).

10. T.W. Moody, F.X. Martin and F.J. Byrne (eds), *A New History of Ireland* (Oxford: Oxford University Press, 1974–87), Vol. IX (1984), p.81, map 98.

11. Edward Larrissy, *Yeats the Poet: The Measures of Difference* (Hemel Hempstead: Harvester, 1994), p.30.

12. W.J. McCormack, *Blood Kindred: W.B. Yeats: the Life, the Death, the Politics* (London: Pimlico, 2005), p.37.

13. Ibid., p.363.

14. Edward Said, 'Yeats and Decolonization', *Culture and Imperialism* (New York: Alfred A. Knopf, 1993), pp.220–38.

15. David Lloyd, *Anomalous States: Irish Writing and the Post-Colonial Moment* (Durham, NC: Duke University Press, 1993), p.68.

16. Ibid., p.74, including quotation from Albert Memmi, *The Colonizer and the Colonized*, trans. Howard E. Greenfield (London: Souvenir Press, 1974 [1964]).

17. Terry Eagleton, 'Politics and Sexuality in W.B. Yeats', *Crane Bag*, 9, 2 (1985), pp.138–42.

18. Marjorie Howes, *Yeats's Nations: Gender, Class and Irishness* (Cambridge: Cambridge University Press, 1996), p.12.

19. David Cairns and Shaun Richards, *Writing Ireland: Colonialism, Nationalism and Culture* (Manchester: Manchester University Press, 1988).

20. Howes, *Yeats's Nations*, p.18.

21. Ibid., p.145.

22. Gloria Kline, *The Last Courtly Lover: Yeats and the Idea of Woman* (Ann Arbor, MI: UMI Research Press, 1983).

23. Elizabeth Cullingford, *Gender and History in Yeats's Love Poetry* (Cambridge: Cambridge University Press, 1993).

24. Ann Saddlemyer, 'Poetry and Possession: Yeats and Crazy Jane', in Richard J. Finneran and Mary Fitzgerald (eds), *Yeats: An Annual of Critical and Textual Studies*, 9 (1991), pp.136–58.; C.L. Innes, *Woman and Nation in Irish Society 1880–1935* (Hemel Hempstead: Harvester Wheatsheaf, 1993), pp.93–108.

25. Anca Vlasopolos, 'Gender-Political Aesthetics and the Early and Later Yeats', in Richard J. Finneran and Edward Engelberg (eds), *Yeats: An Annual of Critical and Textual Studies, 8: Yeats from a Comparatist Perspective* (1990), pp.113–25.

26. Catherine E. Paul and Margaret Mills Harper (eds), *The Collected Works of W.B. Yeats: XIII: A Vision: The Original 1925 Version* (New York: Scribners, 2008), pp.97–102.

27. Declan Kiberd, *Inventing Ireland: The Literature of the Modern Nation* (London: Jonathan Cape, 1995), pp.316–26.

28. Ibid., p.318.

29. Ann Saddlemyer, *Becoming George: The Life of Mrs W.B. Yeats* (Oxford: Oxford University Press, 2002).

30. Margaret Mills Harper, *Wisdom of Two: The Spiritual and Literary Collaboration of George and W.B. Yeats* (Oxford: Oxford University Press, 2006).

31. R.F. Foster, 'Protestant Magic: W.B. Yeats and the Spell of Irish History', *Proceedings of the British Academy*, 75 (1989), pp.243–66. Revised version in *Paddy and Mr Punch: Connections in Irish and English History* (London: Allen Lane, 1993), pp.212–32.

32. Larrissy, *Yeats the Poet*, pp.61–71.

33. Vicki Mahaffey, *States of Desire: Wilde, Yeats, Joyce and the Irish Experiment* (New York: Oxford University Press, 1999), pp.87–141. For 'Celtic Rosicrucianism', see especially pp.108–11.

34. Leon Surette, *The Birth of Modernism: Ezra Pound, T.S. Eliot, W.B. Yeats and the Occult* (Montreal: McGill-Queen's University Press, 1993).

35. Stan Smith, *The Origins of Modernism: Eliot, Pound, Yeats and the Rhetorics of Renewal* (Hemel Hempstead: Harvester Wheatsheaf, 1994).

36. Eugene O'Curry, *Manners and Customs of the Ancient Irish*, 3 vols (London, Edinburgh, Dublin: Williams & Norgate, 1873), Vol. III, p.179.

37. Ibid.

38. Joseph Lennon, *Irish Orientalism: A Literary and Intellectual History* (Syracuse, NY: Syracuse University Press, 2004). See the chapter on 'W.B. Yeats's Celtic Orient' at pp.247–89.

39. Larrissy, *Yeats the Poet*, p.11.

40. Ibid., pp.11–13.

41. For the importance of AE, see also Michael McAteer, *Standish O'Grady, AE and Yeats: History, Politics, Culture* (Dublin: Irish Academic Press, 2002).

42. Lennon, *Irish Orientalism*, p.288.

43. Stephen Regan, 'Poetry and Nation: W.B. Yeats', in Richard Allen and Harish Trivedi (eds), *Literature and Nation: Britain and India 1800–1990* (London: Routledge, 2001), pp.78–94.

44. Elizabeth Cullingford, *Yeats, Ireland and Fascism* (Basingstoke: Macmillan, 1981).

45. David Dwan, *The Great Community: Culture and Nationalism in Ireland* (Dublin: Field Day, 2008), p.137.

46. Fran Brearton, *The Great War in Irish Poetry* (Oxford: Oxford University Press, 2000), pp.74, 80, 82.

47. Steven Matthews, *Yeats as Precursor: Readings in Irish, British and American Poetry* (Basingstoke: Palgrave Macmillan, 2000).

CHAPTER TWO

W.B. Yeats: Biographical Reflections

TERENCE BROWN

In March 1910 the poet and dramatist W.B. Yeats gave a lecture in Dublin in which he spoke of a poet's life. He had good reason on that date to ponder the shape and significance of a life lived in dedication to literary and dramatic art, for a year earlier he had been profoundly affected by the premature death of his friend and co-worker at the Abbey Theatre, the dramatist John Millington Synge, at a moment when Lady Augusta Gregory, with whom he had founded that same theatre, had only recently recovered from life-threatening illness. The lecture, 'Friends of My Youth', clearly suggested in its title that Yeats in 1910 was in autobiographically reflective mood, made aware as he was in his forty-fifth year of his own long-departed youth and of the patterns and fragility of life itself. Indeed the lecture, as Joseph Ronsley has noted,[1] is self-reflectively conscious (in a way that would intensify in Yeats's writings in years to come when auto-bio-graphy would become more and more central to his artistic concerns) that as a poet he belonged to a specific generation which had had to face challenges of particular kinds. And in thinking of these challenges he reached the compelling conclusion:

> A poet is by the very nature of things a man who lives with entire sincerity, or rather the better his poetry the more sincere his life; his life is an experiment in living and those who come after have a right to know it. Above all it is necessary that the lyric poet's life should be known that we should understand that his poetry is no rootless flower but the speech of a man.[2]

The year after Yeats's death on 28 January 1939, the poet and critic

T.S. Eliot summed up the life experiment that Yeats had conducted, and in terms that echoed Yeats's own sense that he had been a representative figure. Indeed Eliot went further when he stated:

> There are some poets whose poetry can be considered more or less in isolation, for experience and delight. There are others whose poetry, though giving equally experience and delight, has a larger historical importance. Yeats was one of the latter: he was one of those few whose history is the history of their own time, who are part of the consciousness of an age which cannot be understood without them.[3]

In 1910 Yeats himself had attempted to see his own generation of English-language poets in the kind of broad historical context that Eliot could the more easily survey after Yeats's representative life experiment had been completed. In fact Yeats in 1910 had been strikingly perspicacious when he had seen his generation as one that had rebelled against the values of high Victorianism as expressed in the works of such poets as Tennyson and Browning who had, as Yeats saw it, 'filled their verse with reasoning, with science, with geology, with the topics of their day'.[4] For his own career can be seen as having its inspirational energies rooted in imaginative reaction against those aspects of modernity that the high Victorians had been willing to include in their writings.

For Yeats this involved a personal rebellion. His own father, the portrait painter John Butler Yeats, embodied the very values that his poet son thought had infected Victorian poetry. John Butler Yeats, the son of a mildly evangelical Church of Ireland clergyman, while at university at Trinity College, Dublin in the late 1850s, had abandoned religious orthodoxy and had substituted for it the then fashionable creed of Comtean positivism.[5] When combined with his genial, ever hopeful personality (he had abandoned a career in the law for the precarious calling of artist, to the chagrin of his much put-upon spouse) this version of scientific, rational optimism was found wholly antithetical by his dreamy, emotionally insecure elder son (born in 1865), the poet-to-be, who later confessed of his youth:

> I am very religious, and deprived by Huxley and Tyndall, whom I detested, of the simple-minded religion of my childhood, I had made a new religion, almost an infallible Church of poetic

tradition, of a fardel of stories, and of personages, and of emotions, inseparable from their first expression, passed on from generation to generation by poets and painters with some help from philosophers and theologians.[6]

Such incipient religious ambition, at odds with his father's sunny agnosticism, an agnosticism undisturbed by the findings of Charles Darwin which such as Huxley popularized, was to bear fruit in the poet's life-long engagement with metaphysical, occult and philosophic enquiry. A break with his father's world-view that on one occasion brought the teenage Willie Yeats almost to blows with his father would over the course of a lifetime bring the poet in contact with many strange personages and groups and involve much wandering in the byways of speculative thought.

Yeats's journey of essentially religious enquiry began in Dublin in the mid-1880s among young men and women who were attracted by occult experiment and eastern religious systems. While studying art in a desultory fashion he joined a Hermetic society and quickly left it for Theosophy, a curious mishmash of oriental philosophic ideas and soaring mystical ambition for transcendent consciousness being propagated in Europe by the improbable figure of a Madame Helena Petrovna Blavatsky (the Madame Sostostris of T.S. Eliot's *The Waste Land*, with her 'bad cold' and 'wicked pack of cards'). When the impecunious Yeats family left Dublin for London in 1887 (where ever-optimistic John Butler hoped to support his family by way of metropolitan success with his paint-brush without too much ungentlemanly labour), Yeats joined the Blavatsky circle, only to find himself expelled from one of its sections by the imperious and fraudulent guru that Blavatsky was, for too great an interest in experimental magic (Blavatsky preferred the kind where proof was not an issue). Fortunately the Order of the Golden Dawn (a Rosicrucian and Kaballistic society that practised ritual magic) had its headquarters close to where the Yeatses had set up home and the poet was initiated into its preliminary mysteries in 1890, progressing to an upper grade in its elaborate hierarchy in 1893. For many years the order (its complement was about 300 largely upper-middle-class persons, many of them women) would preoccupy the poet in a central way, providing motifs and occult images for his symbolist verses and prose tales and a confirmation that the life of the mind in reverie, dream, even drug-induced vision, was a portal to a higher order of being than that investigated by a materialist science. This magical adeptship, which involved Yeats in reckoning his own published and performed poetry as religious acts, gave substance to his own claim of 1892: 'the mystical life is the centre of all that I do & all that I think & all that I write ... I have all-ways considered my self a voice of what I believe to be a greater renaisance [sic] – the revolt of the soul against the intellect – now beginning in the world.'[7]

Up until about 1912 Yeats's near-obsession with magic can be accounted for not only as the revolt of an essentially religious soul (who in the early 1890s had also made the English mystical poet William Blake a major object of study) against the intellect of an age dominated by scientific reductionism, but as a metaphoric expression of the poet's deep fascination for the possibility of transformation in the human personality and in human culture in general. Many of his early poems attend to moments of metamorphosis (alchemy is a recurrent trope) and evoke Celtic Twilight atmospherics as the appropriate ambiance for transformation. They also suggest, however, that the poet's religious nature did not preclude a desire for power; for the early poems, despite the aesthetic delicacy of their verbal and aural effects, also register tones of command and mage-like imperiousness. This association of poetry with authority, in an era when artistic endeavour was increasingly thought to be peripheral to the central concerns of an industrial society in Britain, received augmenting inspiration when Yeats immersed himself in 1902 and 1903 in the headily romantic philosophic outpourings of Friedrich Nietzsche, with their celebration of masterful self-fashioning and the will to power. However, from about 1912 onwards, Yeats became increasingly absorbed by the matter of the soul's survival of death and the nature of the after-life rather than self-transcendence. Attendance at spiritualist seances was increasingly substituted for the liturgical rituals of the Golden Dawn. The poet conducted extensive psychic investigations of paranormal phenomena, engaged in a lengthy exchange of writing with a presumed former incarnation, the ghost of Leo Africanus, first contacted through a medium control, and even allowed himself a period of near-comic credulity when a spiritualist of inventive frame of mind claimed an impressively constructed machine of his could communicate with the dead. All of this

17

came to a remarkable near-apotheosis when in 1917 Yeats married Georgie Hyde-Lees, with whom he had worked among the mystics of the Golden Dawn. On their honeymoon Georgie had discovered a talent for automatic writing (a practice which seems to allow the unconscious mind free written expression in states of significantly reduced self-control) which profoundly affected the poet. He convinced himself at least some of the time that his young bride (he was 51, she 25 when they married) was a conduit to a spirit world, that would provide him with 'metaphors for poetry'[8] at a time in his life when, as literary history suggested, the lyric poet's inspiration could only wane.

Several years of intense psychic interchange between man and wife ensued, which resulted in the publication in 1926 of Yeats's book *A Vision*, with its taxonomy of human psychology and attempt to comprehend the cycles of human history according to a complex geometric symbolism of cones and gyres. The book had apparently been delivered to Yeats from the spirit world, but its general thrust seemed akin to similar explorations of division as an aspect of human personality that could contemporaneously be found in the works of Carl Jung; its pessimistic historicizing and attendant sense of a civilization currently in disintegration, awaiting some new dispensation (the 'rough beast' of Yeats's poem 'The Second Coming') can be seen too as analogous to such works as Oswald Spengler's *The Decline of the West* (1918–23).

Following the publication of *A Vision*, the poet, concerned that in that book he 'had misinterpreted the geometry and in [his] ignorance of philosophy had failed to understand distinctions upon which the coherence of the whole depended'[9] turned away from experimental spiritualism, first to the study of philosophy (with the eighteenth-century immaterialist George Berkeley as a principal interest) and then in the 1930s to explorations of Hindu religious thought, that took him full circle, as it were, to the Theosophical idealism and orientalism of his young manhood. In all of this – the practice of ritual magic with his fellow magicians in the Golden Dawn, the obsessive engagement with spiritualism, the study of philosophy, the immersion in Hindu thought and spirituality (for a time in the 1930s Yeats even had his own personal Swami) – Yeats revealed himself as a man of his age. For throughout, the question and problem of belief kept pressing themselves on the poet's often troubled, if sometimes credulous, mind. And in so doing they high-light how what can seem most idiosyncratic about Yeats's career (all that the English poet W.H. Auden dismissed as the Californian side of Yeats) was in fact a not uncommon, if heroic, attempt to reinstate religious/metaphysical understandings of reality in face of the explanatory force science could muster to discredit orthodox Christianity.[10] If the Romantic poet John Keats in the early nineteenth century had feared that 'cold phi-losophy' (by which he meant what we would understand by the term 'science') could 'clip an angel's wings / Conquer all mysteries by rule and line / Empty the haunted air', Yeats in the twentieth century sensed its chill even more keenly. His life-work as a thinker, in a project he shared with many others – late nineteenth- and twentieth-century philosophers, theologians, poets – can be seen therefore as an effort to save mystery from 'rule and line', from what Keats designated (in the same passage of his poem 'Lamia', quoted above) as 'the dull catalogue of common things'. He hoped to refill the 'haunted air' that science had emptied of sacred meaning. Yet he was perhaps even more a man of his time in that the corrosive power of doubt could never be fully assuaged even when he was at his most religiously ambitious. One notes that in summing up his strange trafficking with the ghost of Leo Africanus in 1915 he concluded of a letter purportedly from Leo to him, as if to put paid to belief in life after death, 'I am not convinced that in this letter there is one sentence that has come from beyond my own imagination ... I think there is no thought that has not occurred to me in some form or other for many years passed ... nothing has surprised me'.[11] And one further notes that in the introduction to the second version of *A Vision*, published in 1937 as a kind of summation of his life-long speculations, Yeats admits of his belief in historical phases in cyclical motion:

> Some will ask whether I believe in the actual existence of my cir-cuits of sun and moon ... To such a question I can but answer that if sometimes, overwhelmed by miracle as all men must be when in the midst of it, I have taken such periods literally, my reason as soon recovered; and now that the system stands out clearly in my imagination I regard them as stylistic arrangements of experience comparable to the cubes in the drawing of Wyndham Lewis and to the ovoids in the sculpture of Brancusi.[12]

In so writing Yeats was indicating that he understood how the psychological and historical system adumbrated in *A Vision* had an essentially aesthetic aspect. The status of its claims to truth was not really the point. Rather *A Vision* offered a way of organizing experience and of investing it with the aura of the numinous that high art could be expected to generate in a degraded time. And in so doing Yeats was attributing to his own work the kind of powers which T.S. Eliot had identified, in a famous review of James Joyce's *Ulysses*, as belonging to a 'mythical method'. There Eliot had accounted for Joyce's organization of a novel about one day in the life of a modern city according to the template of an ancient mythic narrative (Homer's *Odyssey*) as 'a way of controlling, of ordering, of giving a shape and a significance to the immense panorama of futility and anarchy which is contemporary civilisation'.[13]

Eliot in this review was in fact giving expression, with reference to a specific literary work, of a quite widespread, contemporary understanding of the role of myth in human affairs. In this, myth was not to be dismissed simply as collections of legends which had survived from superstitious times that the age of reason and science had superseded. Rather, it was a mode of knowledge. The primitive mind, indeed, with its myth-making capacities, its ability to comprehend reality by way of aesthetically arresting narratives, gave access to orders of truth closed to the mind of modernity, with its materialist bias and its apparent indifference to social chaos.[14]

Yeats as an Irishman was, of course, particularly well-placed to appreciate the special powers of myth in the modern age, for his native land in the nineteenth century, in which he began his literary career, had been revealed as a rich repository of mythology and of mythological material. Yeats as a young man in Dublin had come on the saga material of the early Irish world in the heady writings of Standish James O'Grady in his *History of Ireland* (published in 1878 and 1880). In O'Grady's rhapsodic pages Yeats learned of heroic exploits of a mythological Iron Age hero, Cuchulain, the Hound of Ulster, who would serve as a kind of personal alter ego in his poems and plays for the rest of his life. When he first came upon the works of O'Grady he read them through the lenses of the then fashionable Celticism. And he wrote too of the Irish bards of ancient days, that there throbbed through their work 'one impulse – the persistence of Celtic passion'.[15] Readers of this elevated utterance in

1889 (when it was published) would certainly have thought Yeats was clearly a purveyor of the kind of Celticism that the English poet Matthew Arnold (drawing on such French thinkers as Henri Martin and Ernest Renan) had celebrated in a famous series of lectures delivered in Oxford and published in 1866 as 'The Study of Celtic Literature'. In these Arnold had characterized the Celt, as revealed in his literature, as one 'always ready to revolt against the despotism of fact',[16] one whose affinity for 'natural magic'[17] made him sensitive to a feminized spirit of Nature, a genius of the lyric cry, if incapable of the architectonic structures of great art and self-government. And Arnold's lectures can be read as a kind of manifesto (though that was not their intention) for the Celtic Twilight School of Irish poets of the 1890s (disdainfully dismissed by Joyce in his Dubliners story, 'A Little Cloud') among whom Yeats on a superficial reading might at the time have seemed simply a pre-eminent practitioner.

In fact Yeats's attitude to the concept of Celticism in the 1890s was a developing one. By the end of the decade his writings indicated that even at comparatively early stages of his intellectual development he had a sophisticated sense of how the primitive mind with its mythic consciousness might serve as a viable alternative to the modern Zeitgeist, if its residual energies could somehow be tapped and exploited. This involved a crucial revision of Arnoldian Celticism. Where Arnold had considered Celticism as basically race specific (a possession of certain identifiable peoples) Yeats argued in an essay of 1898 that what was thought of as the Celtic element in European literature was the remnant of a magical, animistic world-view that in pre-history was a universal possession of humankind. In 'The Celtic Element in Literature', Yeats invoked a time when 'Men ... lived in a world where anything might flow and change, and become any other thing' and 'had not our thoughts of weight and measure'[18] and in a daring leap of historical imaging he associated such a primitive capacity with the contemporary European symbolist avant-garde, which had significantly influenced his own belief in the powers of poetry. He wrote:

> The reaction against the rationalism of the eighteenth century has mingled with a reaction against the materialism of the nineteenth century, and the symbolical movement ... is certainly the only

movement that is saying new things. The arts by brooding on their own intensity have become religious.[19]

Tellingly, he links such religio-symbolic art with mythology, for he states that the arts 'must, as religious thought has always done, utter themselves through legends'.[20] And what clearly excites him is that Ireland is the site of such legends, such mythology, as we might say, made available as the smouldering coals of the ancient world-view ready to be fanned into fresh life, for 'the Irish legends move among known woods and seas, and have so much of a new beauty that they may well give the opening century its most memorable symbols'.[21]

A mode of spirituality is inflected here through cultural nationalism as well as through a Yeatsian revision of Celticism. In this Yeats was a man of his age just as much as he was in opposing scientific reductionism. For since the eighteenth century in many parts of Europe poets, artists, thinkers of various kinds, polemicists and politicians had sought to find in the cultural traditions of their individual peoples the inspirational force of a nascent nationalism to set against the universalism of Enlightenment thought and current imperial power. Language was central to this (as, for example, in the case of Czech in the Bohemian lands where Austro-Hungary governed through the medium of German), but cultural nationalism also made much of the 'national' inheritance of mythology, literature, music, indigenous social and religious practice in fostering a sense of national identity that gathered around a near-mystical belief in the spirit of the nation. In this context Yeats's exhilaration at the mythological wealth that lay to hand in the Irish setting seems unremarkable in a period that would for instance see the Finnish composer Jean Sibelius focus in key works on the mythology of his native land and the Hungarian Béla Bartók lay claim to the folk music of Transylvania as a national patrimony. However, in the local Irish context Yeats can be presented as an anomalous figure.

The Yeats family were descendants of a Yorkshireman who probably, as a demobbed soldier, settled in Ireland after the Williamite wars of the seventeenth century. The family since that time had enjoyed some actual political influence and for some of its history had had the benefit of owning significant acreage in a country in which their Protestant religion was essential to membership of the caste that exercised power in the land. The fact that Yeats's great-grandfather and grandfather on his father's side were both Church of Ireland clergymen, and that Yeats's own father inherited some land in Kildare (mortgaged and encumbered as it was until he divested himself of it at an opportune moment), would have made the Yeatses in the eyes of Ireland's Catholic and nationally-minded majority conventional-enough figures in what was termed the Ascendancy (a caste defined more by religious affiliation that by class, since it could include the mighty, landed aristocrat and the humble, impecunious parson). The further fact that Yeats's father had married into a dynasty of merchants and ship-owners in Sligo, in the north-west of Ireland (who had migrated there from the English south east in living memory), when he made Susan Pollexfen his bride, would have added to the expectation that the progeny of such a union would follow convention by being essentially Unionist in politics, even if John Butler Yeats could understand and sympathize with his politician friend Isaac Butt's Home Rule phase.

The poet, however, as a young man not only became an ardent cultural nationalist (the spiritual element of which can be seen to satisfy the propensity for a mystical world-view that his esotericism also evidenced), but also a Republican. By this is meant that from his early twenties he seemed prepared to align himself with the most radical elements in Irish society, those who sought the complete secession of Ireland from the United Kingdom, through revolutionary agitation and, if necessary, through the use of arms. Indeed in the late 1880s Yeats probably took the oath of a secret revolutionary group, the Irish Republican Brotherhood, that traced its origins to the Fenian movement, that had organized a failed rebellion in 1867 and which would play a decisive role in the Easter Rising in 1916.[22]

One may account in fairly simple biographical terms for this curious addition of separatist Republicanism (sporadic and more emotional than ideological as it was) to cultural nationalism in the youthful Yeats's congeries of commitments. In 1887 at a Dublin debating and conversation club he met the old Fenian leader John O'Leary, who had been permitted to return to Ireland after a lengthy term in gaol for seditious activities and a protracted legally enforced exile. Yeats, in rebellion against his own father and in need of a mentor, fell under his spell, admiring O'Leary's stoical hauteur and noble demeanour. It was O'Leary who had introduced Yeats to the work of Irish English-language poetic precursors, who had sung 'to sweeten Ireland's wrong'.[23] And, perhaps as importantly, it was O'Leary's sister who introduced Maud Gonne to the Yeats family. The poet was smitten by the fiery and beautiful young revolutionary who immediately became the object of his unrequited love and also his muse.

Republicanism in the 1890s made the occultist, symbolist and cultural nationalist literary man an unlikely agitator. The high point of Yeats's engagement with such activism was when he was to the fore in preparing for a mass commemoration in Dublin of the United Irish Rebellion of 1798. In preparation for more than a year, it was hoped by the organizers, including O'Leary, Yeats and Gonne, that this event would foment a kind of communal succession from imperial rule (the 'velvet' revolutions of recent Eastern European experience suggest the kind of thing Yeats and O'Leary may have been hoping for; Gonne was much more sanguine about the possible use of force). In the event such hopes proved ill-founded. Democratic Ireland was adjusting in that very year of Republican commemoration and planning to a Local Government Act in the United Kingdom parliament in London that gave substantial powers of patronage at county and district council level to politicians of Irish nationalist hue who were prepared to exploit the opportunities afforded thereby while continuing to support the Irish Parliamentary Party in Westminster with its aspirations for Irish Home Rule within the Empire. Separatist Republicanism on a day of commemoration could summon a crowd, but the majority of the population was unwilling to embrace revolution (even the peacefully achieved version Yeats seemed to think was possible).

Scholarship has engaged for more than three decades in a process that has been more or less coterminous with the consolidation in the academy of Irish Studies as a discipline, with the issue of Yeats's apparently anomalous status as member (along with such figures as his patron and friend Lady Augusta Gregory and the playwright John Millington Synge) of the Ascendancy caste who nonetheless embraced cultural nationalism and, in the poet's case, engaged even with separatist Republicanism. The fact that Irish Studies has largely been constructed as a variant of Post-colonial Studies has meant that Yeats and his confederates have frequently been represented in literary and cultural history as figures whose role in Irish cultural politics can be read as a form of colonial negotiation of an increasingly insecure political environment, in which the power of the Anglo-Irish Ascendancy was in terminal crisis as democratic Ireland asserted its will to power. A key text in this ideological interpretation of the literary and cultural field was Cairns's and Richards' monograph *Writing Ireland: Colonialism, Nationalism and Culture* (1988), which argued that Yeats's 'writing and practice' in the period from the 1880s until 1907 was an 'attempt to enable the fusion of the Anglo-Irish with the people-nation'.[24] In Cairns's and Richards' view Yeats had responded to his awareness that a new Ireland was emerging that would marginalize its former ruling caste by seeking to gain cultural power in the country as Anglo-Irish political power waned. And he had done so by attempting to elevate ancient spiritual values to the level of a national ethos in which political differences could be subsumed. In so doing, it can be further argued that Yeats espoused separatism, because the radical freedom of independence would permit a unifying spirituality to be inscribed on a blank slate, as compared with the sectarian and socially divided Irish status quo that mere Home Rule would sustain.

For the biographer this reading of the Yeatsian motivation in this period presents real difficulty. It is all too easy to fall in with the implied judgement it contains which would indict Yeats's literary and cultural endeavours, for all their aesthetic merit, as cunningly opportunistic and involving the self-interested machinations of a vulnerable ruling caste seeking cultural influence where it would be denied social and political power.[25] And to support the indictment sheet, Yeatsian occultism and supernaturalism can be presented as a symbolic indicator of a political unconscious finding florid expression amid a caste whose insecurity in nineteenth-century Ireland had bred a Gothic tradition of ghost-haunted narratives of decline and fall.[26] Yet the colonial and post-colonial narrative into which Yeats can be neatly fitted seems to this biographer too Hiberno-centred a tale fully to contain the amplitude and European range of the poet's imaginings and ambitions. For him, Ireland, for all his engagement with its quotidian affairs, especially when he was engaged in running a national theatre in Dublin and had to contend with the 'daily spite' of an 'unmannerly town',[27] was a site of a possible religious renaissance of much more than merely Irish significance. As he stated himself in a late prose reflection on his life and career, it had been 'through the old Fenian leader' John O'Leary that he had 'found his theme';[28] but he was

> No nationalist, except in Ireland for passing reasons; State and Nation are the work of the intellect, and when you consider what comes before and after them they are, as Victor Hugo said of something or other, not worth the blade of grass God gives for the nest of the linnet.[29]

Whether Yeats's nationalism (compact of esotericism, a distinctive Celticism and a republican instinct that probably owed something to his Protestant independence of mind) is to be explained solely in an Irish colonial and post-colonial context, or whether it must, as I believe is the case, also involve taking his reactive religio-philosophic project seriously on its own terms, however misguided it can seem, it was in Ireland in the years 1898–1907 that the poet saw his hopes for his nation and for civilization founder. In 1898 the commemoration of the United Irish Rebellion fomented no separatist mass movement. The following year Yeats's play *The Countess Cathleen*, the first offering of the Irish Literary Theatre that Yeats had helped to found as part of his cultural crusade for an aesthetic and spiritual renewal, met with Catholic and Nationalist opprobrium. As did John Synge's play *In the Shadow of the Glen* in 1902, serving notice that an aggressive and exclusive variant of nationalism was in formation in the country. For from 1900 onwards what became known as the Irish Ireland movement would propagate a view of national identity based on the Irish language and Catholicism. It cast Yeats's poetry, his Anglo-Irish literature and the Abbey Theatre (founded in 1904 by the poet among a few others to be a centre of a poetic drama in a land where poetry could still count) as non-national, essentially English phenomena, to be absorbed if not extirpated by the authentic Irish tradition. The riot that met the first production of Synge's play *The Playboy of the Western World* in 1907, when its representation of Irish country folk affronted nationalist *amour-propre*, confirmed Yeats in a conviction that the moment when Ireland might have achieved spiritual leadership in the modern world, had passed.

26

Yeats expressed his alienation from the Ireland that had rejected *The Playboy* in an essay written in the year of that debacle. Entitled 'Poetry and Tradition' it reckoned with a new Ireland, affected by a new class of person, which had come into existence, that would 'change the nature of the Irish movement, which, needing no longer great sacrifices, nor bringing any great risk to individuals, could do without exceptional men, and those activities of the mind that are founded on the exceptional moment'.[30] Subsequent events would seem to confirm that judgement and then apparently challenge it in an overwhelming way. Yeats believed the death of Synge in 1909 was hastened by the hostile reception of his masterpiece and, in following years, the unwillingness of Dublin Corporation to provide an appropriate home in the city for a collection of paintings (including work by the French Impressionists) gifted to it by Lady Gregory's nephew Sir Hugh Lane increased the poet's sense of outrage. The new Ireland was materialist and philistine, rejecting those activities of the mind that could form 'exceptional men' capable of sacrificing themselves at the 'exceptional moment'. All this was more than confirmed in 1913 when Dublin Corporation both baulked at a plan to house the Lane collection in a specially designed gallery in the city and did not seriously confront the employing class in the savage industrial lock-out of that year. In a famous poem/lampoon first published as 'Romance in Ireland' (thereafter 'September 1913') in October 1913, Yeats memorably damned the politics of the new Ireland as the politics of 'the greasy till'.[31] The Easter Rising of April 1916 gave the poet profound reasons to reconsider.

That a small group of intellectuals, poets and political activists had risen in armed rebellion against the might of the British Empire in the midst of a great war in which many thousands of Irish men had rallied to imperial colours suggested that exceptional moments and their demand for heroic sacrifice by individuals had not in fact passed. Yeats's response was the composition of his poem 'Easter 1916' that sought to comprehend how individuals he thought representative of the new unheroic, even degraded, political climate, could have been so transformed. Indeed their apotheosis, wrought by the sacrifice of their lives (fifteen of the ringleaders were executed by firing squad following the Rising's swift suppression) was a metamorphosis in history of near supernatural proportions, the kind of thing Yeats had anticipated in the spiritual sphere as the goal of his occult vocation. 'All changed, changed utterly', the awestruck poet averred, as he gave to the language a phrase to trump for ever the disdainful metonymy of 'the greasy till': 'A terrible beauty is born'.[32]

Terror and beauty were to peel apart in Ireland in subsequent years as, in Yeats's sense of things, the country became victim to the kind of levelling democratic spirit of an age he increasingly came to detest. The republic so quixotically declared by the revolutionaries in 1916 gave way by 1922–23 to a viciously destructive civil war which followed a guerrilla campaign to end British rule in Ireland (1919–21) that sometimes involved unalloyed terror. Then the Ireland that emerged from this imbroglio was far from the liberated isle of beauteous spiritual possibility Yeats had imagined as a young man: it was partitioned into two jurisdictions, the one dominated by a political Protestantism (Northern Ireland), the other (the Irish Free State) largely defined in its social and cultural ethos by the Catholicism of the majority of its inhabitants. Although Yeats was to serve as a Senator of the Free State's legislature between 1922 and 1928, key decisions of that body would intensify his suspicion that democracy could mean the oppression of the exceptional at the whim of the prejudiced mob. The Censorship of Publications Act of 1929 was a final straw in a decade in which Yeatsian elitism and libertarianism had been affronted by policies he thought motivated by base sectarianism. Accordingly the 1930s became for the poet a period when Ireland represented not the possibility of a general spiritual renaissance (as in his youth he had thought it had done) but a place where a 'filthy modern tide'[33] ran with particular virulence. It is in this context that we must seek to understand his late elevation of the Anglo-Irish eighteenth century to a kind of imaginary golden age, his willingness to throw in his lot in 1933 with an incipient Irish neo-fascist movement (the Blueshirt movement quickly collapsed in ignominy) and, as he grew old, his avid interest in eugenic theory and practice. In these activities and preoccupations we can further understand the poet as a man of his time, for reactionary recoil from the conditions of modernity and mass society by intellectuals, writers and artists was a feature of cultural life in many parts of Europe in the 1930s, at its most evident in the English-speaking world in the writings of Wyndham Lewis, T.S. Eliot and Ezra Pound. Yeats, disappointed by a country in which he had vested so much hope, convinced by his occult imagining that history was a cycle of decline and violent rebirth, not a progressive teleology, was easily drawn to the elitist, authoritarian versions of the social order that underpin his late work as poet, dramatist and polemicist.

Yet if Yeats's experiment in living in so many ways made him a quintessential man of the period, the biographer is also struck that so many currents of feeling that helped to define his age flowed through him (as T.S. Eliot noted). A sense of his protean presence in a time of extraordinary transition emerges (and this essay has not had the space to consider how Yeats's complex relationships with the opposite sex also reflected the shift in gender relations that took place in his lifetime, a topic dealt with below), that saw the rise of scientific secularism, industrial warfare, the fall of empire, the establishment of new states and of mass democratic society both threatened by fascism. His representative status implies, I am suggesting a kind of greatness, even if we were to ignore how the life he lived is finally more interesting to us as that of a great poet than as that of a great man.

NOTES

1. Joseph Ronsley, 'Yeats's Lecture Notes for "Friends of My Youth"', in *Yeats and the Theatre*, ed. Robert O'Driscoll and Lorna Reynolds (Basingstoke: Macmillan, 1975), p.61.
2. Ibid., p.74.
3. T.S. Eliot, 'The Poetry of W.B. Yeats', in *The Permanence of Yeats*, ed. James Hall and Martin Steinmann (New York: Collier Books, 1961), p.307. Eliot's lecture was delivered in June 1940.
4. Ronsley, 'Yeats's Lecture Notes for "Friends of My Youth"', pp.66–7.
5. Auguste Comte (1798–1857) was opposed to metaphysical speculation and believed that human enquiry should be devoted to 'positive' facts.
6. W.B. Yeats, *Autobiographies* (London: Macmillan, 1955), pp.115–16.
7. *The Collected Letters of W.B. Yeats*, Vol. 1, 1865–1895, ed. John Kelly, associate ed. Eric Domville (Oxford: Clarendon Press, 1986), p.303.
8. The phrase is attributed by Yeats to the communicative spirits in *A Vision* (London: Macmillan, 1937), p.8.
9. Ibid., p.19.
10. See Janet Oppenheim, *The Other World: Spiritualism and Psychical Research in England*

1850–1914 (Cambridge: Cambridge University Press, 1985) for a wide-ranging study of the impact of these preoccupations on cultural and intellectual life in the period.

11. W.B. Yeats, 'The Manuscript of Leo Africanus', ed. Stephen L. Adams and George Mills Harper, in *Yeats Annual*, No. 1, ed. Richard J. Finneran (Basingstoke: Macmillan, 1982), p.39.

12. Yeats, *A Vision*, p.25.

13. T.S. Eliot, 'Ulysses, Order and Myth', *The Dial*, Vol. LXXV (November 1923), p.483.

14. For an excellent account of the role of myth in early twentieth-century literary culture, see Christopher Nash, 'Myth and Modern Literature', in *The Context of English Literature 1900–1930*, ed. Michael Bell (London: Methuen, 1980), pp.160–85.

15. W.B. Yeats, 'Bardic Ireland', in *Uncollected Prose by W.B. Yeats*, 1: *First Reviews and Articles, 1886–1896*, ed. John P. Frayne (London: Macmillan, 1970), pp.163–6.

16. Matthew Arnold, 'The Study of Celtic Literature', in *The Cornhill Magazine*, Vol. 13 (May 1866), p.543. Arnold derived this phrase from the historian Henri Martin.

17. Ibid., p.546.

18. W.B. Yeats, 'The Celtic Element in Literature', in *Essays and Introductions* (London: Macmillan, 1961; New York: Collier, 1968), p.178.

19. Ibid. p.187.

20. Ibid.

21. Ibid.

22. On Yeats's possible initiation into the IRB see Roy Foster, *W.B. Yeats: A Life*, 1: *The Apprentice Mage 1865–1914* (Oxford: Oxford University Press, 1997), pp.112–13.

23. The phrase comes from Yeats's poem 'To Ireland in the Coming Times': *W.B. Yeats: The Poems*, ed. Daniel Albright (London: J.M. Dent, 1990), p.70.

24. David Cairns and Shaun Richards, *Writing Ireland: Colonialism, Nationalism and Culture* (Manchester: Manchester University Press, 1988), p.66.

25. In a famous essay on Yeats's politics, Conor Cruise O'Brien introduced the notion of 'cunning' as a term appropriate to understanding what he thought were the opportunistic aspects of the poet's career. See Conor Cruise O'Brien, 'Passion and Cunning: An Essay on the Politics of W.B. Yeats', in *In Excited Reverie: A Centenary Tribute to William Butler Yeats*, ed. A. Norman Jeffares and K.G.W. Cross (London: Macmillan, 1965), pp.207–78.

26. For a key essay on this topic see R.F. Foster, 'Protestant Magic: W.B. Yeats and the Spell of Irish History', *Proceedings of the British Academy*, 75 (1989), pp.243–66.

27. The phrase is from Yeats's poem 'The People' (*W.B. Yeats: The Poems*, p.199).

28. W.B. Yeats, 'A General Introduction for my Work', in *Essays and Introductions*, p.510.

29. Ibid., p.526.

30. Yeats, 'Poetry and Tradition', ibid., p.259.

31. *W.B. Yeats: The Poems*, p.159.

32. 'Easter 1916', ibid., p.228.

33. The phrase is from Yeats's poem 'The Statues' (ibid., p.385).

CHAPTER THREE

Early Yeats: 'The Essences of Things'

MICHAEL O'NEILL

My subject is Yeats's early poetry, up to and including *The Wind among the Reeds*, especially the way in which this poetry sighs and sings, and occasionally speaks, with a post-Romantic poetic voice. It is a subject complicated by the fact that we know 'early Yeats' often as he was revised by a much later and rather different poet. Still, the lines of allegiance that run back to Shelley and Blake, in particular, are clear, as Harold Bloom has definitively shown.[1] And yet Yeats may be at his most Romantic (one recalls the Romantic rewriting of Dante and Milton) in his remaking of those Romantic poets in his own image and likeness. The beautiful meditation with which 'The Philosophy of Shelley's Poetry' concludes surely tells us more about Yeats than his great precursor:

> ... voices would have told him how there is for every man some
> one scene, some one adventure, some one picture that is the image
> of his secret life, for wisdom first speaks in images, and that this
> one image, if he would but brood over it his life long, would lead
> his soul, disentangled from unmeaning circumstance and the ebb
> and flow of the world, into that far household where the undying
> gods await all whose souls have become simple as flame, whose
> bodies have become quiet as an agate lamp.[2]

True, Shelley speaks at times, and with most majestic eloquence in *Adonais*, of 'The One'.[3] But he is a poet fundamentally at odds with the serenity envisaged in the concluding cadences of Yeats's meditation. The essay turns prose poem. Licensed by his feelings about Shelley's meanings for him, Yeats offers an evocative apologia for his own practice. Applied to

Shelley, the passage loses touch with the restless dynamism, the commitment to process and becoming audible in virtually every line of the Romantic poet's work. Even when Rousseau enjoins 'the shape all light' in The Triumph of Life to 'Pass not away upon the passing stream', we know that the poem's deepest knowledge is that any 'one image' will, especially when the object of fixated delight or longing, inevitably 'pass away'.

But interpreted as oblique self-description, the passage reads as a powerful gloss on Yeats's poetry up to the end of the 1890s. Poem after poem seeks the 'wisdom' that 'speaks in images', or attempts to imagine the 'soul, disentangled from unmeaning circumstance and the ebb and flow of the world', or sets its heart on 'that far household where the undying gods await all whose souls have become simple as flame' (E&I, p.95). Yet it is also the case that Yeats's longing for rest betrays restlessness, that his admiration for simplicity is all too aware of complexity, and that his wish to disentangle the soul from 'unmeaning circumstance' is rarely uncomplicated. The exquisite remodelling of Ronsard's sonnet 'Quand vous serez bien vieille', 'When You are Old', describes a love that has as its object 'the pilgrim soul in you', and the fourfold repetition of 'loved' in the second stanza suggests a love that divests itself of 'unmeaning circumstance'. Yet the love is the more persuasive because it can imagine the beloved, in her old age, as a person as well as essentialized symbol, 'bending down beside the glowing bars': the bars presumably being the bars in the fireplace where a fire is aflame.[4] The 'pilgrim soul' suddenly leaps into intensified life for being associated with quotidian reality.

'The Lake Isle of Innisfree' shimmers in the space between symbol and delight in particularity for its own sake, as it enumerates the poet's imagined possessions: 'Nine bean-rows will I have there, a hive for the honey-bee, / And live alone in the bee-loud glade'. Very possibly, Yeats recalls the Shelleyan Poet from Prometheus Unbound, Act 1, who watches 'The lake-reflected sun illume / The yellow bees i' the ivy-bloom'. Yet just as his draggingly somnolent and august rhythms revise Shelley's impatient tetrameters, so, unlike Shelley's Poet, Yeats does not write as one content neither to 'heed nor see what things they be'. Neither, one might argue, does the creator of Shelley's Poet in any straightforward way. What fascinates is how Yeats creates the aura of symbolic purpose but backs away from the Platonic pursuit of 'Forms more real than living man' evident in the Shelleyan lyric. Again, in 'The Lover tells of the Rose in His Heart' the drive (caught in the sustained use of two rhymes only in the two quatrains) towards internalization of the beloved into an artistic icon worshipped 'in the deeps of my heart' contends with awareness that the poet is shaping self-consciously an 'image'; he is not intuiting a symbolic presence in any unwilled way. Moreover, the poem memorably distracts itself from any too insistent aestheticizing purpose by evoking the appeal and pathos of the ordinary, 'The cry of a child by the roadway, the creak of a lumbering cart'. Caught up in the poem's long-lined chant, the phrases briefly but unforgettably suggest a quasi-Whitmanian celebration of what is seen, ostensibly, as 'wronging your image'. The foremost meaning of 'wronging' here is 'marring', yet the reader may also feel that 'All things uncomely and broken' are themselves 'wronged' by 'your image that blossoms a rose in the deeps of my heart'. Or indeed, one might feel that, here at any rate, two wrongs make a right, that the image would not newly blossom were it not for the countervailing pressures of 'all things worn and old'.

Incantatory, revolving round a single image, 'To the Rose upon the Rood of Time' illustrates the complex ways in which early Yeats seeks to 'become simple as flame'. If Yeats yearns for such a simplified state, he is also the avid student and co-editor of Blake (with Edwin J. Ellis in 1893) who knows about contraries and oppositions. Looking back, Yeats would write in *A Vision*: 'I never read Hegel, but my mind had been full of Blake from boyhood up and I saw the world as a conflict ... and could distinguish between a contrary and a negation'.[5] For Yeats, the Blakean 'contrary' means a positive opposed to another positive, each needing the other. The Rose is the synthesis of such contraries and the intersection point of their conflicts; it folds within itself history and myth, the personal and the archetypal. In the finest earlier poems the writing allows each contrary to assert itself. When Yeats invokes, in 'To the Rose upon the Rood of Time', the '*Red Rose, proud Rose, sad Rose of all my days!*', he calls up a muse that will guide and protect his mystic, nationalist project: '*Come near me, while I sing the ancient ways*'. I say 'mystic, nationalist project' to suggest how Yeats's indebtedness to Rosicrucianism and Hermeticism with its symbolic disciplines (according to which, as Jeffares glosses the matter, store was laid on 'the conjunction of the Rose (with four leaves) and the Cross, making a fifth element, a mystic marriage') involves itself with emerging and post-Parnellite cultural aspirations.[6] In a note on the poem in *The Countess Kathleen* (1892), Yeats notes that 'The Rose is a favourite symbol with the Irish poets ... and is used, not merely in love poems, but in addresses to Ireland, as in ... Mangan's "Dark Rosaleen".' He goes on: 'I do not, of course, use it in this latter sense' (*VP*, pp.798–9). The note did not reappear, and the poet may have decided that he was too hastily restricting the scope of his symbol.

English and Irish Romanticisms criss-cross: James Clarence Mangan's dark Rosaleen and Shelley's Intellectual Beauty lend their colouring and loftiness to Yeats's symbol, as he embarks on a poetry that 'would call down upon us', as he puts it in 'The Symbolism of Poetry', 'certain disembodied powers, whose footsteps over our hearts we call emotions' (*E&I*, p.157). Here Yeats may demonstrate a calculated relish for his use of a redefining and near-ecstatic critical idiom. But the revolutionary nature of his approach, one that insists on examining everything anew (here poetry's commerce with 'emotions'), is striking. His couplets 'To the Rose upon the Rood of Time' imply a marriage between Rose and singer, 'ancient ways' and 'all my days', the seemingly ephemeral ('all poor foolish things that live a day') and the permanent ('Eternal beauty wandering on her way'). That 'Eternal beauty' should be thought of as 'wandering on her way' suggests Yeats's reluctance to Platonize his ideal too definitely. This reluctance begets another, one sounded at the start of the second paragraph:

> Come near, come near, come near – Ah, leave me still
> A little space for the rose-breath to fill!

That 'little space' is one that allows Yeats not to be subsumed wholly by and within his master-symbol of the Rose. Moreover, the 'rose-breath' turns out to be breathed more by poet than symbol, in a subtle adjustment of the power-dynamics existing between the two. In a similar way, if more assertively, Shelley, seemingly in thrall to and close to being abandoned by the wind with whom he strives in a line of monosyllabic force 'As thus with thee in prayer in my sore need', begins to assume the upper hand towards the close of 'Ode to the West Wind'. Pleadings change their nature and become imperatives: 'Be through my lips to unawakened earth // The trumpet of a prophecy'. Yeats's 'Ah, leave me still' is still less command than entreaty, and yet it is typical of the nuanced form in which his sense of Blakean contraries communicates itself in his early work that he both expresses anxiety 'Lest I no more hear common things that crave' and can imagine himself as being left to 'seek alone to hear the strange things said / By God to the bright hearts of those long dead, / And learn to chaunt a tongue men do not know'.

Shelley, too, as a boy held out 'Hopes of high talk with the departed dead' ('Hymn to Intellectual Beauty'). In however idiosyncratic a form, Yeats restores the 'God' whom Shelley includes among 'the false poison-ous names with which our youth is fed' ('Hymn to Intellectual Beauty'). The early work does not merely reiterate a Romantic humanism; it ques-tions such humanism in the light of Yeats's occult studies, which, for this essay's purpose, serve to demonstrate his quasi-Jungian belief in, or hope to believe in, intersubjective collectivities of symbolic experience, and his refusal wholly to eliminate from his vision the intuition of powers at one with and opposed to human needs and desires. In 1925 he would remark that 'the quality symbolised as The Rose differs from the Intellectual Beauty of Shelley and of Spenser in that I have imagined it as suffering with man and not as something pursued and seen from afar'.[7] But his recollection does less than justice to his earlier ability to see the Rose as at once 'suffering with man' and 'as something pursued and seen from afar' – and, indeed, to Shelley's twinned sense of Intellectual Beauty as experienced within 'human thought or form' ('Hymn to Intellectual Beauty'), even if, possibly and enigmatically, originating elsewhere.

In 'Cuchulain's Fight with the Sea', the poetry contrives finely to work in an idiom and a mode that plaits the exaltedly heroic with the humanly suffering. As in a Greek tragedy, the destined outcome – that Cuchulain will kill his son – is already known. Cuchulain, mythic legend in his own life, is also portrayed as vulnerably human, in need, one might suppose, of the admiration of his 'young sweetheart' who 'Stared on the mournful wonder of his eyes, / Even as Spring upon the ancient skies, / And pondered on the glory of his days'. The marmoreal stillness of these sculptured rhythms deliberately misleads in its suggestion of a life that can evoke only elegiacally 'mournful wonder'. Cuchulain's story is not yet over; one grim twist of the plot remains. In all his later poems, one wonders whether Yeats ever managed to depict event and feeling quite so adroitly as in the account of the battle between Cuchulain and the young man who turns out to be his son and believes that 'The dooms of men are in God's hidden place'. It is a place that remains hidden from Cuchulain. In his grave couplets, often setting rhyme and sense in a tensed relationship, Yeats depicts his hero's ineluctable destiny in a scene hard not to allegorize as a meeting of young and old poets, one in which the young Yeats cedes victory to his predecessors and masters them in the process:

> But now the war-rage in Cuchulain woke,
> And through that new blade's guard the old blade broke,
> And pierced him.
> >   'Speak before your breath is done.'
>
> 'Cuchulain I, mighty Cuchulain's son.'
>
> 'I put you from your pain, I can no more.'

That penultimate line works cunningly to identify the son as a version of 'Cuchulain' himself, before the speaker makes clear that he is 'Cuchulain's son'. In breaking through 'that new blade's guard', Cuchulain's 'old blade' has broken itself; the father slaying his son has slain himself, and is left desolately to engage in heroic, futile struggle with 'the invulnerable tide'. The poem speaks of early Yeats's fascination with warring contraries and his proleptic awareness of the necessary defeat of the poet who would maintain a heroic stance amidst modernity: an awareness that lends poignancy to much of his later work.

Style is a means of ennobling tragic defeat in this poem and more widely in many poems in *The Rose*. Yeats's revisions may spring from the understandable but possibly incorrect feeling that that he had been insufficiently alert to the possibilities of heroism. The *locus classicus* of his revisionary practice is 'The Sorrow of Love', reworked by Yeats in the interests of a more 'clamorous', impersonal sense of the tragic. Quarrelling sparrows grow more vociferously as well as singularly 'brawling'; a proto-modernist 'image' seeks to invigorate a more ethereally fin-de-siècle 'cry'; the moon is no longer 'crumbling' but 'climbing'; and 'you' turns into a 'A girl' (all variants quoted from *VP*). The reader experiences a sense of increased mastery, but wonders whether 'mastery' was quite the effect this poem, to speak of it as a singular event, requires. Here is the second stanza as it appeared in *The Countess Kathleen and Various Legends and Lyrics* (1892):

> And then you came with those red mournful lips,
> And with you came the whole of the world's tears,
> And all the sorrows of her labouring ships,
> And all the burden of her myriad years.

The revised version runs:

> A girl arose that had red mournful lips
> And seemed the greatness of the world in tears,
> Doomed like Odysseus and the labouring ships
> And proud as Priam murdered with his peers ...

In the later version, mythological reference is both more explicit (we hear of Odysseus and Priam) and complex (the Helen of Troy-like subject is compared with a Greek survivor and a Trojan victim). In the first version, borne along on subtly wavering rhythms, 'you' simply and unfathomably 'came'; in the second, more apocalyptically, 'A girl arose'. The first version shows Yeats's youthful capacity to slide from the personal into the universal; the second his mature determination to arrest through towering dramatization. In the first version relative modesty of inflection coexists with surprising ambitiousness, as in the line, 'And with you came the whole of the world's tears': 'the whole of the world's tears' is characteristic of the early verse in its readiness to net the 'whole' of the world in its alliterative sweep. By contrast, the revised 'And seemed the greatness of the world in tears' has about it, for all its grandeur, a lurking circumspection. This Yeats is a poet who knows about 'seemed'. Moreover, 'the greatness of the world's tears' is rhetorically splendid, but less intent on making the 'girl' bear the weight of 'the world's tears' than the first version. Arguably, the revision seeks to retain vulnerability ('A girl' is probably intended to emphasize such vulnerability), even as it enhances tragic resonance. But its very stylistic sheen gives it an aura of distanced invulnerability that changes the relationship between that very human 'you' and her burden of significance.

The relationship between early Yeats and later Yeats is finer than that of contrast. *The Wind Among the Reeds* can seem the apogee of artifice and symbolist obscurity. But even amidst the mists of the Celtic Twilight an energy pulses through the verse that transcends anything in, say, Dowson, and reminds us of the resolute extremism of Shelley, Keats and Blake. 'The Hosting of the Sidhe' with which the volume begins has a power which comes across most fully when the poem is read, as it demands to be, as an exultant chant, albeit one tempered by questioning and residual terror:

> The host is riding from Knocknarea
> And over the grave of Clooth-na-Bare;
> Caoilte tossing his burning hair,
> And Niamh calling *Away, come away*:
> *Empty your heart of its mortal dream.*
> *The winds awaken, the leaves whirl round,*
> *Our cheeks are pale, our hair is unbound,*
> *Our breasts are heaving, our eyes are agleam,*
> *Our arms are waving, our lips are apart;*
> *And if any gaze on our rushing band,*
> *We come between him and the deed of his hand,*
> *We come between him and the hope of his heart.*
> The host is rushing 'twixt night and day,
> And where is there hope or deed as fair?
> Caoilte tossing his burning hair,
> And Niamh calling *Away, come away*.

The whole poem, especially the italicized lines voicing Niamh's call towards another world, moves with present-tense urgency. This has much to do with the use of verbs such as 'is riding' and 'are waving' that make of the present a state of tumultuous process; and, complicating this, of a hurried series of appositional clauses that blend both dynamic movement and what feel like permanent states of visionary emotion ('*Our cheeks are pale*', '*our eyes are agleam*'); and, complicating this even further, the mixture of appeal and threat in the voiced invitation: '*And if any gaze on our rushing band, / We come between him and the deed of his hand, / We come between him and the hope of his heart*'. Should Niamh's call be heeded, the lines almost say, the heeder will forfeit all capacity for act, all his deepest hopes. The tug is away from '*mortal dream*' towards a world that is more real but frighteningly so. The Sidhe will '*come between*', in the entrancing, cold menace of that repeated phrase, the gazer and his '*deed*' and '*hope*'. Yeats's movement is from the world of maya into the world of super-natural tumult, from the world where 'nothing is, but all things seem'[8] towards a strange state of unimagined being. If this is escapism, it is escapism with a quietly terrifying apocalyptic twist. The poem, Rilke-like, instructs us, implicitly, to change our lives, but tells us that, in seeking to do so, we may destroy ourselves; hence the Shelleyan device of the rhetorical question that turns out to work in a not wholly rhetorical fashion ('And where is there hope or deed as fair?'). The world of the Sidhe is the world of the imagination conceived as a rebuke to late-Victorian getting and spending, but it is less a Nirvana or elfin grot than a condition of imaginative activity that throws down a gauntlet to all empirical values, and has no particular brief for the indirectly desirable consequences of the Romantic imagination, as Coleridge and Shelley theorize them. The poem leaves us with a repeated invocation of its Irish mythological figures – Caoilte and Niamh – as though to suggest we have been in the presence of male and female archetypes. Embodiments of warrior-like courage and entrancing beauty, they detach themselves from the host, almost like Paolo and Francesca in Dante's episode, moving in their present participial form through the reader's imagination, prin-ciples (and principals) of some intensified mode of being.

The *Wind Among the Reeds* is a poetic challenge to contemporary history made in the name of ancient Irish myth, a revaluation of values that masks itself as quasi-languorous escapism. Quasi-languorous: the book is animated by frictions evident in Yeats's poetics of the period, memorably summarized in 'The Autumn of the Body', among other places. Throughout the essay, there is a distinct twist given to ideas purportedly transmitted from others. So, Yeats concludes by quoting Symons approv-ingly for affirming the Mallarméan notion (as Yeats conceives it via his friend) that 'poetry will henceforth be a poetry of essences, separated one from another in little and intense poems' (E&I, pp. 193–4). Such a description might well be applied to Yeats's early collections, especially The *Wind Among the Reeds*. But his next sentence indicates his wish to remake the world as well as to crystallize moods: 'I think there will be much poetry of this kind, because of an ever more arduous search for an almost disembodied ecstasy, but I think we will not cease to write long poems, but rather that we will write them more and more as our new belief makes the world plastic under our hands again' (E&I, p.194). *The Wind Among the Reeds* does not contain 'long poems', but a concern that it shares with *The Wanderings of Oisin* (Yeats's one major venture of this kind) is the quest to make the 'world plastic under our hands again'.

Preferring the phrase 'the autumn of the body' to describe 'what many call "the decadence"', Yeats speaks of himself as believing that 'the arts lie dreaming of things to come' (E&I, p.191). Those 'things to come' may sound, in the essay, as though composed of Hermetic lore and arcane wisdom, but the emphasis on the poet as growingly self-acknowledged legislator of the world is evident: 'The arts are, I believe', writes Yeats in the wake of Matthew Arnold, 'about to take upon their shoulders the burdens that have fallen upon the shoulders of priests, and to lead us back upon our journey by filling our thoughts with the essences of things, and not with things' (E&I, p.93). Those 'burdens' involve coming to terms with the view, itself expressed through a hesitant syntax, that 'We are, it may be, at a crowning crisis of the world' (E&I, p.192), marked by 'a weariness that will not end until the last autumn, when the stars shall be blown away like withered leaves' (E&I, p.193). The note of *tedium vitae* cannot disguise the Shelleyan lineage, and the 'withered leaves' are blown into Yeats's essay by way of the conclusion of the Romantic poet's 'Ode to the West Wind', where Shelley writes, 'Drive my dead thoughts over the universe / Like withered leaves to quicken a new birth'. Yeats's early poetry, too, is inspired by the 'breath of Autumn's being' ('Ode to the West Wind'), even if it imagines an intensification of the autumnal as the prelude to apocalyptic change.

'Dreaming of things to come' is suggestive of the poetry's approach to reverie. In 'A Philosophy of Shelley's Poetry', Yeats links the Romantic poet's account of 'reverie' in his essay *On Life* with an imputed (and very Yeatsian) sense that 'an image that has transcended particular time and place becomes a symbol, passes beyond death, as it were, and becomes a living soul' (E&I, pp.79–80). As is indicated by that final allusion to Wordsworth's 'Lines Written a Few Miles above Tintern Abbey', in which the Romantic poet imagines how we 'become a living soul',[9] Yeats saw this capacity to transmute image into symbol as a means of inner regeneration and near-quietist insight: but it is a quietism that might bring about the fall of empires. Or such is the implication of one of the most millennial of Yeats's poems in *The Wind Among the Reeds*, 'The Valley of the Black Pig'. In this poem, Yeats assumes the posture of lyric visionary, not only recounting but enacting the experience of vision:

> The dews drop slowly and dreams gather: unknown spears
> Suddenly hurtle before my dream-awakened eyes,
> And then the clash of fallen horsemen and the cries
> Of unknown perishing armies beat about my ears.
> We who still labour by the cromlech on the shore,
> The grey cairn on the hill, when day sinks drowned in dew,
> Being weary of the world's empires, bow down to you,
> Master of the still stars and of the flaming door.

Yeats's note remarks on the 'political force' (*VP*, p.808) possessed by the myth of the Valley of the Black Pig where a battle was supposed to take place in which Ireland's enemies would be routed. The 'we' who are 'weary of the world's empires' includes poets such as Yeats 'fusing occultism and advanced nationalism', as R.F. Foster remarks of the poem originally published as 'Apologia addressed to Ireland in the coming days'.[10] In that poem, Yeats marries his occult devotion to '*the red rose bordered hem / Of her whose history began / Before God made the angelic clan*' (variants from *VP*) to his sense of belonging to '*that company / Who sang to sweeten Ireland's wrong, / Ballad and story, rann and song*', the very music of the lines, along with the word '*rann*',[11] affirming his allegiance to Ireland's visionary '*company*' of poets. 'The Valley of the Black Pig', by contrast, avoids polemic or outright assertion; it chooses, rather, the hieratic authority of images that 'have transcended particular time and place', even as it implies a kinship between the poet's magus-like 'labour' and the origins of history denoted by the 'cromlech' and 'grey cairn'.

This labour is both unrelated and related to the dream battle occurring in the Armageddon-witnessing valley. The 'shore' and 'hill', locations of artistic endeavour, are far removed from the valley of the title. Yet it is to such labourers that the opening vision of historical dissolution, figured by the image of dew, and featuring 'fallen horsemen' and 'unknown perishing armies', discloses itself. The poem plays subtly with contrast between planes of awareness. A micro-instance occurs in the disjunction between 'slowly' in the first line and 'Suddenly' in the second, a disjunction pointed up by the draft's change from 'dreams come' to 'dreams gather'.[12] The revision sharpens a sense of the gap yet link between the slowly gathering dreams and the suddenness of the images that 'hurtle before my dream-awakened eyes'. There is, too, an element of interplay between the fact that the spears like the armies are 'unknown' and the description of 'dream-awakened eyes', itself a quietly paradoxical adjective. Moreover, the poem moves without explicit explanation from the visionary subjectivity of the start to the collective consciousness of the 'We' in line 5, and the mood shifts from a startled if stately onrush of images to an account of the ongoing labour of those, who, seemingly indifferent to history, may in some not wholly disclosed sense hold the key to it. If they do so, it is through their submission to a force that seems like a God conceived in the image and likeness of a symbolist poet, one who is 'Master of the still stars and of the flaming door'. The 'stars' are 'still', and yet 'We ... still labour', a repetition that underlies a signal difference between images symbolic of the Master's power and the need 'We' have to go on working, if only to recreate and uncover that power. Yeats's 'flaming door' may have possessed occult significances, but it also calls to mind the 'flaming brand' (Milton, *Paradise Lost*, XII, 643) by which Michael bars the way back to the Garden of Eden.[13] The Master's 'flaming door' sounds perilous, but it is a 'door'; there is hope, the poem suggests, of some way forward that might take us beyond 'the world's empires' towards some new wisdom: the wisdom found in and by poets.

Such a 'wisdom' has looked highly suspect to many readers. 'What are we to say', asks Auden's Public Prosecutor in 'The Public v. the Late Mr. William Butler Yeats', 'of a man whose earliest writings attempted to revive a belief in fairies and whose favourite themes were legends of barbaric heroes with unpronounceable names, work which has been aptly and wittily described as Chaff about Bran?' Auden's Counsel for the Defence in the same work offers an answer; the poems 'express a sustained protest against the social atomisation caused by industrialism, and both in their ideas and their language a constant struggle to overcome it'.[14] Moreover, Yeats was 'looking for a world religion'.[15] Auden's words of support evidently represent his own attempt to overcome his repugnance to aspects of Yeats's earlier work, and Richard Ellmann's brilliant chapter on his response to Yeats in *Eminent Domain* contains an imaginary dialogue that draws on the writers' texts to pinpoint the fault-lines running between the two poets' positions. Especially relevant to the current essay is the following excerpt:

YEATS: Truth is the dramatic expression of the highest man, of the poet as hero.

AUDEN: The poet no longer fancies himself a hero; he is an explorer of possibility.

YEATS: Say impossibility rather.

AUDEN: All that is passé with the romantic movement, thank God. Crying has gone out, and the cold bath has come in.

YEATS: The whale is extinct and the little fish lie gasping on the strand.[16]

The final allusion is to 'Three Movements', Yeats's terse, three-line account of 'Shakespearean', 'Romantic' and present eras, published in *The Winding Stair*. There, Yeats writes, 'Romantic fish swam in nets coming to the hand', before asking, 'What are all those fish that lie gasping on the strand?' The poem tells a tale of diminishment and difficulty. But if for Yeats, as Ellmann ventriloquizes him, 'Truth is the dramatic expression of the highest man, of the poet as hero', both in the early and the later work the operative word is 'dramatic'; the 'poet as hero' is an idea, and ideal, that is the subject of an endless drama, 'a constant struggle', in the words of Auden's Counsel for the Defence. If the poet as hero required for his validation a 'world religion', then the early poetry gives the sense of 'looking' for, rather than easily finding, such a religion. Heroic gestures can be found in early Yeats; one thinks of the speaker in 'He thinks of those who have Spoken Evil of his Beloved', where, like Shakespeare reassuring the young man of the sonnets that he will be eternized in poetry, Yeats says to Maud Gonne:

They have spoken against you everywhere,
But weigh this song with the great and their pride;
I made it out of a mouthful of air,

Their children's children shall say they have lied.

The control of metre is vital for the effect of technical and emotional mastery here. These four decasyllabic lines contain a mixture of two- and three-stress feet that lends weight to the poet's carefully paced counter-statements. Yeats trumps the notion of insubstantiality conjured by the 'mouthful of air' by suggesting its impact on subsequent generations in the last line, which achieves a quasi-biblical force as it prophesies the response of 'Their children's children'. Yet this heroism depends on our sense of the risky loneliness of the 'I' and his making.

Elsewhere in the early work, there is a less of a gap between the 'poet as hero' and the 'explorer of possibility' than is allowed for in Ellmann's trenchant summary of the difference between Yeats and Auden. Yeats/Oisin may conclude *The Wanderings of Oisin* in a state of defiance, asserting his opposition to religion ('I throw down the chain of small stones' [III], he cries, referring to the rosary) and commitment to nationalism (he will 'dwell in the house of the Fenians, be they in flames or at feast' [III]). But the poem as a whole has spoken of the inability to escape or transcend 'the grey wandering osprey Sorrow' (I), and while it may be the case, as Harold Bloom has it, that 'Oisin is a hero, and his failed quest is Yeats's own',[17] the poem is unnervingly alive to all that challenges its heroic hopes. Of 'The Song of Wandering Aengus', Edward Larrissy, in the course of a fine reading, argues that the 'hazel wand' with which Aengus is fishing has 'magical' associations'; it might be said, therefore, that Aengus is 'asking for something magical to occur – something which will answer to the "fire" of desire in his head'.[18] The poem, as Larrissy has shown, is alive with movement, and this movement, in the end, speaks as subtly of desire unfulfilled as of desire satisfied. Certainly, it imagines a fulfilled state, one seemingly clinched by the internal rhyme between 'long dappled grass' and the 'apples' of moon and sun in the last two lines. But this state is very much one that is imagined. The poem's active verbs have, it is true, managed to spark events that exceed expectation; in the second stanza, after 'I went to blow the fire aflame', 'something rustled on the floor, / And some one called me by my name'. But even so, the possibility of shape-changing illusion cannot wholly be discounted; the 'glimmering girl' mate-rializes and de-materializes in the same moment, as she 'faded through the brightening air', where verb and adjective construct, through their interplay, a miniature version of the poem's subliminal conflict between the aura of promise and the fact of vanishing.

At the close, Yeats makes his scene of fulfilment conditional on endlessly deferred search: 'I will find out where she has gone'. 'I will' bears witness both to the will to find, true to the quietly forceful way in which desire is voiced in the early poetry, and to the fact of futurity. It sets itself against, but has knowledge of, the third stanza's opening sub-clause, 'Though I am old with wandering / Through hollow lands and hilly lands', a sub-clause that posts a warning. Admittedly, the final collocation of 'The silver apples of the moon, / The golden apples of the sun' sounds like a triumph. But in terms familiar from Romantic poetry, the triumph is strictly imaginative, virtual, textual.

Early Yeats wanted to believe that words could shape or overcome or replace worlds. 'A symbol', writes Yeats in 'William Blake and His Illustrations to the *Divine Comedy*', 'is indeed the only possible expression of some invisible essence, a transparent lamp about a spiritual flame'. By comparison with 'allegory', defined 'as one of many possible representations', symbol is 'a revelation', not 'an amusement' (E&I, p.116). Yeats has learned his Coleridgean lesson well, but his symbols are often less forms of revelation than a means of searching, or embodying his search, for revelation. The close of 'The Secret Rose', for example, a poem that revisits the central symbol of the grouping that Yeats would retrospectively (in 1895) call *The Rose*, is among his boldest symbolic adventures. The rose encloses in its 'great leaves' a roll-call of mythological figures, who sweep in proud procession through the poem's flowing couplets. Noticeably unafraid of mixed metaphor when it is expressive of visionary emotion, Yeats endows the rose with the properties of Shelley's West Wind. Bloom notes that 'though he echoes Blake, Yeats ends the poem more in Shelley's skeptical if fierce spirit',[19] and the poem sustains a fine balance between ardently awaiting 'The hour of thy great wind of love and hate' and refusing wholly to commit itself to any apocalyptic 'revelation' to be brought about through its central symbols, symbols that magnetize question-marks to themselves in the conclusion:

> When shall the stars be blown about the sky,
> Like sparks blown out of a smithy, and die?

Surely thine hour has come, thy great wind blows,
Far-off, most secret, and inviolate Rose?

As indicated above, the study of Blake had taught Yeats about Blakean contraries, without which there is no progression. Yet here the progress is towards revelation of inner contradiction. On one hand, Yeats forces Shelley's image of his words as 'Ashes and sparks' ('Ode to the West Wind') to take on an apocalyptic significance. Shelley's sparks will kindle readerly fires where they fall. Yeats's sparks are momentarily emblematic of a world that will fade from sight when the poet's ambivalent belief that 'Words alone are certain good', as he puts it in 'The Song of Sad Shepherd', incarnates itself as Logos-like refashioning of reality. But not until then, the poem says under its subtextual breath. That 'Surely' is 'already more of a question than an assertion',[20] because the poet wishes to keep his words within the realm of representation. Were the 'Far off, most secret, and inviolate Rose' to undergo metamorphosis into, say, a nationalist or political sword, poetry would be obliged to yield up the peculiarly expressive post-Romantic territory it occupies in early Yeats: between highly aestheticized inwardness, and the desire to voice what he took to be the only half-created consciousness of a nation in waiting.

NOTES

1. See Harold Bloom, *Yeats* (London: Oxford University Press, 1970), esp. Chapters 4 and 5, but also *passim*. On the topic of Yeats and Romanticism, see also George Bornstein, *Yeats and Shelley* (Ithaca, NY: Cornell University Press, 1970) and the same author's *Transformations of Romanticism in Yeats, Eliot, and Stevens* (Chicago, IL: University of Chicago Press, 1984) and his 'Yeats and Romanticism', in *The Cambridge Companion to W.B. Yeats*, ed. Marjorie Howes and John Kelly (Cambridge: Cambridge University Press, 2006), pp.19–35; see also Edward Larrissy, *Blake and Modern Literature* (Basingstoke: Palgrave, 2006), and Michael O'Neill, *The All-Sustaining Air: Romantic Legacies and Renewals in British, American, and Irish Poetry since 1900* (Oxford: Oxford University Press, 2007). For an illuminating overview of Yeats's early work that comments on 'the powerful synthesis of Aestheticism, nationalism, and occultism at work in Yeats's early conception of poetry', see Stephen Regan, 'Yeats and the *fin de siècle*', in *Yeats in Context*, ed. David Holderman and Ben Levitas (Cambridge: Cambridge University Press, 2010), p.27.

2. W.B. Yeats, *Essays and Introductions* (London: Macmillan, 1961), p.95; hereafter referred to in the text as E&I.

3. Quoted, as are all Shelley's writings, from Zachary Leader and Michael O'Neill (eds), *Percy Bysshe Shelley: The Major Works* (Oxford: Oxford University Press, 2003; reissued with corrections 2009).

4. Yeats's poetry is quoted from Peter Allt and Russell K. Alspach (eds), *The Variorum Edition of the Poems of W.B. Yeats* (New York: Macmillan, 1957); hereafter *VP*.

5. W.B. Yeats, *A Vision* (London: Macmillan, 1962 [1937]), p.72.

6. *Yeats's Poems*, ed. and annotated A. Norman Jeffares with an appendix by Warwick Gould (London: Macmillan, 1991 [1989]), p.496.

7. *Yeats's Poems*, ed. Jeffares, p.495.

8. Yeats quotes these words from the 'Conclusion' to Shelley's 'The Sensitive Plant' in 'The Philosophy of Shelley's Poetry', *E&I*, p.73.

9. Quoted from Michael O'Neill and Charles Mahoney (eds), *Romantic Poetry: An Annotated Anthology* (Malden, MA: Blackwell, 2007).

10. R.F. Foster, *W.B. Yeats: A Life: 1: The Apprentice Mage: 1865–1914* (Oxford: Oxford University Press, 1997), p.122.

11. The OED derives the word from 'Old Irish'. Jeffares notes that 'rann' is 'a verse of a poem in Irish, not the whole poem': *Yeats's Poems*, ed. Jeffares, p.506.

12. W.B. Yeats, *'The Wind Among the Reeds': Manuscript Materials*, ed. Carolyn Holdsworth (Ithaca, NY: Cornell University Press, 1993), pp.114–15.

13. Quoted from Stephen Orgel and Jonathan Goldberg (eds), *John Milton*, Oxford Authors (Oxford: Oxford University Press, 1991).

14. Edward Mendelson (ed.), *The Early Auden: Poems, Essays, and Dramatic Writings, 1927–1939* (London: Faber, 1977), pp.391, 393.

15. Ibid., p.393.

16. Richard Ellmann, *Eminent Domain: Yeats among Wilde, Joyce, Pound, Eliot, and Auden* (New York: Oxford University Press, 1967), pp.122–3.

17. Bloom, *Yeats*, p.99.

18. Edward Larrissy (ed.), *W.B. Yeats*, Oxford Authors (Oxford: Oxford University Press, 1997), p.xvi.

19. Bloom, *Yeats*, p.132.

20. Ibid.

CHAPTER FOUR

Middle Yeats: In the *Seven Woods* (1903) to *Responsibilities* (1914)

VICKI MAHAFFEY and JOSEPH VALENTE

The critical line on Yeats's middle period developed out of a review of *Responsibilities* by that 'queer creature' and 'solitary volcano' Ezra Pound.[1] What people remember from this review is Pound's appreciation of Yeats's 'change of manner', his argument that Yeats's new poetry has a 'greater hardness of outline' (CH, p.188). The 'hard light' of the middle period has replaced what Pound referred to as the 'glamour' of Yeats's early poems, the magical, misty shimmer of the Celtic twilight. Pound stresses that he has 'not a word against the glamour as it appears in Yeats's early poems', but he claims to be tired of the 1890s style, and even more tired of Yeats's many imitators, with their 'pseudo-glamours and glamourlets'. What Pound celebrates in *Responsibilities* is a change he saw beginning with 'No Second Troy': an engagement with 'things as they are' (p.189).

What is less often remembered is Pound's use of a musical metaphor to describe this modulation in Yeats's work, the emergence of a 'manifestly new note' (p.187). Pound explains that 'with the appearance of "The Green Helmet and Other Poems" one felt that the minor note – I use the word strictly in the musical sense – had gone or was going out of his poetry' (p.188). What is the 'minor note' that Pound referred to as disappearing? First and foremost, it is the note of poignancy, illustrated visually through an always lost, otherworldly beauty, a strain that Pound stresses he admired. But the change is more than a change of tone and style (defiantly asserted in 'A Coat'), and it is even more than a change of key. The most important change affects the structure of reality as it is reflected in Yeats's poems. In his earlier work, Yeats strove to integrate opposite extremes such as darkness and light, time and eternity: such mingling is what produced the impression of twilight and what gave it its distinctively haunting aura. In the middle period, however, Yeats accents the disjunction of opposite extremes, and in this new space between opposing values there is room for irony and even humour. In place of poignancy, we find a vigorous celebration of what is high and low, the extraordinary and the common, and an impatience for anything in the middle: especially the middle class. Yeats's middle period, then, is marked by a disdain for mediation, and a refusal of compromise. The 'middle ground' has dropped away.

By 1910, with the appearance of *The Green Helmet and Other Poems*,[2] Yeats had completed this about-face. Instead of erotic dreaming, we find business; where extremes once mingled and dallied, they have now polarized, and the result is a new briskness and a preference for laughter over longing. This altered mood is nowhere signalled more strongly than in the play *The Green Helmet: An Heroic Farce*, which concluded the first edition of *The Green Helmet and Other Poems*.

Yeats had been used to position Cuchulain as a tragic hero – the inverse of Oedipus who unknowingly destroys the future in the person of his son, and thereafter wars fruitlessly against time itself as embodied by the tide.[3] But in *The Green Helmet* Cuchulain comes to embody the laughing hero, who is nonetheless honourable as well as daring. As the Red Man declares at the end of the play, when Cuchulain has fought his way past Emer to offer his head as a sacrifice, 'I have not come for your hurt ... I choose the laughing lip / That shall not turn from laughing, whatever rise or fall'. As the title implies, the play – unlike the portions of Lady Gregory's *Cuchulain of Muirthemne* on which it is based – is not about determining who is the most powerful champion, but about what kind of individuals should be at the helm of Ireland, and why.[4] Moreover, Yeats's Red Man is compounded of two characters in Lady Gregory's volume: Bricriu, who engenders discord, and Curoi, whose aim is to 'try the heroes through his enchantments', which he does in the guise of Uath, the Stranger, when he claims to be searching for 'a man that will keep his word and will hold to his agreement with me'. In Yeats's play, the redness of this compound figure (especially in contrast to the green clothing of the other characters in the play) suggests England. Allegorically, Yeats implies that England jestingly provokes Ireland to spar with it, but Ireland cannot 'kill' England, even by beheading it. The other way England debilitates Ireland is by instigating 'contests' or championships among the Irish. Those contests destroy Irish unity, which is replaced with infighting made bitter by cowardice and lack of confidence. As Yeats hereby recalls, Irish nationalists had long charged England with a divide-and-conquer strategy, specifically with sowing discord along ethnic and sectarian lines.

A brief précis of the play may help illustrate its farcical concern with leadership – specifically leadership of Ireland – which it symbolizes through the motif of heads. The Red Man is a very tall, red-headed spirit dressed completely in the colour red, although he wears a horned green helmet on his head, as befitting an English power at the helm of Ireland. In contrast, all the other characters (with the exception of the Black Men, who wear dark purple with eared caps) are dressed in various shades of green, like the 'luminous' sea. For example, Cuchulain, the great hero of the Red Branch cycle of Ulster tales, wears 'a long green cloak that covers him up to the chin'. The play begins with two men, Laegaire and Conall, apprehensively waiting for the Red Man to reappear and cut off their heads. They tell Cuchulain that two years ago, they were half-drunk with ale and at the stroke of midnight in came 'a wide, high man with a red foxy cloak, / With half-shut foxy eyes and a great laughing mouth' who was ready to drink the sea (associated through its greenness with Ireland). The three drank and sang and danced together, and then the Red Man offers to show them the best game that ever had been, which he calls 'whip off my head! / Then one of you two stoop down, and I'll whip off his'. He laughs 'as though his sides would split' until Conall gets angry and 'whips off his head at a blow'. The Red Man takes up his head in his hands and walks into the sea. A year to the day after that the Red Man runs up from the sea with his head on his shoulders and demands that Conall and Laegaire pay him his debt. He promises to come again in another twelve-month, which is up that night. The question the men face is 'How can you fight with a head that laughs when you've whipped it off? ... Or a man that can pick it up and carry it out in his hand?'

The allegorical meaning of this farce is fairly clear. England has the wherewithal, the power and the plenty, to treat the struggle with Ireland as a kind of sport, in which any sacrifice or expense can be recompensed from economic and military reserves so vast as to appear magical. Frustrated by the lack of such material abundance, and inflamed by drink, the Irish cannot but regard the struggle as a fight to the death, a fight for survival, a fight they must and yet apparently cannot win. Just as the Red Man is proof against death, England is proof against defeat. The Red Man picks up his head and goes back into (or over) the sea, promising that he'll be back for the head of one of the Irishmen. Analogously, imperial England withdrew its forces again and again upon receiving the debt of fealty from Irish chieftains (the historical compeers of the mythic Cuchulain), and England always returned – under the Tudors, under Cromwell, under George III, under Victoria.

But Yeats, like Curoi in Lady Gregory's version of the tale, is also staging a conflict among the Irish themselves, framed as an agon between two kinds of hero. Conall and Laegaire are fractious, warlike men easily moved to anger and violence (Conall claims he has cut off a hundred heads of cat-headed men from Connaught before daybreak). Even their wives compete over status; they fight about who has the right to take precedence over the others when they come through the door, and dispute over whose man is better than the others. In contrast to these bickering men are the Red Man and also, surprisingly, Cuchulain himself. The Red Man insists that his game was a joke and a juggler's feat, and he himself a kind-hearted Shape-Changer, 'the drinker's friend', who makes the time go quickly'. Instead of cutting off one of their heads, he brings them the gift of the Green Helmet 'for the best of you all to lift'. The helmet represents leadership: not only does it belong on the head, it also suggests being at the helm, or steering a ship, and its greenness associates it with Ireland. The question then becomes, who should lead Ireland? Which of the three is the bravest? Laegaire and Conall start competing for the prize, but Cuchulain fills it with ale and passes it around, saying, 'the Red Man gave it for one, / But I shall give it to all – to all of us three or to none'. He proposes that they drink until they '[s]troke into peace this cat that has come to take our lives', in sharp contrast to Conall, who would cut off the heads of the cat-men, as he cut off that of the Red Man. Cuchulain's proposal is to share power instead of fighting; the novelty of this idea is highlighted when they hear a great noise as 'the charioteers and the kitchen and stable boys' all begin shouting at one another. They, too, are fighting about whose master is best. When the wives wrestle to determine 'who'll be first in the house' Cuchulain refuses to let any of them through the door, instead commanding that they break down the walls of the house so that each wife can come in at her own door, for 'One is as fair as the other, each one the wife of a king'. Strangely, in light of his reputation as a lone fighter whose allegiance cannot be bound by oaths, Yeats here presents Cuchulain's leadership as democratic. He advocates that the men and their wives and their servants all work together to keep the Red Man (or England) from inciting them to strive against one another.

The Red Man demands that some man kneel down and let him cut off his head, and Cuchulain does so. He then leavens his bravery with verbal humour, referring to the Red Man as 'old radish', and the Red Man returns the favour, giving Cuchulain's sacrificial gesture a punning significance. Instead of decapitating the Hound, he crowns him with the Green Helmet, thus suggesting that he who is willing to part with his head for the sake of the community is worthy to become the head of that community. He symbolically puts Cuchulain at the helm of Ireland, making him an embodiment of Yeats's new vision of what the Irish could (and should) be like, and how they might work together with a strong and not entirely ill-intentioned England to create an Ireland not handicapped by internal bickering.

This revamped, green-helmeted Cuchulain epitomizes the turn in Yeats's values in the middle period, emphasizing the premium he placed on energy, inventiveness, humour and adherence to principle without anxiety over the outcome. Cuchulain is part of an elite (there are very few like him), but he is not an elitist; it is the fractious 'common' warriors like Conall and Laegaire and all the wives and servants who worry and even fight about who is 'best', who should come first in public exhibitions of importance and prestige. Cuchulain is not only democratic, he is concerned with creating harmony among those jockeying for dominance, which he does by creating doors for all to be equal and by turning the Green Helmet, the prize for the best man, into a drinking cup they can share. His desire to foster a cooperative community does not make him a middle man, however; unlike the middle class, he

is heedless about profit or loss, and he does not compromise his principles. This image of a strong, daring, laughing Cuchulain dressed all in
green, offering his head to the enemy to save his country from 'wrack',
represents Yeats's new poetic vision for Ireland. Announced in his first
great essay of the middle period, 'Poetry and Tradition', this embrace of
a vitalizing 'recklessness' illuminates the tone of the middle poems,
especially those in *The Green Helmet and Other Poems* and *Responsibilities*.

The Cuchulain of *The Green Helmet* helps us formulate the crucial
difference between the common good and the common way. Cuchulain
is a champion of the common good, but he cannot implement it by
following the common way, because the common way is too concerned
with personal profit and the competition it engenders to promote the
common good. Understood in relation to the new Cuchulain, Maud
Gonne's symbolic meaning also undergoes a change: as a modern Helen
of Troy, she emerges as Cuchulain's counterpart and antithesis, promoting
(in the name of the common good) a divisiveness that could produce
widespread destruction.[5] Yeats captures his twin admiration for, and horror
of, Maud/Helen as a noble but destructive force in his incomparable sonnet, 'No Second Troy'. Maud would overturn the world order, hurling 'the
little streets upon the great'; her ways are not small, middle-class ones;
she is uninterested in compromise and she, like Cuchulain, does not
reckon up the consequences. Like him, she is not common: the taut
weapon of her beauty, poised to send forth a deadly arrow, her fiery
nobleness, her high, lone sternness are 'not natural in an age like this'.
But unlike the green-helmeted Cuchulain, she lacks the humour that can
interrupt bitterness or the leadership that abolishes faction. Instead, she
tries to teach 'to ignorant men most violent ways'. The entire poem represents Yeats's attempt not to blame her for 'being what she is', while
retaining his own passionate conviction that violence and destruction
can never produce a common good.

In 'No Second Troy', Maud/Helen, like the poet-speaker(s) elsewhere
in the volume, is both high ('high and solitary and most stern') and low
(identified with the 'little streets' she would hurl upon the great). She,
too, knows no 'middle' way. Similarly, Yeats aligns himself with what is
high and what is low, chafing when forced to chart a middle path. In 'The
Fascination of What's Difficult', he identifies himself (and his poetic

inspiration) with Pegasus, 'our colt' with 'holy blood' that 'on Olympus leaped from cloud to cloud'. With wonderful clanking rhymes (on '-cult', 'colt', 'jolt', 'dolt' and 'bolt'), the speaker deplores the way his winged horse is weighed down, lashed and made to do dull work, to 'Shiver under the lash, strain, sweat and jot / As though it dragged road-metal'.⁶ He identifies this work with managing the Abbey theatre, cursing 'plays / That have to be set up fifty ways' along with 'the day's war with every knave and dolt'. In the final couplet, he asserts his determination to set his colt free to fly again: 'I swear before the dawn comes round again / I'll find the stable and pull out the bolt'.

In contrast to 'The Fascination of What's Difficult', and its desire to fly free of the conflicts that weigh down inspiration, the poem that most emphatically embraces lowness is 'All Things Can Tempt Me'. Here, it is 'the craft of verse' rather than the challenge of staging plays that is the 'accustomed toil'. In this poem, what he wants is not to set his inspiration free to fly unrestrained, but to lie low and be mute, declaring that 'could I but have my wish, / [I would be] Colder and dumber and deafer than a fish'. Strikingly, there is a new comedy apparent in these poems: the vision of Yeats longing for the peace of a cold, deaf-and-dumb fish is wryly humorous, as are the clanking rhymes in his sonnet-complaint against theatre work. There is even something faintly comic in the repeated phrase 'knave and dolt' as an old-fashioned, punchy denunciation of rogues and fools. What we see in *The Green Helmet and Other Poems* is greater perspective, a growing intellectual distance from the 'middle way'.

The 'high' extreme in *The Green Helmet* is most often associated with things that fly: not only with Pegasus, the winged horse of inspiration, but also with the eagle that can stare unblinking and laughingly at the sun, as we can see most clearly in 'Upon a House Shaken by the Land Agitation'. The question Yeats asks in this poem – and it *is* a question, even if a rhetorical one – is how would the world be luckier if Lady Gregory's house at Coole Park went to ruin? He begins with the plausible tenet that freedom from economic worry promotes laughter, sweet thought and easeful writing, a position not so different from that of Virginia Woolf in *A Room of One's Own*. What is bred in such surroundings are 'laughing eagle thoughts that grow / Where wings have memory of wings'. The poem circles around the distribution of 'luck' and 'gifts'; in this house, inhabitants have enjoyed 'the gifts that govern men', as well as 'gradual Time's last gift, a written speech / Wrought of high laughter, loveliness and ease', but even if the house were to fall, thereby making the '[m]ean roof-trees' of peasant cottages sturdier, could it make them lucky? The poem suggests that those 'high' gifts that allow someone to govern and to write are gifts of fortune, in both senses of the term: luck and money. In the big house, people have long enjoyed the privilege of a passion united with precision, and in some instances that privilege helps them to look without blinking on the sun, and to laugh at its destructive power, much like Cuchulain when offering his head to the 'old radish' that the others fear.

What Yeats resists in 'Upon a House' is the discourse that would place all things 'at one common level', that would not only find a middle ground, but would reduce everything to it. In order to clear out this level space or space of levelling, however, Yeats elided the social and economic 'medium' that already existed between the cottages and the Big House, treating them as if they occupied parallel universes, the one fortunate and the other less so. In his focus on hierarchy and the social distance it creates, he occults the persistent connection between these high and the low estates, a connection grounded in political and economic power and the material fruits thereof. His poem forgets that to 'govern men' is not just an exercise in god-given or natural 'gifts', but a means for securing and enhancing all manner of social gifts – style, leisure, 'loveliness and ease', even the laughing insouciance he so prizes. It would not be too much to say that the aristocracy receives such benefactions in part from the tenant-farmers themselves, in the form of service, rent and reflected glory. Moreover, luck and money combine into good fortune, not by contingency alone, but through the social institution of inheritance ('where wings have memory of wings'), the restricted transmission of private property and cultural capital – like Coole Park itself – which ensures the reproduction of class dominance and dependency. So if the 'mean roof-trees' made 'sturdier' by a levelling wind can never, as Yeats assures us, compass the 'luck' of the genteel mansions, it is because no group can be counted on to buttress them as the peasants themselves have buttressed the Big House.

Yeats is on considerably sounder footing when he defines the middle specifically as the middle class, who lack the constancy and daring that Yeats increasingly found in both the nobility and the folk:

> Aristocracies have made beautiful manners, because their place in the world puts them above the fear of life, and the countrymen have made beautiful stories and beliefs because they have nothing to lose and so do not fear … The [middling] others, being always anxious, have come to possess little that is good in itself, and are always changing from thing to thing, for whatever they do or have must be a means to something else.[7]

It is the fickleness of a middle-class audience, that 'Proteus / That turns and changes like his draughty seas', that Yeats would 'bridle'. As he complains (in the rhythm of Ronsard)[8] in 'At the Abbey Theatre', their audience is irrationally oppositional, protesting when the plays are 'high and airy', but when presented with an 'art of common things', they complain that the subject matter isn't higher, as if 'they longed to look / All their lives through into some drift of wings'. Yeats identifies his enemy as 'the merchant and the clerk', who 'Breathed on the world with timid breath' ('At Galway Races'). In short, Yeats is looking for the carefree daring he attributed to Cuchulain in The Green Helmet, and spurning the calculating, timid, divisive spirit that is always on the lookout for its own advantage.

When Yeats turns to Responsibilities,[9] importing several poems from The Green Helmet and Other Poems into this new volume, he leaves the heroic ideal (epitomized by a careless, laughing, but true-to-his-word Cuchulain) behind him. Instead of making the hero an embodiment of his values, Yeats instead embraces the outcast, especially the fool, the beggar and the ghost. In Responsibilities, Yeats is less interested in leadership than in meaning, and that meaning is here more spiritual than heroic, encompassing not only the natural world but also the supernatural. In this volume, Cuchulain's symbolic place is taken by the sky and its inhabitants: the bird, especially the eagle, the ghost, and even the angel. Yeats's enemy is materialism, avarice and the narrow-mindedness he sees them as fostering. In Responsibilities, Yeats looks up to the heavens and down to fools and beggars in a sustained attempt to expose the deception involved in sleeping with the 'foul witch' of riches ('The Witch') or consorting with the over-cautious, thrifty and sometimes spiteful Biddys and Paudeens.

Instead, he embraces 'the pride of the eye' symbolized by the peacock, celebrating the man whose gay ghost cares nothing for riches, because even in desolate rocky surroundings, he can find feathers to furnish his imagination. Yeats spurns a world in which all his *priceless things / Are but a post the passing dogs defile*' (closing rhyme), talking instead to the spirits of past and future, looking everywhere for a wild and unmediated conjunction of highest and lowest, an 'uncontrollable mystery on the bestial floor' ('The Magi').

Responsibilities is in several respects a counterpart to Joyce's *Dubliners*, published the same year (1914). Both target the prevalence of timidity, hopelessness and greed – the attempt to market what is spiritual and therefore unable to be owned or transferred – but Joyce has more distance on his Dublin (literally as well as figuratively; he was living in Italy), and that distance allows for a steadier compassion, free from anger, for the lower-middle-class characters whose blindness nonetheless entraps them. Yeats, writing amid the fray, is feeling attacked, and he therefore satirizes and diminishes the smallness of his attackers, reducing them to stereotypes that 'fumble in a greasy till' and live only to 'pray and save' ('September 1913'). With characteristic fairmindedness, however, he also reprimands himself for his irritation at them, reminding himself that 'There cannot be ... / A single soul that lacks a sweet crystalline cry' ('Paudeen').

On first reading, *Responsibilities* seems closely engaged with worldly controversies – with current events, such as Hugh Lane's proposed gift of art for the Dublin Municipal Gallery and the controversy that ensued from it, or the lockout of strikers that prompted Yeats to respond with 'September 1913', the riots over Synge's *The Playboy of the Western World*, or Yeats's annoyance with his imitators ('A Coat'). But what actually unifies the volume is an exhortation to live more intensely – but peacefully, without wrangling, protest and violence. Yeats champions vitality, a fearless, laughing willingness to take on the most difficult challenges, while weighing 'lightly' what one gives ('September 1913'). His ideal Irishman denies nothing, entertaining the most extreme aspects of human existence – irrational and poetic as well as rational – with the same passionate attention.

In *The Hour-Glass*, the one-act play bound with the poems in the first edition of *Responsibilities*, the fullness of life becomes apparent to the reputed 'Wise Man' only when he learns he has one more hour to live. An angel appears to the man who had argued against the existence of God, announcing that both heaven and purgatory are barred to him because he denied their existence; instead, the Wise Man's eternal lot is hell, which is the knowledge of having denied the possibility of happiness and the hope of purgation. The Wise Man had successfully convinced everyone around him, including his pupils, that 'there is no God and no soul';[10] but the play refutes his position: not through argument and scientific proof, but with visions and images. Interestingly, the play suggests that the spiritual world exists in diametrical opposition to the earthly one, like Tir na nOg, the Country of the Young, in Irish mythology. This is the meaning of the passage the students choose for their lesson with the master, written by a beggar upon the walls of Babylon, a passage that displeases him: 'There are two living countries, one visible and one invisible, and when it is summer there, it is winter here, and when it is November with us, it is lambing-time there' (CPl, p.197). The fool treats the passage as an obvious truth: he knows that, to quote Oscar Wilde, 'a truth in art is that whose contrary is also true'. The Wise Man has twice dreamed about this passage, which if true would mean that 'all we have done would be undone, / Our speculation but as the wind' (p.198). But he has denied the truth of dreams, and in so doing disputed the contra-dictory structure of reality, thereby losing its poetry as well as its folly. He cannot see the daily miracles that for Teigue (whose name means 'poet' in Irish) are commonplace, such as the fall of night, which Teigue describes as black-dressed men who diurnally spread great black nets over the hills to catch the feet of the angels (p.200). As the angel puts it, the Wise Man has lost his soul, which is why he fears death. Soul cries out in joy, 'laughing on its lonely precipice'; it 'trembles with delight' (p.202). The Wise Man dies, but regains his soul, which flies from his mouth as a butterfly, and Teigue, who can 'hear the wind a-blow', and 'hear the grass a-grow' refuses to tell his what he knows, and runs away.

What the inclusion of *The Hour-Glass* with the poems of *Responsibilities* helps to show is the meaning of the epigraphs: 'In dreams begins responsibility' and 'How am I fallen from myself, for a long time now / I have not seen the Prince of Chang in my dreams' (attributed to

Khoung-Fou-Tseu). Pound was right when he said that 'the minor note' was disappearing from Yeats's poetry, but when he says that Yeats is engaging with 'things as they are', he can easily be misinterpreted as attributing to Yeats a new realism. This is a misinterpretation because it fails to specify how Yeats approaches the real: he embraces a different, newly bare and rocky landscape, which seems to signify a less comfortable reality, but he nonetheless sustains a determination to balance worldly responsibility with dream. He looks at reality through two lenses: that of the sceptic, but also (with full awareness that these two views are incompatible) that of the poetic fool and mystic.

The love of life that emerges in *The Hour-Glass* through the prospect of imminent death continues to express itself through the two poems addressed to dead men with which *Responsibilities* begins. In the initial framing rhyme, '*Pardon, old fathers*', Yeats asks his dead ancestors to pardon him for not having given biological life to a child that would 'prove your blood and mine', explaining that he has instead poured his life into 'a book'. Then, in the next poem, 'The Grey Rock', Yeats offers a complexly framed story designed to illustrate his commitment to a life that is both imagined and real, mythological and lived. Addressing himself to the now-dead poets of the Rhymers club who met at the Cheshire Cheese in London in the 1890s to discuss their poetry, he declares his faith in peace over war, in 'passion / That has more life in it than death'. In his poem, Yeats celebrates the vitality of 'wine, women, and song' in a darker and more complex way than was immortalized by Dowson, one of Yeats's addressees, in his 'Villanelle of the Poet's Road'. Paradoxically, Yeats is speaking to ghosts about the importance of life, which he presents as far preferable to 'sword-strokes'. He explains that these dead compatriots and fellow-writers will better understand his theme than his Irish contemporaries, so he proposes to tell them a story he has remade. His tale is a retelling of an episode in Lady Gregory's *Gods and Fighting Men* about Aoibheal of Craig Liath in Clare, whom Yeats renames Aoife of the Grey Rock. It may be significant that Yeats takes Aoibheal, a banshee, and gives her the name of Aoife, the woman who bore Cuchulain his only son, whom Cuchulain subsequently killed, because it keeps the unseen world of mythic Irish heroism at play behind the tale of battle – here the battle of Clontarf – that he is about to relate.

Again, as in 'Pardon, old fathers', an underlying issue is the lack of an heir, here for the High King of Ireland, since the story told in the poem concerns the death of Brian Boru and his son Murchad (here Murrough) in the Battle of Clontarf in 1014. The death of both Boru and his son – which left the throne of the High King empty – threw the Irish back into fractiousness and disunity (recalling the problems with leadership Yeats addressed in his play The Green Helmet). In the poem, Aoife exhorts the Celtic gods at Slievenamon to help her dig up, mock and then harry the dead man she loves, who betrayed her by dying in the battle. She had tried to save her lover by making him invisible (by pushing a pin into his shirt), which helped Ireland win by frightening the Danes into a retreat. However, her lover refused to remain unseen (and therefore invincible) when he met Murrough and saw his wounds. Aoife mourns, 'He claimed his country's need was most', thereby breaking her heart and igniting her desire to revenge herself upon his corpse. The gods drench Aoife with Goban's wine, which clears her memory and restores her gladness of heart, so that she 'Stare[s] at the gods with laughing lip'.

What makes the poem difficult, though, are the many layers of identification Yeats builds into it. First, he identifies himself as the antithesis of Aoife's dead lover, who was lured by solidarity with the other fighters and his country's need into lethal fighting. Unlike that man, whom Aoife believed to have betrayed her, Yeats declares that he has 'kept [his] faith, though faith was tried', to her and her 'rock-born, rock-wandering foot', a faith he kept by preferring lover's music to sword-strokes. This has meant he is 'in no good repute' with the martial masses, 'that loud host before the sea'. Second, he identifies himself with those who can envision – in death or in dreams – that aftermath of such a god-banquet, which includes Maud Gonne and his now-dead 'tavern comrades'. He reminds his hearers that to see it would daze and terrify the viewer, because a vision of the sidhe will empty 'all our days to come'. This is the effect it had on the woman he recalls, whom 'none could please, Because she dreamed when but a child / Of men and women made like these'. By implication he too has been seduced by a bigger, more heroic vision of godlike humans, and he suggests that maybe his old friends, being dead and therefore free of 'bone and muscle', have encountered such visions in the spirit world. Although they died young, they, too, shared the speaker's values: they 'never made a poorer song / That

[they] *might have a heavier purse, / Nor gave loud service to a cause / That [they] might have a troop of friends.'* What makes these friends his real compatriots is not only that the world has forgotten them, but more importantly that they *'kept the Muses' sterner laws, / And unrepenting faced [their] ends'.* Because of what all dreamed, they were as steady as rocks in their devotion. And that devotion was above all to life and laughter, not to mortal combat.

Responsibilities ranges in tone from bitterness and anger to defiance and even ecstasy. The poet's strongest allegiances are to the rocks and the wind, despite the fact that they can be hard and cruel, respectively. The end of the volume is peopled primarily by hermits and beggars, sleepers and idlers, as well as the cranes, eagles, rooks and peacocks of the sky. Perhaps the most sought-after desire is to achieve the exultation the speaker recommends to Lady Gregory in 'To a Friend whose Work has come to Nothing':

> Bred to a harder thing
> Than Triumph, turn away
> And like a laughing string
> Whereon mad fingers play
> Amid a place of stone,
> Be secret and exult,
> Because of all things known
> That is the most difficult.[11]

A version of this same isolated, unobserved, determined joy is again celebrated in 'The Three Hermits' in the person of the third hermit, who, 'Giddy with his hundredth year, / Sang unnoticed like a bird'. It emerges yet again in 'Running to Paradise', in which the speaker appreciates his 'friend' the wind, a connection underscored by rhyme, because it is 'old and still at play' and 'nobody can buy or bind' it (*CW* I, p.115, although wind also makes a 'monstrous crying' that expresses disillusionment and loss, p.121). Books and paintings by men who imagine and dream of fantastic beauties and terrors, 'dolphin-drawn / Sea-nymphs in their pearly wagons' can 'awake a hope to live / That had gone / With the dragons' (p.119).

At the other extreme from joy in isolation is bitterness at the world's disappointments. In 'To a Shade', the ghost of Parnell is evoked and then dismissed; he is advised to return to his grave and pull up his 'coverlet' of earth in Glasnevin cemetery, because the Irish who caused him sorrow are at their old tricks (p.109). Although the immediate impulse behind the poem is anger at the unnamed William Martin Murphy, an old enemy of Parnell who also opposed Hugh Lane's gift of art to Dublin (a failed effort that Yeats deplores in several poems), it nonetheless acknowledges the visionary generosity of people of Parnell's 'own passionate serving kind' who care for the future, hoping to give 'their children's children loftier thought' and 'Sweeter emotion' (p.109). The crowds who rioted at the performance of Synge's *The Playboy of the Western World* are compared to eunuchs in Hell running to stare upon and rail against Don Juan's 'sinewy thigh' (p.110), and Yeats ruminates on how he could have warned the 'Child dancing in the Wind' against the inevitability with which the world betrays the innocent and joyful (p.121).

Another theme that runs through *Responsibilities* is, of course, the theme of desire, which becomes increasingly prominent as the volume progresses. In 'The Three Beggars', Yeats frames his poetic narrative with two comments by the old crane of Gort that highlights its moral about desire: 'men who least desire get most' (p.111). The wet and hungry crane hopes that she shall take a trout if she does not 'seem to care'; the beggars, in contrast, opine that 'They get the most / Whom man or devil cannot tire'. In other words, they believe that those who most desire get the most, but King Guaire proves them wrong by promising a thousand pounds to the one who falls asleep first. In practice, the three beggars 'cannot tire'; the first night they are kept awake by 'The exorbitant dreams of beggary', and thereafter they keep each other awake, each trying to prevent the others from winning the reward. The danger of wanting *too little*, however, is illustrated by 'The Hour before Dawn', when another beggar finds a sleeper in a hole, drunk on the beer of the sidhe, near where Queen Maeve's home had been 'long years ago'. This man has given up on life altogether, since it must end, and the beggar pummels him, covers up the hole with stones, and gives God thanks that he has escaped.

A cluster of ecstatic poems about Maud Gonne – 'A Memory of Youth', 'Fallen Majesty', 'Friends', 'The Cold Heaven' and 'That the Night

Come' – recall and renew the power of his admiration and desire for her, as he maps the brilliance of their 'high' love in relation to the heavens. As many commentators have noted, 'A Memory of Youth' is a rewriting of 'Adam's Curse'. Instead of the weary-hearted 'hollow moon', Yeats describes Love's moon as 'marvellous', telling how it had been 'hid away' by 'A cloud blown from the cut-throat north' and how they 'could find / Nothing but darkness overhead'. As they 'sat silent as a stone', about to be 'savagely undone', they hear the 'cry / Of a most ridiculous little bird', whereupon Love 'Tore from the clouds his marvellous moon' (CW I, p.122). In 'Fallen Majesty', Yeats's hand records a memory of Gonne as 'a burning cloud' that walked the streets, and in 'Friends' he appreciates her 'eagle look' that still shows. Memory of his love is awakened in 'The Cold Heaven' by gazing at the winter sky, and the speaker himself is 'Riddled with light'.

Gonne's disdain for 'The common good of life' in 'That the Night Come' is used to explain the 'storm and strife' in which she lived, impatient 'For what proud death may bring'. This poem initiates a defiant, prolonged poetic climax in which Yeats repeats his major themes: disdain for 'the tame will', the 'timid brain', and 'heavy knitting of the brow'; the spiritual and animal revelation made possible through dream and sky-watching ('The Magi'); the tension between life and its imitators ('The Dolls'); the announcement of a new, bare style ('A Coat'); and finally the bitterness of the poet's feelings about being considered 'Notorious', with all 'his priceless things' reduced to 'a post the passing dogs defile' ('Closing Rhyme').

Yeats's middle period is defined by a disdain for mediocrity and the calculated timidity, greed and fractiousness he associated with it. His commitment is to the bold and carefree, whether those virtues are embodied by the young, the penniless, or the birds, who sing (poet-like) from the heights or who stare unblinking at the sun. Both Cuchulain of *The Green Helmet* and the fool of *The Hour-Glass* epitomize the willingness to use imagination and dream to revitalize the world and to steer it towards peace and forgetfulness of past wrongs. Most strikingly, perhaps, Yeats in *Responsibilities* identifies himself with a certain kind of audience: he reviles the audience who hated Synge's play (the eunuchs of hell) as well as the portion of his own audience that imitated the fashion of his poems, identifying instead with laughing, trembling or intense watchers of the heavens. His (dead but hard-living) companions of the Cheshire Cheese, a name that cannot be said without a smile given its associations with Lewis Carroll's Cheshire Cat and the way the word 'cheese' causes the mouth to broaden, comprise one such audience. Maud Gonne, who like him formed her expectations for the future on her visions of mythological heroes of the past, is another. Yeats himself, looking at the 'cold and rook-delighting heaven' until heart and imagination are driven wild, or experiencing sweetness flowing from his heart's root until he shakes from 'head to foot' at break of day, is yet another. When dolls catch sight of the doll-maker's baby, they scream in protest, objecting to its vitality as 'filthy'; this is a bitter parody of the kind of audience Yeats spurns. His ideal audience might be identified as ancient yet contemporary Magi, waiting in the 'blue depth of the sky' in the hope of finding once more that startling conjunction of bestial, human and divine: 'The uncontrollable mystery on the bestial floor'. Tapping into a tradition that the Magi who visited the infant Christ might have been astrologers, Yeats describes them almost like human stars themselves. According to a commentary on the book of Matthew,

> the magi are extraordinary visitors ... Magos designated originally a member of a priestly caste of the Medes and Persians (Zoroastrians) who specialized in interpreting dreams ... Later the word came to be used of those who possessed superior knowledge and ability, including astrologers, oriental sages, and soothsayers in general ... it also became a label for all 'sorcerers' and 'magicians' ... and finally for 'quacks', 'deceivers', and 'seducers'.[12]

Yeats's Magi anticipate, and in some ways oppose, the ancient Chinamen in 'Lapis Lazuli'; instead of being small, they are large; instead of gay, they are 'pale' and 'unsatisfied'. In 'stiff, painted clothes', their heads encased in 'helms of silver', their 'ancient faces like rain-beaten stones', they search for something far below them, something as new, vital, animal and energetic as they are old and stiff. According to Matthew, the Magi were inspired to begin their journey by a dream; their unexpected discovery of a divine infant surrounded by beasts was the fulfilment of that dream. This is the kind of audience Yeats yearns for: one that is wise in a way that some might call foolish, one comprised of visionaries (who might be dismissed as deceivers), one that refuses compromise and is unsatisfied by death ('Calvary's turbulence'), but proudly and tirelessly seeks to find a rebirth of contradictory, uncontrollable life.

NOTES

1. Yeats described Pound as a 'queer creature' in October 1909; he characterized him as a 'solitary volcano' to Mrs Shakespear and Dorothy (later Dorothy Shakespear Pound) on 11 May 1914. See A. Norman Jeffares (ed.), *W. B. Yeats: The Critical Heritage* (London and Boston, MA: Routledge & Kegan Paul, 1977), p.186; hereafter referred to in the text as CH followed by page number.

2. W.B. Yeats, *The Green Helmet and Other Poems* (Dundrum: Cuala Press, 1910).

3. See 'Cuchulain's Fight with the Sea', in Richard J. Finneran (ed.), *The Collected Works of W.B. Yeats*, I, *The Poems*, 2nd edn (New York: Scribners, 1997), pp.29–31; and *On Baile's Strand*, in David R. Clark and Rosalind E. Clark (eds), *The Collected Works of W.B. Yeats*, III, *The Plays* (New York: Scribners, 2001), pp.151–74.

4. See 'Bricriu's Feast, and the War of Words of the Women of Ulster' and 'The Championship of Ulster' in *Cuchulain of Muirthemne*, in: W.B. Yeats and Lady Gregory, *A Treasury of Irish Myth, Legend, and Folklore* (New York: Gramercy Books, 1986), pp.392–425.

5. This view of Yeats's relationship with Maud Gonne in *The Green Helmet and Other Poems* runs counter to those who emphasize Raymond Lully (Ramón Llull) and his Wife Pernella as a model for the Yeats–Gonne 'mystic marriage'.

6. To 'fascinate' is to bewitch, enchant. Yeats's inspiration has been bewitched by the difficulty of managing the theatre.

7. W.B. Yeats, 'Poetry and Tradition', in *Essays and Introductions* (New York: Collier, 1968), p.251.

8. The French poet, Pierre de Ronsard (1524–85), was known for his metrical inventiveness.

9. W.B. Yeats, *Responsibilities* (Dundrum: Cuala Press, 1914).

10. David R. Clark and Rosalind E. Clark (eds), *The Collected Works of W.B. Yeats*, III, *The Plays* (New York: Scribners, 2001), p.196; hereafter referred to in the text as CPl followed by page number.

11. Richard J. Finneran (ed.), *The Collected Works of W.B. Yeats*, I, *The Poems*, 2nd edn (New York: Scribners, 1997), p.108; hereafter referred to in the text as CW I, followed by page number.

12. Dale C. Allison and W.D. Davies, *Matthew: A Shorter Commentary* (New York: Continuum, 2004), p.21.

CHAPTER FIVE

The Wild Swans at Coole (1919) and Michael Robartes and the Dancer (1921): Gender, History and the Esoteric

EDWARD LARRISSY

It verges on the fatuous to speak of particular volumes of poems by Yeats as 'transitional'. This is a poet who wishes constantly to move forward, discovering new topics and new ways of addressing and framing old ones. To put it another way, Yeats's philosophy of conflict militates against standing still. For contrary or conflictual principles do not always stay the same or always repeat the same battle: out of the conflict new states are constantly being created, and these become the stage for a new range of creative conflict. Nevertheless, in contemplating the two volumes, The Wild Swans at Coole (1919) and Michael Robartes and the Dancer (1921), one is struck by the extremity of the contrast with the Yeats of twenty years previously, and one also notes, as we shall see, the development of characteristics that were to remain in place for the rest of his life. It is understandable that Eliot should have cited the style of the title poem of the first volume as evidence of a profound change. Yet it is not only a matter of style. These are volumes in which Yeats's principle of juxtaposing poems of contrasting tendency and content produces some of the starkest and most unexpected effects. On reflection, this is not entirely surprising, for they are volumes in which Yeats's esoteric interests start to find explicit expression, sometimes in a manner which verges on the expository, as in 'The Phases of the Moon' or 'The Double Vision of Michael Robartes', from The Wild Swans at Coole. These are both expositions of the esoteric system which was to find expression in *A Vision*, the substance of which derived from automatic writing produced by his wife George, beginning in the days shortly after their marriage in 1917. These poems share a volume with 'An Irish Airman Foresees his Death', Yeats's most direct treatment of the Great War. In *Michael Robartes and the Dancer*, 'Easter 1916', his celebrated poetic response to the republican insurrection in Dublin, shares a volume with 'Solomon and the Witch' and 'An Image from a Past Life'. This various and many-faceted character was thenceforth to remain typical of Yeats, but it is worth pausing to ponder the impression this might have had on readers who first encountered it. It must have produced a startling and bold effect, verging on the discordant, and perhaps here there is another indication of Yeats's affinity with aspects of modernism. At the same time, the juxtaposition of poems on the esoteric with poems on contemporary political or military events suggests that the latter can be seen in a remote and large-scale historical perspective, as part of a pattern covering many centuries. This is a point which has sometimes been made about the presence of 'The Second Coming'[1] in *Michael Robartes and the Dancer*: this poem about the apocalyptic fate of western civilization, of which contemporary revolution and anarchy are harbingers, is printed a few pages after 'Easter 1916', which is a particular example of one such revolution. But I am also claiming that the effect is created even where the content of a poem with esoteric connections is not directed at contemporary history: the point lies in the juxtaposition with poems of more apparently mundane tendency.

As should be clear from a passing knowledge of his interests prior to 1917, which included membership of the Golden Dawn, an interest in Theosophy and attendance at seances, the esoteric did not suddenly appear in Yeats's life with *A Vision*. One should really think of Yeats's occult writings as the expression of a constantly developing set of speculations. For that matter, *A Vision* itself exists in two different versions, published in 1925 and 1937. As it happens, one of the most memorable and striking of the expository poems about esoteric beliefs in *The Wild Swans at Coole*, 'Ego Dominus Tuus', dates from 1915, before the intervention of the spirits who directed Mrs Yeats's automatic writing. In fact, it expounds ideas to be found in a prose discourse on occult matters which Yeats had been meditating back then, *Per Amica Silentia Lunae*, which was published in 1917. This is divided into two sections, 'Anima

Hominis' ('The Soul of Man') and 'Anima Mundi' ('The Soul of the World'). The poem offers an account of the essence of the thinking to be found in 'Anima Hominis'. This analyses the soul of man in terms of two opposed elements, the self and the anti-self (or antithetical self). To the latter, Yeats gives the name of 'Daimon' (a spirit), and indeed, the essay perpetuates the notion Yeats first developed in seances, that man is haunted by a guardian spirit who represents the inversion of all the characteristics of the given self. The 'Daimon', being a spirit, resides in the 'Anima Mundi' – a repository for spirits and images, both of which have the same subtle bodies, composed of 'animal spirits'. A fundamental aspect of the relationship between self and anti-self lies in the striving of the self to adopt the characteristics of the anti-self: this is the origin of Yeats's mature concept of the Mask, codified in *A Vision*, whereby the self seeks to become like the anti-self by adopting its nature. The chief gain for the artist, or other creative types, is that the conflict and difficulty are the sources of creativity. As he famously said in *Per Amica*, 'We make out of the quarrel with others, rhetoric, but of the quarrel with ourselves, poetry.'[2] The 'quarrel with ourselves' is the conflict between self and anti-self.

'Ego Dominus Tuus' dramatizes this conflict by representing it as a dispute between 'Hic' and 'Ille': that is, the Latin demonstrative pronouns for 'this' and 'that' (*CW* I, pp.161–4). 'Hic' represents the self, 'Ille' (being in another place, so to speak) the anti-self. Yeats's example of the way this kind of conflict might work in the life of a poet is that of Dante. 'Ille' speculates that it was hunger for the anti-self which fashioned the appearance of Dante's gaunt and 'hollow' face. The title of the poem itself comes from Dante's *La vita nuova*, in which at one point Love in a vision shows Dante his own bleeding heart and then makes Beatrice, Dante's beloved, eat it. The suggestion is that the relationship of lover and mistress is demonic, in the sense that she will represent in ideal form the qualities that he lacks, and that in pursuing her he will lose his own original self – productively, in the inventions of his writing. The close relationship between 'Daimon' and the beloved woman is a topic developed at greater length in the first version of *A Vision*, though subsequently Yeats seems to have found this description in sexual terms to be too limiting a conception of the 'Daimon' or 'Daemon'.

The other really notable expositions of occult learning, 'The Phases of the Moon' (CW I, pp.164–8) and 'The Double Vision of Michael Robartes' (pp.172–4), take their subject matter from *A Vision*. The first expounds the master image of the whole system. This is predicated on the idea that human history and individual human existence are incarnated in forms which can be imaged in terms of the twenty-eight phases of the moon. In other words, one takes one's personality from the qualities supposedly associated with each of the different phases, as if in a version of the astrological determination of character. A further structural principle is provided by the quality of the moon's light. The light of the moon symbolizes subjectivity (or the 'antithetical tincture', as Yeats calls it), the dark of the moon objectivity (or the 'primary tincture'). The antithetical is so called because it rejects the given (which is an overtone of the word 'primary') and seeks to go imaginatively beyond it. Indeed, this is what it is doing in courting the anti-self, which is a related term. Thus the character of each phase is partly determined by the relative quantities of dark and light. There can be no human incarnation, however, at the full or the complete dark of the moon, for these symbolize perfect subjectivity and perfect objectivity respectively, and there can be no perfection in what the Middle Ages called the 'sublunary' world of mutability and physicality. The other poem, 'The Double Vision of Michael Robartes', describes a vision of a girl associated with the full moon, the 'fifteenth night': 'being dead it seemed / That she of dancing dreamed'. For the phase of absolute subjectivity is not of mortal life, and is associated both with dream and art. She is guarded on either side by a sphinx and by the Buddha, the former representing intellect, the latter love.

While the poems with their origins in occult learning share a volume with others on the Great War or the demesne of the Gregorys, they are not printed next to each other. Poems like 'The Phases of the Moon' or, indeed, 'The Cat and the Moon', are to be found towards the end of the book, as if in this manner Yeats were indicating a gathering profundity of speculation. The book begins with 'The Wild Swans at Coole' (CW I, pp.131–2), a haunting and technically perfect meditation on ageing. On the principle that the ordering of poems in Yeats's books is significant, this contrasting positioning means that the volume moves from the particular to the general, from time in the individual's life to time on the historical scale. The poem reckons time past and passing by referring to counting: on the water of the lake there are 'nine-and-fifty swans'; it is the 'nineteenth autumn' since the speaker first 'made [his] count'. The activity of counting is mimicked by the regular sound of the swans' wings and by the sound of the speaker's foot-steps. He recalls the 'bell-beat of their wings above my head' when he 'Trod with a lighter tread' – lines which deploy alliteration and the adjustment of metre to onomatopoeic effect. At the same time, the apparent immortality of the swans (they look and behave as they did nineteen years ago) allows them to become emblems of immortal beauty – of that timeless realm which according to Yeats's esoteric doctrines is both distinct from, and in constant interaction with, our mortal existence.

It is fitting enough, then, that the next poem in the book should be 'In Memory of Major Robert Gregory' (CW I, pp.132–5), for here we have the combination of a memorialization of death with a meditation on the values that inform a life and transcend any individual who embodies them. The poem commemorates the death of Lady Gregory's son, who had died as a fighter-pilot in the war. He, indeed, is the 'Irish Airman' of the celebrated poem. 'In Memory' hints at a tension in the rationale of the commemoration. On the one hand, Gregory is repre-sented as a kind of paragon of the paternalist virtues of the rooted and responsible aristocrat – 'Soldier, scholar, horseman, he' – and thus the loss is lamented of one whose care for the land and the people has also been lost. On the other hand, his volunteering to go off and fight is pre-sented as symptomatic of a different kind of aristocratic virtue (if such it be): a kind of daring, Byronic free spirit: 'Some burn damp faggots, others may consume / The entire combustible world in one small room'. In the end, Gregory, because of the impulsive daring of his choice, seems more like a quick burner than one who could ever have settled for the slow and unimpressive business of estate management. This tension really does correspond to a tension within Yeats's own ideas of the aristocratic personality, by turns respecting the traditional and supposedly eternal relation of the noble and the beggarman, and all the customary arrangements that go with it; but then praising the unpre-dictable individuality which makes aristocratic society receptive to the ideas of the innovative artist.

In 'An Irish Airman' (CW I, p.135), composed in 1918, the focus is on the impulsive and unfettered daring of the young warrior. 'A lonely impulse of delight' motivated him, and in comparison the years before and after – in other words, the time in which the unexciting demands of a mundane existence might have occurred – seemed 'waste of breath'. Indeed, even the ethical principles which might have motivated other men to join up do not appear to guide Gregory in Yeats's interpretation: 'Those that I fight I do not hate, / Those that I guard I do not love'. The more one ponders the poem, the more Gregory's motives appear to verge on the irresponsible. And three years later, responding to the Black and Tan atrocities of the British forces during the Irish War of Independence, Yeats, in 'Reprisals', bitterly reckoned up the consequences for Gregory's tenants of their abandonment by one who could have been their advocate and defender: 'Half-drunk or whole-mad soldiery / Are murdering your tenants there'.[3] The poem opens with straightforward sarcasm about Gregory's 'last exciting year', but in the end accords him at least the honour of joining 'the other cheated dead'. The concise scorn of this poem reminds one of how genuinely horrified by violence and injustice Yeats was capable of being, despite his philosophical acceptance of the necessity of warfare. The line about the 'cheated dead' has wider implications, however, pointing to angry dissatisfaction at a social order which could slaughter millions and offer them nothing in return. This dissatisfaction is comparable to that which his friend Ezra Pound had expressed in 'Hugh Selwyn Mauberley' (1920).

Moving deeper into the volume, however, we find that Yeats's unifying imagination brings together a lament for Robert Gregory and the fruits of his own occult discoveries and researches. For 'Shepherd and Goatherd' (CW I, pp.142–6), a pastoral elegy, ends with the goatherd predicting the life of Gregory's soul after death, a life in which he will unwind the conflicts and contradictions of existence ('He unpacks the loaded pern [i.e. spindle]'). This is a process which is described in the second version of A Vision (1937) as 'The Dreaming Back'. Yeats had already begun to introduce, indirectly, the matter of A Vision, with a concealed reflection on the automatic writing produced by his wife: 'Solomon to Sheba' (CW I, p.138) celebrates the feminine wisdom which has the power to instruct even that wisest of monarchs. This reminder balances the more demonic representation of feminine influence implied in 'Ego Dominus Tuus', though in both cases the implication is that feminine and masculine wisdom are different and complementary.

This is the topic with which *Michael Robartes and the Dancer* opens, for the title-poem (*CW* I, pp.177–9), a dialogue where Robartes and 'the Dancer' are significantly given the parts of 'He' and 'She', shows the former arguing that women should banish 'every thought' unless 'The lineaments that please their view / When the long looking-glass is full, / Even from the foot-sole think it too.' That is, they should banish every thought that does not both arise from, and represent, the wholeness of their physical being when it is at the pitch of beauty. This is not the same thing at all as saying that women should not think; and it is in the light of this realization that one needs to interpret the opening line of the poem about how 'Opinion is not worth a rush'. Opinion is the superficial exercise of an inferior form of reasoning that does not arise from the whole self. While it may be that men are more attuned to the ambitious exercise of reason, both sexes are vulnerable to the temptations of superficial opinionatedness. Furthermore, the exercise of female wisdom seems to offer a lesson for the poet, even if not for the philosopher or scientist. For the wisdom that arises out of the whole being, not conceived simply as nature, but adorned with artifice (ready for the 'looking glass') sounds like a way of describing the poet's art.

Perhaps unexpectedly, this perception can offer a point of entry to 'Easter 1916' (*CW* I, pp.182–4) in the same volume. The kind of reading that notices only the respect Yeats accords to the leaders of the insurrection is simply inadvertent. The word 'changed', which echoes throughout the poem, refers in part to a radical change of perception on the part of the speaker. He had spoken mockingly of these political activists, thinking that they but lived 'where motley is worn', that they were actors in the 'casual comedy'. And the mockery becomes almost savage when it pauses at the figure of the Countess Markievicz: 'That woman's days were spent / In ignorant good will, / Her nights in argument / Until her voice grew shrill.' Opinion, like some arid spectre, has destroyed the fine wholeness of being in part represented by the sweet voice of her youth when she 'rode to harriers' back at Lissadell. It is, I think, by implication an affliction of all the insurgents, but to Yeats seems particularly damaging in the case of this once-comely aristocrat. But the transformation wrought by all the insurrectionists is one in which they move from comedy to tragedy. And their role in the tragedy is heroic, not only because of the sublimity of their sacrifice of their own lives, but also because, in order to achieve it, they had for years damaged their existences in the service of a cause dominated by political sloganizing and manoeuvring. In becoming martyrs, they have fashioned themselves into images for the Irish people, and thereby have done far more than could be achieved by discursive argument. They have made themselves fit matter for many a poem. While at first they cannot be said to have learnt from 'the Dancer', it seems, at last, almost as if they had done so. This is a good example of the fundamental unity which is so often to be discovered below the surface of Yeats's books. To return to the apparent dissonance among the poems in these volumes, palpable though this is, it needs to be held in the balance with that fundamental unity. The effect of discord of matter and manner, which nevertheless can be referred to the poet's fundamental idea of truth, is characteristically modernist, and points to the naturalness of using that description of Yeats.

'The Second Coming' puts this particular insurrection in a long perspective – the longest. History, as we noted before, follows the pattern of the phases of the moon, and alternating periods of lunar dark and light, objectivity and subjectivity. Yeats's system sees these periods in blocks of 2,000 years, and states that the Christian era, associated by him with objectivity, morality and social concern, is to be replaced by a new era of subjectivity, of imagination, of aristocracy and the domination of powerful individuals. The onset of this era will be marked by some brutal intervention: hence the rough beast slouching towards Bethlehem. In accordance with his mixed feelings about conflict when he actually encountered it in real life, his poem 'A Prayer for My Daughter' (CW I, pp. 190–2) displays great anxiety about the anarchy and disorder threatening the world Yeats has known, with its care for innocence. It sounds like a Christian virtue, and Yeats fears for the fate of his little daughter in the world that is coming to be.

NOTES

1. Richard J. Finneran (ed.), *The Collected Works of W.B. Yeats*, I, *The Poems*, 2nd edn (New York: Scribners, 1997), p.189; hereafter referred to in the text as *CW* I, followed by page number.

2. W.B. Yeats, *Mythologies* (London: Macmillan, 1959), p.331.

3. Peter Allt and Russell K. Alspach (eds), *The Variorum Edition of the Poems of W.B. Yeats* (New York: Macmillan, 1957; rev. 1966), p.791. Yeats never included this poem in one of his collections out of sensitivity for the feelings of Lady Gregory.

CHAPTER SIX

Later Poetry

STEPHEN REGAN

In the prolific fifty-year period between *The Wanderings of Oisin* (1889) and *Last Poems and Two Plays* (1939), Yeats surpassed the early ideals and ambitions of the Irish Literary Revival and gave to modern Irish literature a far-reaching international significance and appeal. The publication of *The Tower* (1928) was crucially important in establishing Yeats as a major modernist poet in the company of T.S. Eliot and Ezra Pound, but the most powerful burst of creative energy was still to come. One striking indication of the dramatic transformation in Yeats's career, from the late nineteenth-century romantic nationalist to the mid-twentieth-century cosmopolitan modernist, can be found in his changing conception of the heart as the guarantor of deep feeling and the primary source of poetry. In the early lyric, 'The Lover Tells of the Rose in his Heart' (1892), there is an urge towards transcendence and transformation, a desire to protect the image of love and beauty from 'All things uncomely and broken, all things worn out and old'. The speaker longs to 'sit apart' from the world of change and to contemplate artistic permanence in the shape of 'a casket of gold'.[1] Forty years later, in 'Vacillation' (1932), there is a new aesthetic credo founded on the acceptance of fierce antinomies and on the perpetual destruction and rebuilding of artistic achievements. Now, the heart has learned 'remorse' (p.300), but there are intimations of the 'tragic joy' that will come to the fore at the very end of Yeats's life.

The imaginative terrain of Yeats's early work is aptly summed up in the title of one of his earliest and most successful plays, *The Land of Heart's Desire* (1894), and many of the early poems speak from the heart or appeal to the heart as a way of announcing their own authenticity. The exilic yearning for Ireland in 'The Lake Isle of Innisfree' is given both magical suggestiveness and physical rootedness in the memorable 'nine bean rows', but what generates the passionate longing for return is the sound of lake water lapping and the intense experience of being able to 'hear it in the deep heart's core' (p.60). If the heart is an emblematic reminder of the persistent romantic legacy in Yeats's poetry, it is also a sensitive barometer of the uncertain political climate of the times. In that early, impassioned declaration of his commitment to the revival, 'To Ireland in the Coming Times', the aspiring poet pledges his dual allegiance to Ireland and the Rose of Beauty with a heartfelt flourish: 'I cast my heart it into my rhymes, / That you, in the dim coming times, / May know how my heart went with them / After the red-rose bordered hem' (p.71). There is a purposeful ambivalence here, with the main verb simultaneously suggesting hazardous throwing and artistic fashioning. Nationalist and aesthetic priorities compete for attention, and the continuing effort to reconcile them is evident in the 'terrible beauty' of the Easter Rising. 'Easter 1916' cautions against the over-zealous endeavours of hearts with one purpose alone, even at the risk of appearing to undermine the prevailing symbolism of death and resurrection: 'Too long a sacrifice can make a stone of the heart' (p.229).

The violence and brutality of the ensuing War of Independence and the Civil War are regarded in *The Tower* as a perversion and coarsening of the heart: 'We had fed the heart on fantasies, / The heart's grown brutal from the fare' (p.251). A defining characteristic of the late poetry of Yeats is its ultimate acceptance of the heart's impurity and capacity for hatred. A new and distinctive note can be heard in *The Winding Stair and Other Poems* (1933), a strange and uneasy mixture of deep remorse and bold defiance:

> Out of Ireland have we come.
> Great hatred, little room,
> Maimed us at the start.
> I carry from my mother's womb
> A fanatic heart. (p.305)

For all its confident rhetorical brio, there is uneasiness here about the emergence of Irish poetry, a perverse undoing of Wordsworth's intimations of immortality: 'not in utter nakedness, / But trailing clouds of glory do we come'.[2] There is a declaration of shared beginnings, but any secure sense of national tradition is undercut by suggestions of deformed birth. The poem looks back on the early nationalist ideals of 'To Ireland in the Coming Times', sceptically countering the younger poet's wish to 'sweeten Ireland's wrong' with a sombre acknowledgement of the actuality of hatred (p.70). The assertion of fanaticism is mitigated to some extent by the uncertain stress in the final line. Yeats claimed that his own pronunciation of 'fanatic' was 'the older and more Irish way, so that the last line of each stanza contains but two beats'.[3] Even in his most extravagant declarations in the late poems, Yeats remains an impeccable stylist, conscientiously alert to the nuances of every syllable.

'Remorse for Intemperate Speech', from which the lines quoted above are taken, declares that the poet cannot 'rule' his fanatic heart, yet the consummate verbal and rhythmic control of passionate speech is precisely what makes the late poems of Yeats so powerfully imposing and provocative. Remorse is one of the complicated emotional keynotes of the later Yeats, colouring the memories out of which late poems like 'The Circus Animals' Desertion' are fashioned. The other side of this self-lacerating late Yeats is the imperturbable nihilist who looks on coldly and unconcernedly as all things perish and decay. The complex interaction of these different perspectives on the passing of time and the experience of loss creates a new kind of elegiac writing markedly different from either 'Easter 1916' or 'In Memory of Major Robert Gregory', both of which had drawn on conventional codes of mourning and consol-ation. Now, the loss is starkly registered and the traditional search for consolation is supplanted by a stoical letting go, or (more disturbingly) by an unconcealed delight in destruction.

The Winding Stair and Other Poems opens with an effulgent elegy, 'In Memory of Eva Gore-Booth and Con Markiewicz'. This poem is not as formally contrived or elaborate as the earlier elegy for Robert Gregory, but its brevity, its subtle quatrains, its brisk tetrameter lines and its immediate present tense address all fittingly convey the fragile, transient beauty of the sisters and their cultural vogue. The opening is beautifully atmospheric, with the dying light leading on to the brilliant climactic blaze at the end, and the syllables in the name of the country house in Sligo, Lissadell, hinting at the cultivated gentleness and delicacy of a whole way of life. The extravagance and exoticism of the imagery are all the more effective in view of the remorseless destruction of beauty that will follow.

As so often with Yeats, the involvement of women in politics is seen to hasten the withering of beauty. The accusation levelled at Constance Markiewicz for her part in Easter 1916 and the political upheavals that followed – 'conspiring among the ignorant' (p.283) – echoes the charge against Maud Gonne in 'No Second Troy' that she had 'taught to ignorant men most violent ways' (p.140). The poet who had once wished for the cloths of heaven now castigates the younger sister, Eva, for her vague utopian politics. The opening verse paragraph repeats the image of two girls in silk kimonos, almost as a refrain, effectively conveying both the ruminating quality of the ageing poet and the instinct to preserve a particular memory. What makes this an especially poignant elegy is Yeats's touching address to the sisters as shades who now have knowledge of the afterlife: 'Dear shadows, now you know it all' (p.283). In other respects, the elegy is deeply unconventional, calling on the sisters to rise, only that they might inspire in the poet a vision of fiery destruction. With devastating insight, the poem acknowledges that we ourselves have constructed the great gazebo of time and that we spend our lives seeking redemption from the guilt of the past. In a striking departure from her usual resistance to historical readings, Helen Vendler argues persuasively that the gazebo refers to the 'folly' of Anglo-Irish culture, and that the guilt acknowledged here is the specifically political guilt that Yeats shares with the sisters, of 'entering into the fight against the "common" wrongs or rights of their day'.[4] For all its apocalyptic suggestiveness, the closing line's powerful exhalation is a testimony to the renewed vitality and vehemence of Yeats's poetry in his later years: 'Bid me strike a match and blow' (p.284).

The elegiac impulse shapes two decorous tributes to Augusta Gregory, 'Coole Park, 1929' and 'Coole and Ballylee', both written in *ottava rima*, a much favoured form in the later years of Yeats's career. What makes these unusual elegies is that they were composed some time before Lady Gregory died in 1932, and therefore function as premature obituaries. They give a renewed urgency to fears about the ruin of Coole Park and the consequent cultural decline that Yeats had first expressed in the 1909 poem, 'Upon a House Shaken by the Land Agitation'. In the event it was casual neglect rather than political agitation that brought about the demise of Coole Park. The pervasive influence of Matthew Arnold's *Culture and Anarchy* can be detected in 'Coole Park, 1929', with its commendation of the dreaming air and intellectual sweetness fostered by the great estate, and there are further Arnoldian echoes to be found in Yeats's writing at this time.[5] The opening meditation upon a swallow's flight is sustained and expanded throughout the poem, inviting thoughts of Lady Gregory's visitors as migratory birds, but also quietly anticipating the last summer at Coole Park. The final stanza has a strange proleptic power, enforced by the curiously suspended diction of the closing lines. The call to 'traveller, scholar, poet' to 'take your stand' suggests an attitude of spectatorial detachment rather than concerted resistance, and the poem seems to beckon, rather than simply mourn, the impending desolation: 'When all those rooms and passages are gone, / When nettles wave upon a shapeless mound' (p.293).

'Coole and Ballylee, 1931' draws on the well-established elegiac convention of streams and tributaries connecting the living and the dead, but here the fierce water races from heaven's view into darkness and re-emerges as a flooded lake. The literal darkening at the outset takes on a disturbing metaphorical significance at the end of the poem in the ominous image of a darkening flood. The flow of water initially connects Yeats and Lady Gregory with the blind poet Raftery (their common endeavour to create 'the book of the people'), but the poem moves towards a desolate realization of cultural stagnation and emptiness, the loss of inheritance, and the reversal of all that was initiated by that other blind poet, Homer. The stately *ottava rima* is interrupted with questions and interjections that have to do with the poet's own capacity for philosophical reflection and metaphor-making: 'What's water but the generated soul? ... Another emblem there!' Revisiting and rewriting that earlier and calmer elegy, 'The Wild Swans at Coole', Yeats now accentuates and explicates his own symbols, including the mysterious swan: 'like the soul, it sails into the sight / And in the morning's gone' (p.294). The final admission that 'all is changed' looks back to 'The Wild Swans at Coole', and before that to 'Easter 1916', but now there is a steely gaze as the swan 'drifts' upon the flood. The 'high horse riderless' suggests a lack of inspiration and a lack of control. Pegasus seems to metamorphose here into the wild and energetic horses in the paintings of the poet's brother, Jack B. Yeats (p.295). The traditional sanctity and loveliness of Yeats and 'the last romantics' reaches back to the mid-eighteenth century, but the vision of chaos and catastrophe ahead is characteristically modernist (p.294).

The elegiac forms in which Yeats gathers his memories of people and places in the west of Ireland are complemented by a series of meditations on death which look out to Africa, India and the East for philosophical truths, as if preparing the soul for the afterlife. 'At Algeciras – A Meditation upon Death' and 'Mohini Chatterjee' (originally published as 'Two Meditations upon Death') both look back to the poet's vanished boyhood and send out the imagination in search of compensating wisdom. In the first of these, written towards the end of 1928 when Yeats was recovering from illness in southern Spain, migratory birds once again portend the passage of the soul from life to death, this time crossing the narrow straits between Europe and Africa. In the second meditation, the Brahmin Mohini Chatterjee, whom Yeats had heard lecture in Dublin in 1885, instructs the poet on the doctrine of reincarnation. The poem adds a commentary that queries the passivity of Chatterjee's words and asserts the importance of living life to the full within each cycle of existence: 'Men dance on deathless feet' (p.297). The most impressive and accomplished of these meditations on death is 'Byzantium', which Yeats wrote towards the end of 1930 as a more intense exploration of the afterlife than he had achieved in 'Sailing to Byzantium', the opening poem of The Tower. Here, the gross physical sensations of day have receded, and the metaphysical reigns supreme: 'A starlit or a moonlit dome disdains / All that man is, / All mere complexities, / The fury and the mire of human veins' (p.298). As Daniel Albright comments, the poem offers a more elaborate guided tour of the afterlife than the earlier poem permitted, fastening upon a series of mesmerizing images: a walking mummy, a bird of hammered gold, mysterious flickering flames, and dolphins transporting the spirits of the dead to paradise.[6] Even while striving to construct befitting emblems of the afterlife, the poem concedes the impossibility of its own endeavours in the rhythmic and syntactical complexities of a baffling hallucinatory verse: 'Before me floats an image, man or shade, / Shade more than man, more image than a shade' (p.298).

That Yeats's late poetry could not easily resolve its own fierce oppositions, that it largely depended upon the continued raging of 'all complexities of mire and blood', is strongly evident in the boisterous, lustful lyrics included in the sequences, 'Words For Music Perhaps' and 'A Woman Young and Old', incorporated in *The Winding Stair and Other Poems* in 1933. Louis MacNeice admired the 'zest' of these late poems and shrewdly noted Yeats's subtle handling of a light verse that seemed to sanction the sexually explicit subject matter.[7] It might be, as Marjorie Howes claims, that the erotic frankness of the poems was, in part, a combative response to the social and sexual conservatism of the Irish government, but it is also the case that Yeats was intent on discovering the creative possibilities of extremity, of setting up new kinds of dialogue between the body and soul.[8] There is undoubtedly provocation in having Crazy Jane talk with the Bishop, but part of the fascination of these poems is that Crazy Jane discovers wisdom through her body, speaking a kind of Blakean aphorism ('Love is all / Unsatisfied / That cannot take the whole / Body and soul'), while the Bishop is surprisingly frank and vigorous in his speech: 'Those breasts are flat and fallen now, / Those veins must soon be dry' (pp.307, 309).

The sexual vigour and explicitness of the Crazy Jane poems have a troubling political corollary in Yeats's growing interest in eugenics in the 1930s. His deep distaste for modern civilization, commercialism and democracy found vehement expression in the inflammatory tract, *On the Boiler*, published by his own Cuala Press in 1939. Recalling a mad ship's carpenter who ranted from the top of a large rusted boiler in his Sligo boyhood, Yeats constructs a vicious persona to convey his provocative views on discipline, war and selective breeding. There is a Swiftean vehemence and extremity in the writing, and it spills over into some of the later poems, including 'Under Ben Bulben', without any apparent wearing of a mask, prompting some difficult questions about Yeats's politics in the final years. His involvement with the Irish Fascist Blueshirts in 1933–34 is usually described as a 'flirtation' or 'enthusiasm'. While acknowledging the actual extremity of Yeats's politics at this time, it is important to understand the particular context in which they developed.

Jonathan Allison offers a thoughtful, measured account of Irish fascism in the 1930s, claiming that Yeats's attraction to the Blueshirts had more to do with widespread fears of an overthrow of legitimate government by the losing side in the recent civil war than any ambitions for a European fascist state. In this respect, 'Yeats was a pre-Holocaust fascist for a season, but only in local terms.'[9] In terms of literary output, the fascist flirtation was disappointing, producing only 'Three Marching Songs' (revised between 1934 and 1938), whose creaking rhythms were never likely to inspire a multitude of followers.

There are times when the vehemence and sexual daring of the late poems seem to function as a prompt for a poet who fears that his creative energies might be flagging. The short poem titled 'The Spur' (written in 1932) is disarmingly explicit about the ageing poet's source of inspiration: 'You think it horrible that lust and rage / Should dance attendance upon my old age' (p.359). Yeats claimed that one of his most powerful poems on modern Irish politics, 'At Parnell's Funeral' (published in *A Full Moon in March* in 1935), was a rhymed version of a lecture he had given in America. Whether versified lecture or not, the poem has a crucial place between *The Winding Stair* (1933) and *New Poems* (1938), combining deep political disillusionment with a bracing and brazen rhetorical frankness ('I thirst for accusation'), and ushering in a new and urgent sense of epochal change in Ireland and beyond ('An age is the reversal of an age'). Yeats sees the period of Irish history between Daniel O'Connell and Charles Stewart Parnell as a turning from casual comedy to tragic drama. These are the terms in which he also views the events leading up to Easter 1916, of course, but now the drama is intensified as a modern version of Greek tragedy and the ritualistic blood sacrifice is seen through the lens of J.G. Frazer's *The Golden Bough* (1890). Just as James Joyce in *A Portrait of the Artist as a Young Man* depicted Ireland as 'the old sow that eats her farrow', so Yeats contemplates an Ireland intent on devouring itself.[10] A decisive historical shift has taken place with Parnell's death, but the bitter wisdom Parnell learned from Swift has not been passed on to a modern Ireland which now seems stagnating and atrophied, lacking inspiration and direction. As with 'The Circus Animals' Last Desertion', the poem is alert to the dangers of treating life too intently as drama on 'a painted stage'. If the deaths of earlier Irish patriots (Emmet, Fitzgerald, Tone) seemed like a historical pageant, the death of Parnell was all too real and near: 'nor did we play a part / Upon a painted stage when we devoured his heart'. 'Parnell's Funeral' marks a turning-point in Yeats's career in other ways, as well. Its conviction that 'An age is the reversal of an age' takes on a climactic international significance, while the phrase 'what matter' (used critically here to describe an attitude of unconcern) comes increasingly to signify an outlook of defiant stoicism, and even joyous celebration, in the face of catastrophe and ruin (p.329).

'The Gyres' (initially titled 'What Matter') opens *New Poems* (1938) with exhilarating power, calling on 'Old Rocky Face' (a conflation of the Delphic Oracle and the poet's mask of stoical wisdom) to look forth on a world of tumultuous change.[11] Yeats had invoked the gyres, the spinning cones which he sees governing and propelling the cycles of historical succession, in 'The Second Coming' (1919), in a fearful vision of Christianity supplanted by an antithetical order. Now, in the very midst of chaos, the impulse is to rejoice. The poem vividly conveys an impression of turning gyres, juxtaposing a present-tense apprehension of tragic events in classical Greece ('Hector is dead and there's a light in Troy') with an appalling acknowledgement of violent destructiveness in its own era: 'Irrational streams of blood are staining earth'. 'What matter?' might seem a crassly insensitive response to these nightmare visions, except that it derives from a fundamental conviction that a revolutionary transformation will take place, with the declining aristocracy (represented by lovers of horses and of women) supplanted by a renewed and invigorated social hierarchy ('The workman, noble and saint'). The ultimate power of the poem derives, however, from the pressurized formal containment of entropic breakdown and dissolution. The perception of exhausted cultural and intellectual resources is conveyed with what Helen Vendler has aptly termed, 'The incantatory power of reduplicative language': 'Things thought too long can be no longer thought / For beauty dies of beauty, worth of worth' (p.340). In the same way, the poem's vision of discord is given force and concentration through the structural coherence of the modified *ottava rima* stanzas. As Vendler notes, Yeats succeeds in prising the *ottava rima* stanza away from its Renaissance associations, bringing it 'forcibly into modernity'.[12]

The final burst of creative energy in the late poems of Yeats brings with it a plethora of complicated emotional responses and aesthetic attitudes, fittingly encapsulated in the paradoxical concept of tragic joy. Blissful gaiety is strangely mixed with the sublime apprehension of suffering and loss. If exhilaration in the face of destruction is prompted by Yeats's conviction that the turning gyres are bringing about a new social order, it is also informed by a continuing tendency to look on life as an unfolding drama of both casual comedy and terrible beauty. Now, however, the attitude is one of lofty spectatorial detachment and apparent coldness: 'We that look on but laugh in tragic joy' (p.340). The late poems turn to Shakespearean tragedy in search of an enabling wisdom and dramatic form with which to confront catastrophe, but they also reveal their modernist credentials in their cold aesthetic attitude. Two years before his death, in 'A General Introduction for My Work' (written for a collected edition that was never published), Yeats explained his fascination for an art that was at once cold and passionate. 'The heroes of Shakespeare', he maintains, are able to 'convey to us through their looks, or through the metaphorical patterns of their speech, this sudden enlargement of their vision, their ecstasy at the approach of death.' But, he insists, 'all must be cold; no actress has ever sobbed when she played Cleopatra'. Recalling Lady Gregory saying that 'Tragedy must be a joy to the man who dies', he goes on to claim that the tragic persona 'must be lifted out of history with timeless pattern' and 'carried beyond feeling into the aboriginal ice'.[13]

Like Ezra Pound, Yeats was to discover a compelling instance of this cold aesthetic detachment in the art of the East, and his own peculiar romantic modernist orientalism can be seen at work in late poems such as 'Meru' and 'Lapis Lazuli'. Strategically positioned as the final offering in a series of 'Supernatural Poems' in *Parnell's Funeral and Other Poems* (1935), 'Meru' looks back to the civilized ways of Coole Park and forward to 'The Gyres' and other late poems of tragic joy. Civilization is 'hooped together', both in the spiralling gyres of time and as a temporary, man-made artefact, sustained by 'manifold illusion'. The poem adopts the Shakespearean sonnet form with skilful assurance, countering the desolation and terror of the West with the cold wisdom of 'Hermits upon Mount Meru or Everest / Caverned in night under the drifted snow'. In a poetic form long dedicated to themes of transience (Shelley's sonnet, 'Ozymandias', is briefly echoed here), Yeats bids farewell, not just to the glory and monuments of places like Coole

Park, but to mighty empires and entire civilizations, too: 'Egypt and Greece good-bye, and good-bye, Rome' (p.339).

The snowy scene of 'Meru' is transplanted to the Chinese stone carving that epitomizes the attitude of tragic joy at the end of 'Lapis Lazuli'. The Chinese musicians who 'begin to play' at the end of the poem act as a counterpoint to the prevailing images of destruction and destitution, their serenity providing an instructive contrast to the hysteria and alarm with which the poem opens. At the same time, the transcendent mood of tragic gaiety attributed to the Chinamen in the closing line is seen throughout the poem to be a condition that can be aspired to and achieved by all. Once again, all the world is a stage, and the poet-director looks down on a cast of aspiring actors: 'All perform their tragic play, / There struts Hamlet, there is Lear, / That's Ophelia, that Cordelia' (p.341). In the middle of the closing fourteen-line verse section, however, the poet plays a more involved role as he turns to contemplate the figures in the lapis lazuli carving: 'and I / Delight to imagine them seated there; / There on the mountain and the sky' (p.342). The carving is itself the model for a certain kind of art – hard, cold, unsentimental – but it also provides the opportunity for the poet to imagine an extended narrative, to bring the carving to life, as it were, and allow the figures to look out with him upon the tragic scene. The present-tense animation might, for a moment, suggest a parallel between Yeats's lapis lazuli carving and Keats's Grecian urn, but the significant difference is that the Chinese carving seems more of a piece with life's uncertainties and disappointments, recording the passage of time as well as its own seeming durability. Edward Larrissy sums this up superbly well, when he writes of the lapis lazuli art work 'embodying in its shape the beautiful brokenness of this world: "Every discolouration of the stone, / Every accidental crack or dent"'.[14]

In contrast to the violent destructiveness envisaged in 'The Gyres' and 'Lapis Lazuli', a number of late poems offer an elegiac counterweight, withdrawing momentarily into the stillness of the past, as if in an act of renewed contemplation. It is almost as if Yeats cannot yet loosen his grip on the particularity of things, even if 'all things run / On that unfashionable gyre again' ('The Gyres'), and even if 'All things fall and are built again' ('Lapis Lazuli'). The quality of thought in 'Beautiful Lofty Things' seems to contend with the earlier suggestion that 'Things thought too long can be no longer thought / For beauty dies of beauty, worth of worth' (p.340). As Michael O'Neill has argued, the poem offers 'a different version of tragic acceptance' from that found in 'The Gyres' and 'Lapis Lazuli', replacing the theory of cyclic recurrence with 'elegiac celebration of the unique beauty and nobleness of individuals', emphasizing in each case their 'heroic singleness'.[15] The poem functions as a series of sculptural vignettes or busts, recalling all those prominent Irish figures – John O'Leary, John Butler Yeats, Standish O'Grady, Augusta Gregory and Maud Gonne – who have now achieved an Olympian elevation, moving from memory into myth. Significantly, this is the only poem by Yeats in which Maud Gonne is named, her transformation into Pallas Athene touchingly preceded by the mundane detail of her waiting a train. The poem's hexameter lines and its repetition of certain words in place of conventional rhyme create a fitting impression of rumination and reminiscence. The closing half line, 'a thing never known again', is delicately poised between absence and presence, between possession of the thing and its certain loss (p.350). The curtailment in this line is reminiscent of the sudden inarticulacy at the end of the elegy 'In Memory of Major Robert Gregory', where speech is apparently overwhelmed by feeling: 'but a thought / Of that late death took all my heart for speech' (p.184).

Robert Gregory and Coole Park are remembered in another elegiac late poem, 'The Municipal Gallery Revisited'. This, too, provides an artistic tableau of Yeats's friends and collaborators, with the gallery serving as an architectural metaphor of memory. This time, the poem enacts both the overpowering and the recovery of the heart (which is also a recovery of speech, as the wordplay implies), as the poet looks upon images of the dead in paintings by John Lavery and other notable artists: 'Heart smitten with emotion I sink down, / My heart recovering with covered eyes' (p.367). The emotional effect here testifies to the power of images, and the poem acknowledges how paint both records and transforms history, setting standards of excellence that might be emulated by future generations. If Yeats pays an elegiac tribute to his friends, he also reflects upon the making of himself and the achievements by which he will be judged after his death. Other poems are more explicit about the poet's old age and about his frustration with his own mental faculties and the incompleteness of his artistic ambitions: 'Here at life's end / Neither loose imagination, / Nor will of the mind / Consuming its rag-and-bone, / Can make the truth known' (p.348). Despite its suggestions of the poet's superannuated grazing, 'An Acre of Grass' calls for 'an old man's frenzy' that will 'Shake the dead in their shrouds' (p.349).

New Poems (1938) was the final volume of poems that Yeats saw through to publication, but he clearly had plans for another collection, which was published posthumously with The Death of Cuchulain and Purgatory as Last Poems and Two Plays in 1939. The main preoccupation of these last poems, from 'Under Ben Bulben' to 'The Circus Animals' Desertion', is with the making and remaking of the poet's own identity, and with the fierce struggle between completeness and incompleteness on the way to poetic immortality. Daniel Albright claims that Last Poems moves from tragic joy to 'ferocious humility', reiterating an idea already entertained in the Crazy Jane poems, 'that the most sublime matters embody themselves in the lowliest, even the filthiest, forms'.[16] Elevation and debasement, ascension and descension, are among the primary organizing principles in the volume. 'Under Ben Bulben' takes us from the cold, mountainous landscape of 'Lapis Lazuli' to the wintry mountains of Yeats's own boyhood Sligo to confront the supernatural horsemen and learn from their completeness. The brisk, modified trochaic tetrameter of the verse recalls the charms of the witches in Macbeth, but also the clamorous making of Blake's Tyger. There are echoes of Hamlet, too (in the 'grave-diggers' toil', for instance), though Yeats's allusiveness is akin to Eliot's in its ironic alignment of high culture and its modern context of reception, as with Michael Angelo and the roof of the Sistine Chapel, 'Where but half-awakened Adam / Can disturb globe-trotting Madam / Till her bowels are in heat'. The deflationary impulse here has a comic potential reminiscent of Eliot at his bathetic best. Behind Yeats's stylistic allusions, however, is an unshakeable belief in the 'Profane perfection of mankind' (p.374).

The call to Irish poets to 'learn your trade, / Sing whatever is well-made' seems innocuous enough, except that the command is quickly followed by an extension of that formalist aesthetic to a hatred of the ugly and misshapen in the human sphere: 'Base-born products of base beds'. The aesthete and the eugenicist now contrive to produce a different kind of nationalist revival from that which inspired the fin de siècle Yeats. The fervent hope 'That we in coming days may be / Still the indomitable Irishry' echoes the early nationalist manifesto 'To Ireland in the Coming Times', but the vision of the future now rests on an uncompromising political alliance of 'the peasantry' and 'Hard-riding country gentlemen' (p.375). The poet who had 'cast' his heart into his rhymes adopts a more imperious attitude in the fashioning of his own epitaph: 'Cast a cold eye / On life, on death. / Horseman, pass by!' (p.376). Originally conceived as a quatrain beginning 'Draw rein; draw breath', the curtailed epitaph leaves death unrhymed. It also demonstrates its own avoidance of 'conventional phrase' by ignoring the traditional Christian instruction to stop at a grave and pray, offering instead 'a modernist and skeptical haughtiness, together with a modernist asymmetry of form'.[17]

In 'The Circus Animals' Desertion', written over a period of nearly a year, between November 1937 and September 1938, Yeats returns with compelling power to the ideas of completeness, perfection and accomplishment that had prompted 'Under Ben Bulben', but this time striving for an impression of personal candour and confession. Originally titled 'Despair' (at finding a new theme for poetry), 'The Circus Animals' Desertion' is Yeats's De Profundis, a final stripping away of the mask to reveal a broken man, though the poem intimates that this apparent exposure may be yet another trick. The prevailing idea of the poet as retired ringmaster, with his poetic images and devices as circus animals 'all on show', is brilliantly maintained. The ottava rima stanzas offer spacious accommodation for the ageing poet's retrospective view of his career, while a tripartite structure introduces and then concludes a narrative sequence, also consisting of three stages, marked by three representative works: The Wanderings of Oisin, The Countess Cathleen and On Baile's Strand. In each case, the poet's imaginative conceptions are seen to appropriate and monopolize the love that stirs in the human heart. One of the extraordinary features of Yeats's late work is that it should return, after all its political and philosophical excursions, to the enduring image of the heart: 'Now that my ladder's gone / I must lie down where all the ladders start / In the foul rag and bone shop of the heart' (p.395). Michael O'Neill has argued with impressive conviction that 'there is celebration as well as exhaustion in the final line's strongly stressed monosyllables', and that 'to end such a last-testament-like poem with a rhyme involving "start" is itself an arrestingly self reflexive effect'.[18] Of course, another self-reflexive effect is evident in those closing lines in the echo of the Echo in the preceding poem, 'Man and the Echo' – 'Lie down and die' – though it might be argued that this dark undercurrent only strengthens the poem's commitment to regeneration (p.393). In the same way, the closing poem, 'Politics', echoes the sentiments of that old anonymous English lyric, 'Western Wind', pitting love and desire against the wind and the rain: 'But O that I were young again / And held her in my arms' (p.395).

The ironic and mildly provocative 'Politics', with its rueful reflection on lost youth, is in many ways an appropriate 'signing off' by Yeats, but the poem that seems to resonate most powerfully as a summation of his career is 'The Statues', written during the spring of 1938, but probably not completed until September of that year. Looking back to Walter Pater and the high aesthetic ideals of the 1890s, but also facing the darkness in a late phase of decadence reminiscent of Oswald Spengler's Decline of the West (1918–22), the poem foresees for Ireland a new dawn of civilization akin to that of ancient Greece. The poem's fierce commitment to artistic renewal based on extreme authoritarian politics has not been to every critic's taste. For Harold Bloom, 'The Statues' is simply a 'bad' poem, a combination of 'Pythagorean fascism' and 'creaking' verse, but Helen Vendler astutely observes the broken perfection in Yeats's final, agitated use of the ottava rima stanza.[19] The poem gives startling realization to ideas about form and beauty that Yeats had mused over for many years, seeing in the perfection of Greek sculpture an embodiment of measurement and calculation that made the workmen 'greater than Pythagoras'. If the poem celebrates the triumph of European art and civilization over 'Asiatic vague immensities' (p.384), it also suggests the extent to which that disciplined art has determined standards of bodily perfection, and it offers a theory of the migration of art and its implication in colonial politics, seemingly underwritten by Alexander's transportation of Greek ideals to India and their subsequent influence on Buddhist aesthetics. All of this, as Roy Foster shrewdly notes, makes it 'a poem where not only eugenicism but xenophobia and anti-democratic contempt lurk only just below the surface of oracular Platonic injunctions'.[20]

The poem returns from its travels in the East to an Ireland that has witnessed revolution, and with a sudden, thrilling shift of perspective fastens its attention on Patrick Pearse and the declaration of Irish independence in the General Post Office in Dublin in Easter 1916. The stirring image of Pearse summoning 'Cuchulain to his side' is prompted by the recollection of heroic Gaelic ideals among the rebels, but also by the unveiling of Oliver Sheppard's statue of 'Dying Cuchulain' in the GPO in 1935. The nation among which Yeats can now claim his birthright is one that looks back to ancient Greek and Gaelic achievements, but one that has still to supplant the filthy, formless shape of contemporary civilization:

> We Irish, born into that ancient sect
> But thrown upon this filthy modern tide
> And by its formless spawning fury wrecked,
> Climb to our proper dark, that we may trace
> The lineaments of a plummet-measured face. (p.385)

Throughout his career, Yeats had imagined historical change, not just in the abstract philosophical patterns devised in *A Vision*, but in the palpable, physical imagery of gestation and birth, as with the 'terrible beauty' that is 'born' in 1916 (p.228), and the rough beast of 'The Second Coming' slouching towards Bethlehem 'to be born' (p.235). This new birth is founded on a myth of belonging and identity that conveniently bypasses the commercial middle class that Yeats so despised. It is here, in the revulsion from the present and the recourse to older cultural models awaiting revival, that Yeats's credentials as a modernist poet might be found. As Stan Smith has argued,

> The origins of Modernism may be sought by enquiring into those ancient sects and sources, and everywhere in the poetry of Yeats, as of Eliot and Pound, we are encouraged to seek them there. But what we find, on enquiry, is an 'address not known' that returns us to the 'filthy modern tide' of contemporary history.[21]

Smith argues impressively that the key volume for understanding the turn to modernist ideas and perspectives in Yeats's career is *The Green Helmet*, but *Last Poems* has an unprecedented and culminating intensity that derives from political hatred coupled with an unquenchable thirst for artistic perfection. At the close of 'A General Introduction for my Work', Yeats is chillingly explicit about the political sentiments that later inform 'The Statues', both declaring his hatred of modernity and announcing the onset of violent change:

> When I stand upon O'Connell Bridge in the half-light and notice that discordant architecture, all those electric signs, where modern heterogeneity has taken physical form, a vague hatred comes up out of my own dark and I am certain that wherever in Europe there are minds strong enough to lead others the same vague hatred rises; in four or five or in less generations this hatred will have issued in violence and imposed some kind of rule of kindred[22]

There is a striking development to be observed here, from Yeats's 'own dark', with its suggestions of personal psychology, antagonism and uncertainty, to 'our proper dark', which invokes the phases of the moon and ushers in a new art paradoxically born out of the contemplation of death and destruction. Even more striking, however, is the distance travelled by the poet who, in that great symbolist volume of poems, The Wind Among the Reeds (1899), had wished for the cloths of heaven, 'Of night and light and the half-light'. Now he stands in 'the half-light' of a modern city, on a bridge that symbolizes his own imminent crossing into the dark, with the tender dreams of that early lyric having turned to hatred.

NOTES

1. Daniel Albright (ed.), W.B. Yeats: The Poems (London: J.M. Dent, 1990), p.73. All further quotations are from this edition of the poems, and page numbers will be incorporated within the text.

2. E. De Selincourt and Helen Darbishire (eds), The Poetical Works of William Wordsworth (Oxford: Clarendon Press, 1947), p.281.

3. Albright (ed.), W.B. Yeats: The Poems, p.729.

4. Helen Vendler, Our Secret Discipline: Yeats and Lyric Form (Oxford: Oxford University Press, 2007), p.229.

5. Edward Larrissy quotes a letter from the 1920s in which Yeats tells Olivia Shakespear, 'Once out of Irish bitterness I can find some measure of sweetness and of light'. See Yeats the Poet: The Measures of Difference (Hemel Hempstead: Harvester, 1994), p.9.

6. Albright (ed.), *W.B. Yeats: The Poems*, p.717.

7. Louis MacNeice, *The Poetry of W.B. Yeats* (London: Oxford University Press, 1941), p.158.

8. Marjorie Howes and John Kelly (eds), *The Cambridge Companion to W.B. Yeats* (Cambridge: Cambridge University Press, 2006), p.16.

9. Jonathan Allison, 'Yeats and Politics', in *The Cambridge Companion to W.B. Yeats*, ed. Marjorie Howes and John Kelly (Cambridge: Cambridge University Press, 2006), p.202.

10. James Joyce, *A Portrait of the Artist as a Young Man*, ed. Seamus Deane (Harmondsworth: Penguin, 1992), p.220.

11. As Michael O'Neill points out, 'Old Rocky Face' might also be derived from Shelley's Ahasuerus in *Hellas*. See Michael O'Neill, *The Poems of W.B. Yeats* (London: Routledge, 2004), p.172.

12. Vendler, *Our Secret Discipline*, pp.109, 289.

13. W.B. Yeats, 'A General Introduction for My Work', in *Essays and Introductions* (London: Macmillan, 1961), pp.522–3.

14. Larrissy, *Yeats the Poet*, p.186.

15. O'Neill, *The Poems of W.B. Yeats*, p.175.

16. Albright (ed.), *W.B. Yeats: The Poems*, p.808.

17. Vendler, *Our Secret Discipline*, p.97.

18. O'Neill, *The Poems of W.B. Yeats*, pp.88–9.

19. Harold Bloom, *Yeats* (London: Oxford University Press, 1972), p.444; Vendler, *Our Secret Discipline*, p.270.

20. R.F. Foster, *W.B. Yeats: A Life*, II: *The Arch-Poet* (Oxford: Oxford University Press, 2003), p.617.

21. Stan Smith, *The Origins of Modernism: Eliot, Pound, Yeats and the Rhetoric of Renewal* (Hemel Hempstead: Harvester, 1994), p.214.

22. Yeats, 'A General Introduction for my Work', p.526.

CHAPTER SEVEN

W.B. Yeats as Dramatist

MICHAEL McATEER

Whatever the contested nature of Yeats's reputation as dramatist, there can be no doubting the energy and commitment he brought to Irish theatre as its international profile grew at the start of the twentieth century. Founding member of the Irish Literary Theatre and co-director of the Irish National Theatre Society as the Abbey Theatre came into being in 1904, his role was critical not only to the short yet stunning career of Synge in the 1900s but also to the creation of a platform for lesser known playwrights like Padraic Colum, George Shields and W.J. Henderson. The arrogance and condescension he displayed in disagreements with others at the Abbey has come in for much critical scrutiny over recent decades, yet it would be foolish to underestimate the enormous imprint he left on the character and development of Irish drama from the 1900s. Through the relationships he formed with Augusta Gregory, Florence Farr, Mrs. Patrick Campbell, Annie Horniman, Ellen Terry and Edward Gordon Craig in the 1890s, he was instrumental to the initial success in getting the Abbey Theatre off the ground and developing a movement that would come to international attention through Abbey Theatre tours in England and America, as well as through the popular successes of plays like Gregory's *Spreading the News* and Synge's *Riders to the Sea* in Ireland.

Yeats's early drama is best viewed in the first instance as a contribution to this movement, an effort to fashion a distinctively Irish drama that was in immediate contact with developments in continental European theatre during the 1890s. Following the notable impact of *The Land of Heart's Desire* and *The Countess Cathleen*, plays greeted with curiosity in London and a degree of controversy in Dublin, Yeats went on to write a series of plays during the 1900s in dialogue with the work of Gregory and Synge, but distinct in their form as poetic drama. These included *Cathleen ni Houlihan* of 1902, written in collaboration with Gregory, *The King's Threshold*, first staged in 1903 with Synge's *In the Shadow of the Glen* at Dublin's Molesworth Hall, and *Deirdre*, first performed in 1906.

Despite the scepticism greeting his first poetic plays, audiences picked up on a certain quality that distinguished them from the verse dramas of Tennyson and Browning earlier in the nineteenth century. For all the frivolity of its fairy theme, for example, *The Land of Heart's Desire* proved remarkably popular. Along with *Cathleen ni Houlihan*, written mostly by Gregory, it was the only early Yeats play to be repeatedly revived and reprinted in later years. This was due to the simple, fresh and vivid nature of the settings offered to London audiences that had, perhaps, become somewhat too familiar with the lavish interiors of Wilde's comedies by the mid-1890s. *The Land of Heart's Desire* presented its London audience of 1894 with a setting that was at once naturalistic and esoteric; the interior of a rural Irish cottage, a somewhat ephemeral wild Irish girl, a Catholic priest and a strange fairy child. He succeeded here in combining lyricism and strangeness that would carry a certain exotic appeal in London, particularly for those interested in the work of the new Belgian dramatist Maurice Maeterlinck that was coming from Paris.

Achieving recognition in Ireland through this form of drama would require a more pronounced attachment to the theme of national awakening. The first Yeats play to be staged in Ireland was *The Countess Cathleen*, performed at the Antient Concert Rooms in Dublin in May 1899. It failed to make any lasting impact, instead simply arousing the ire of Frank Hugh O'Donnell, leading member of the Irish Parliamentary Party, who took great exception to the representation of the Irish peasantry as materialistic and superstitious. Initially composed in the aftermath of Yeats's first encounter with Maud Gonne in 1889 and developed under the influence of Phillipe Auguste Villers de l'Isle-Adam's *Axël* that Yeats attended with Gonne in February 1894, *The Countess Cathleen* was ambitious in its scale. Presenting the tale of a landowner who offers her souls to demons in order to save those of the peasantry on the brink of starvation, the play was heavily weighted with occult symbolism that Yeats encountered in *Axël* and the idea of mystical correspondence he learnt from Emmanuel Swedenborg and William Blake. Aiming to cultivate a sense of symbolical intensity through slow deliberate movement that had become the hallmark of Wagnerian opera in the nineteenth century, the play failed to create an energy that might have drawn a sympathetic audience into its vision. Its treatment of the subject of famine was insufficiently sensitive to the historical experience of famine in nineteenth-century Ireland for the play to enact a movement of national awakening, but it did at least suggest the possibilities for an Irish theatre movement vitalized by exposure to developments in European theatre.

Heeding the advice of Frank Fay writing in *The United Irishman* in 1901, Yeats was encouraged by the potential others saw for his plays in Ireland while also obliged to admit the limitations of his work in the 1890s.[1] Rejecting plot-laden drama full of movement and colour such as that produced by Boucicault earlier in the century, Yeats was aiming at an emotional subtlety created through simple staging, poise and concentration of voice in delivery. The purpose was to conjure a mood in which foreboding supernatural presences would acquire an aura of reality. There are moments in which he succeeded in achieving this, like that of the young Mary Bruin's death at the end of *The Land of Heart's Desire* or the first appearance of the demon merchants in *The Countess Cathleen*. The latter was marred by a conclusion that was unconvincing theatrically, in which the Countess is redeemed by an angel at the last moment, and Yeats's attempts to write dialogue in poetic form appears for the most part stilted. Aware of these shortcomings, he collaborated with Gregory for the play that became *Cathleen ni Houlihan*. Structured according to the frame of *The Land of Heart's Desire*, the instant success of the play in April 1902 was due largely to the real connection to lived experience in rural Ireland Gregory made through dialogue and character delineation. Placed against this backdrop, the poetry delivered by Cathleen made an impact not possible through the verse forms of *The Countess Cathleen*. The result was that the quality of estrangement Yeats sought through his Ideal theatre made a deep impression on his Dublin audiences, amplified by the nationalist overtone of the play. For once collaboration proved successful; Yeats's co-authorship of *Diarmuid and Grania* with George Moore in 1901 was an abject failure, and Gregory's rewriting of Yeats's *Where There Is Nothing, There Is God* in 1907 as *The Unicorn from the Stars* fared no better.

Spurred on in part by the success of *Cathleen ni Houlihan*, his hostility to the general commercialization of theatre, and the possibilities opened up by the acquisition of a permanent home for the Irish Literary Theatre with the purchase of the Abbey Theatre under the patronage of Annie Horniman in 1904, the 1900s was a period of continuous experiment for Yeats. The development of poetic speech in performance was taken to a new level when he undertook a voice experiment with Florence Farr in 1902 to the accompaniment of a new version of the psaltery, designed by Arnold Dolmetsch. Here he sought a mode of articulation capable of transcending the division between speech and song with a view to altering the sound-patterns to which modern theatre audiences had become accustomed. Yeats derived this aspiration from a belief that the experiment with Farr and Dolmetsch would rediscover for Western audiences the capacities of the human voice to awaken a range of feelings without recourse to the complex tonal variations of song. He had in mind something close to the simple patterns of Tibetan and Arabian music, and imagined that Homer had once spoken his verses to a harp.[2]

Many of the conflicts with which Yeats became involved in the 1900s were related to his efforts to translate the experiment into performance. Working with an amateur group of actors in Dublin presented obvious difficulties, but Yeats had equal reservations when it came to working with professionally trained actors from London. These matters were compounded by the national status the Abbey directors accorded the theatre, given political circumstances in Ireland at the time, in particular the irreversible diminution of influence exercised by the Irish Protestant landowning class with the enactment of George Wyndham's Land Bill of 1903. Yeats found himself in persistent wrangling with the Fay brothers, Frank and Willie, regarding the direction, casting and acting style for his plays. This was exacerbated by the continuous interference of Annie Horniman, who despised the Fays and any nationalist colouring lent to what she regarded as her theatre of art. The impact of the voice experiment was qualified by the fraught circumstances at the Abbey Theatre where Yeats was trying to develop it, yet some element of estranging power comes through in the women's chorus of his 1903 play, On Baile's Strand and, more markedly, in the speech-patterns of Deirdre, first performed in Dublin in 1906 with Mrs Patrick Campbell in the leading role. In these statuesque plays, action is kept to a minimum, each element acquiring the aspect of a moment in a rite of passage to an interior landscape of the soul. In sharp contrast to the Kiltartan dialect of Gregory's plays or the unique rhythms of Synge, Yeats sought a spartan discipline in the mode of delivery, aiming away from plot development and towards the creation of a single tragic moment.

Recent criticism has called into question the presumption that, in the pursuit of a stylized theatre of art, Yeats sought to free cultural life in Ireland from political division and acrimony. Adrian Frazier and Lionel Pilkington have forcefully demonstrated the extent to which, as a national institution, the Abbey Theatre could not remain immune from fractious political affairs. Challenging earlier critical narratives of the Abbey Theatre as instrumental to a broader political movement towards Irish independence, Pilkington debunks one gesture supporting such a view: the decision not to cancel Abbey performances as a mark of respect at the death of King Edward VII on 11 March 1910. This had led to Horniman finally withdrawing her subsidy to the Abbey. Pilkington points out, however, that the Abbey remained opened by accident; on the basis of a letter of apology that appeared in the Irish Times on 13 March, it appears that had the directors found out in time, the Abbey would indeed have been closed.[3] The clash between claims for artistic freedom and political loyalties was most clearly dramatized in the disturbances following the opening performance of Synge's The Playboy of the Western World in January 1907. Adrian Frazier points out that the traditional view of the riots as a clash of art and politics overlooks the extent to which political motives lay as much with those defending Synge's play as with those attacking it. Frazier draws attention in particular to William Boyle's shock at the glee with which Horniman greeted events, expressing her vitriolic hatred for Irish nationalism, leading Boyle to withdraw his plays from the Abbey.[4]

In their combination of verse form, the aspiration to aesthetic subtlety, and the recurrent theme of a spiritual otherworld, Yeats's plays of the 1900s appeared not only devoid of any explicit political interest, but deliberately set against the kind of Shavian theatre of ideas for which politics was the central preoccupation. The obvious exception was Cathleen ni Houlihan but, even then, the emphasis lay heavily on the spiritual. Some of Yeats's own comments were significant in shaping that view of the Abbey Theatre struggles of the 1900s as a conflict of art and politics. In his preface to the 1906 version of The King's Threshold, he commented on how the play had first been written when the Irish National Theatre Society was struggling for the recognition of 'pure art' in an Irish society 'of which one half was buried in the practical affairs of life, and the other half in politics and a propagandist patriotism'.[5] The subject of The King's Threshold, derived from a fifteenth-century tale from Co. Galway but owing much to the influence of Shelley's An Apology for Poetry, marks an opposition between the poet and his society that appears to reinforce that distinction Yeats made between art and politics in several important poems subsequently, particularly 'On Being Asked for a War Poem' and 'Politics'. Yet the play treats a subject that would have a critical and emotive impact on Irish political history in the twentieth century – hunger strike. Often dismissed as of little relevance for contemporary experience and devoid of any engaging action, the play shows itself to be quite complex in its treatment of poetry and its place in political affairs. His position at the Court of King Guaire having been terminated at the request of the Bishop and the Mayor, Seanchan lies on the steps of the palace in protest, refusing to heed the pleading of the King, the Mayor and his students to end his fast.

All elements in The King's Threshold, including the use of an inner proscenium designed in collaboration with Edward Gordon Craig, were intended to represent an artistically autonomous play in the classical Greek style. But this same autonomy comments upon the figure of Seanchan himself, separated from those around him and gradually withdrawing into his own poetic imagination as the play moves to its conclusion. It is important to acknowledge it formally and thematically as a protest play; the presentation of Seanchan's devotion to the vocation of poet through a stylized poetic medium was a gesture of defiance against the society of Yeats's own day, particularly in regard to the commercialization of theatres, but also against the subordination of the arts to particular political ends. This protest form explains the ease with which Yeats could draw on the play, for all its sense of poetic elevation, in protest against the British Government in the aftermath of the death by hunger strike of Terence MacSwiney, Lord Mayor of Cork, in 1920. Simply changing the conclusion from the original version – in which

king and poet are reconciled – to have Seanchan die before an unrelent-
ing king and the state he represented, Yeats converged the theme of artistic and political protest this time in sympathy with the course of radical
Irish nationalism.

The King's Threshold is one example of the political complexity of Yeats's
drama in the 1900s, performed as the popularity of Gregory's plays and
the controversy of Synge's were distinguishing the Abbey repertoire in
Dublin and abroad. The theme of the artist figure in conflict with his age
recurs in Where There Is Nothing, On Baile's Strand and The Green Helmet. The first
of these is one of Yeats's most intriguing if uneven plays of the decade,
presenting the character of Paul Ruttledge who rejects his respectable
middle-class background to live first among a community of travellers,
then among a community of monks, before preaching a sermon of spiritual anarchism that splits this community apart. Ruttledge's family suspect him of madness and in the end he is beaten to death by a mob. The
play appears to be a strong influence on Synge's The Tinker's Wedding, published two years later in 1904. It is also strongly indebted to the ideas of
Nietzsche that Yeats learnt through his friend Arthur Symons; Yeats was
to become absorbed in Nietzsche's work after John Quinn presented
him a three-volume edition early in 1903.[6] Most of all, however, the play
marks the earlier influence of William Morris on Yeats in the 1890s, a
man who, like Blake, sought a movement for political freedom according central prominence to art in shaping a vision of a new society. Not
political in any programmatic sense, Where There Is Nothing nonetheless
addresses the revolutionary impact of the artist-type on his society and
the disturbance following his wilful assertions of creative freedom. The
idea is taken up again in On Baile's Strand and The Green Helmet, the first of
his five plays on Cuchulain. These were mythical interpretations of the
heroic personality out of line with the trend towards intellectual con-
formity that Yeats discerned in his own day in the power of the press to
form public opinion.

Richard Ellmann has suggested that Yeats's drama of the 1900s was
fatally undermined by his partiality for theories of theatre that got in the
way of what might have been compelling productions.[7] There is some
truth in this, but two observations are worth bearing in mind. The Irish
Literary Theatre emerged not simply from the desire to represent Ireland

as 'the home of an ancient idealism', as the movement's inaugural state-
ment put it.[8] It had also grown out of a feeling of immense dissatisfaction
within bohemian intellectual circles of London and Paris towards the end
of the nineteenth century at the state of contemporary theatre. This had
given rise to new movements abroad, in particular Naturalism, Symbolism
and Alfred Jarry's Ubu Roi of 1896, the earliest example of what would later
be coined Surrealism. The experiments Yeats undertook in the 1900s were
part of that search for a new theatre that might recover a sense of its own
artistic values and challenge contemporary popular taste. Bringing his
belief in magic and the supernatural into the structure of performances,
Yeats was aiming to renew interest in Celtic mysticism conceived as part
of a universal arcane knowledge common to all ancient civilizations.
Somewhat paradoxically, this required completely new forms of theatrical
production and performance with which contemporary audiences would
be unfamiliar.

The performance of Deirdre of 1906 was the one instance where the
balance between – in Eagleton's phrase – the archaic and the avant-garde
achieved a measure of success.[9] Here Yeats drew on the final moments
from one of the most poignant and popular tales of Irish mythology, the
story of Deirdre and the Sons of Usna, previously treated by Samuel
Ferguson, Standish O'Grady, Augusta Gregory and George Russell.
Primarily through the crisp poetic dialogue delivered according to the
method of the psaltery experiment, Yeats succeeded in harnessing all
theatrical elements to the single tragic instance of Naoise's death and
Deirdre's consequent suicide. The solemnity of the piece showed
through the general influence of Wagner and, more directly, the conclusion to Villers de l'Isle-Adam's Axël, in which the suicide of the lovers
represents the apex of symbolic movements through which their love
achieves its highest intensity. In its verse form and stylized solemnity the
play was indebted to classical and Elizabethan theatre, yet it was equally
anticipating the obsessive preoccupation with theatrical self-reflection
that characterized continental European drama from the 1920s, particularly the work of the Sicilian dramatist Luigi Pirandello.

This is most evident in the chess game the lovers play immediately
before their deaths, a game that not only binds their fate to that of an
earlier mythic pair who met the same end, Lugaidh Redstripe and his

wife, but also shows the play itself as a game in which the lovers become ensared (*VP1*, p.373). Likewise, while the equipoise of poetic speech in the play is undoubted testimony to Shakespeare's influence, Yeats was also anticipating, however inadvertently, new developments in the philosophy of language that would exert a profound influence on literary developments in Europe subsequently. In Gregory's prose version of the story of Deirdre and the sons of Usna, the king of Ulster's seer, Levarcham, is sent to spy on Deirdre and Naoise after they have arrived at the House of the Red Branch of Ulster. There she finds the lovers playing chess and reports the beauty of Deirdre back to King Conchubar.[10] In Yeats's play, this incident is transformed into the formal structure of the tale as a tragedy in which Deirdre and Naoise enter into the realm of myth. In the process, the play itself becomes a game of chess, the poetry of the lovers' speech a tapestry of their destiny. Language and gesture denote nothing other than a ceremonial enactment of the fate realized in the performance. Theories of language that would prove hugely influential for the writers and dramatists of the modernist era bear no relation to the classicism and poignancy of *Deirdre*. Nonetheless, both Wittgenstein and Saussure identified in chess the purest image of language as they conceived it. Furthermore, in drawing analogies between the operations of language and the rules of chess on the basis of *custom* as a governing principle, their ideas were not nearly as remote from the manner in which the chess game is used in *Deirdre*, for all its esotericism and archaism of word and image.[11] The verse form of *Deirdre* was certainly intended to recover a tradition of poetic speech in performance, yet it also contributed to a new movement for intellectual theatre in which what Yeats regarded as the slovenly lyricism of melodrama and the turgid rhetoric of stage realism would be exchanged for a concentrated treatment of the linguistic medium itself as the subject of performance.

Yeats's experiments with theatre space were another dimension to this search for a new form of theatre capable of reviving the imaginative and spiritual power of drama in performance. Edward Gordon Craig, son of the London actress Ellen Terry, was a crucial influence here. Yeats had known Craig and his sister Edith since the 1890s, and Edith had invited him to write verses for a lament in Edward's 1903 production of Ibsen's *The Vikings of Helgeland*, which ran at the Imperial Theatre from 15

April to 14 May 1903. Feeling Yeats's verses for Örnulf's funeral chant over his seven dead sons in Act IV of the play to be too unlike Ibsen, however, Craig decided to stick with William Archer's original translation (CL3, pp.323–6). Their collaboration made its most formidable impact when Craig's screens were first employed at the Abbey Theatre during 1910–12. These were used in 1911 as the basis for a new spatially oriented interpretation of Yeats's 1903 play, The Hour-Glass, along with Gregory's new play, The Deliverer, and a revised version of The Countess Cathleen.[12] Craig's development of mobile architecture for performance aimed at a total synaesthetic effect: space, light, movement and speech harmonized to a single dramatic purpose. Above all, Craig desired a theatre of artifice in defiance of what he saw as the clumsy combination of organic and inorganic elements in contemporary theatre.[13] Many of the striking experiments in theatrical form that distinguished Yeats's plays from 1916 were anticipated in the ideas for a new theatre that Craig promoted through his Florence-based journal, The Mask, and his works On the Art of the Theatre and Towards a New Theatre from the 1911–13 period.

Craig's influence on Yeats bore fruit in the first of his plays written in the style of Japanese Noh theatre, At the Hawk's Well, performed at Lady Cunard's London drawing-room in April 1916. The narrative is stripped to its barest elements in this play. There is virtually no movement, save for the hawk dance of the Guardian of the Well. A development of those ideas of theatre space Yeats had been working out with Craig since the late 1900s, the play also looks back to the Symbolist drama of Maurice Maeterlinck from the 1890s, drama that was striking for its effective manipulation of stage space. Yeats emphatically rejects the painted landscapes of melodrama and naturalism here. Seeking instead to conjure the presence of spirits through the situational immediacy of performance, he offers as the stage for the play 'any bare space before a wall against which stands a patterned screen' (VP1, p.398). Yeats's adaptation of the Noh style for At the Hawk's Well coincided with the publication by Macmillan of Ernesto Fenellosa's translations of several Noh plays in the 1916 volume, Noh, Or Accomplishment, co-authored with Ezra Pound. Interest in Japanese art within London bohemian culture stretched back to the 1890s. The Dome, for example, reprinted works by the eighteenth-century Japanese artists Utagawa Hiroshige, Katsushika Hokusai and Kitagawa Utamaro in issues from 1897 and 1898, when the magazine was also printing Yeats's poems, 'The Desire of Man and of Woman', 'Aodh to Dectora', 'Song of Mongan', as well as his influential essay, 'The Theatre'.[14] One of the features that most attracted Yeats to the Noh form was its use of masks. Not only did this prevent any clumsy movement between the naturalistic and the artificial – the complaint of Craig – it allowed expression to become concentrated on a single idea or purpose. This in turn heightened the feeling for the supernatural in performance, the primary function of the mask in Noh theatre, as Donald Keene notes: 'Noh begins with a mask, and within the mask the presence of a god.'[15]

At the Hawk's Well presents its audience with the figure of an Old Man who has been waiting for years beside a dried-up well in the hope that its waters would flow one day, believing that these waters granted immortality. The Guardian of the Well stands static and mute beside it, indifferent to the Old Man's bitter laments. A Young Man appears wearing the mask of Cuchulain, derides the Old Man for his folly, and determines to achieve immortality through the waters. At the cry of a hawk the Guardian awakens to perform the hawk dance. During the dance, the waters flow and the Young Man falls into a trance, following the Guardian off-stage after the dance has been completed. The Old Man awakens from sleep to discover that the waters had flown, and curses his fate. This action is framed by the songs of musicians at the start and the end, sung for the unfolding and folding of a black cloth with a gold pattern suggesting a hawk. No details are given as to the characters of the Old Man and the Young Man; the songs of the musicians reflect on fate as a universal condition rather than the particular fates of these men. The three figures in the play are archetypes and what little narrative there is remains purely mythical.

The lack of any character development and the thinness of plot suggest that this Noh experiment has little enduring theatrical quality. Furthermore, as a medium for evoking a sense of supernatural presences through the structure of myth, the play seems far removed from the dominant sensibility of western theatre as it has evolved since the early twentieth century, particularly in its preoccupations with a loss of religious faith and the struggle to find durable values in modern society.

Remoteness was certainly a quality Yeats sought to achieve in his poetry and drama, but criticism has tended to confuse this with indifference. Furthermore, in painting through the songs of the musicians a landscape suggesting the Sligo of Yeats's childhood, and taking as its subject one of the most famous figures of Irish mythology, *At the Hawk's Well* appears rooted in the sensibility of Irish Romanticism, for all the esotericism of its form. Remoteness in this sense conjures a sense of the otherworld specific to the traditions and beliefs of the west of Ireland, removed from the complexities and anxieties of contemporary urban life.

The absence of character or plot development in *At the Hawk's Well* and subsequent dance plays – *The Only Jealousy of Emer*, *The Dreaming of the Bones*, *Calvary* and *The Death of Cuchulain* – was consistent with a belief Yeats shared with Craig that modern theatre was losing the sense of its own artistic values in addressing social issues as they arose, pandering to public taste, or attempting to represent scenes too realistically on stage. In fact, the Noh experiment Yeats began with *At the Hawk's Well* was one of the earliest examples of anti-theatre, a species of theatrical experiment that would mark its presence most forcefully in the years after the First World War, particularly through the drama of Pirandello. These plays refused all the conventions of mainstream theatre of the time in the attempt to address what was felt to be a deep-rooted crisis of value in western culture. This sense received its most controversial and influential expression in Oswald Spengler's *The Decline of the West*, first published in 1918, a work in which the author argues that western culture was in its last phase, the 'de-souling of the human being' likely to set in around 2000.[16] While a belief in the reality of supernatural power is evident in all the dance plays Yeats wrote from 1916, spiritual redemption is frustrated in all instances. Yeats may have engaged religious forms and themes here, but the outcome is always damnation and loss, or even mockery of the God, as in *Calvary*.

The achievement of the dance plays lay not in a successful presentation of cosmic and mythic visions of antiquity but in the controlled delivery of a concentrated vision of human alienation. Little has been made of the fact that Yeats intended the actors to move in the manner of marionettes for *At the Hawk's Well*, *The Only Jealousy of Emer*, *The Dreaming of the Bones* and *Calvary*. This was important in locating the Noh experiment in relation to the theatrical developments of Paris in the 1890s; both Maeterlinck and Jarry engaged the marionette acting style in addressing spiritual loss. In Jarry's case, this style was in part intended to deride the stilted convention of contemporary social mores through exaggerated imitation; in Maeterlinck's drama of the interior, it expressed the spiritual paralysis of an entire culture. Yeats's preference for this style also owed much to Craig's experiments and the ideas proposed in pieces like 'The Actor and the Übermarionette'. This marionette style was to be concentrated in the Hawk dance, first performed in 1916 by the Japanese dancer, Michio Ito. Yeats's vision of the dance here and its role in theatrical performance was far from the lascivious sensuality of Salomé's dance in Wilde's play of 1895. Adapting the almost mechanical movements of the hawk, the dance drew on Japanese (and Egyptian) traditions to convey the state of the automaton, the figure stiffened under the power of a hidden will. In this way, the marionette style and the dance form of these plays participated in the vision of the primitive to come through in the cubist rigour of Picasso and Braque. To this end, Yeats's dance plays were complex responses to processes of mechanization made violently manifest in the First World War, representing these through a primeval identification with the totem. This subject had become an obsession in the late nineteenth century through the work of Andrew Lang, Alfred Nutt and Max Müller – in Sir James Frazer's *The Golden Bough*, the generation of Yeats and Eliot found a rich source of primitive rituals, customs and totem practices through which what they sensed as a crisis of value in western culture could be addressed artistically.

With the exception of *The Words Upon the Window-pane* (1930) and *Purgatory* (1938) Yeats's late drama has remained largely inaccessible to audiences, mired in the obscurity of the Automatic Script from which the esoteric system of *A Vision* first evolved. In a play like *The King of the Great Clock Tower* it seems as if the drowsy Emperor of 'Sailing to Byzantium' had finally nodded off. This is compounded by the sense that Yeats was writing for a cognoscenti audience, reinforcing the aloof figure of the ageing poet withdrawn to his Galway tower. The decision to reject *The Silver Tassie* in 1928 was critical to the profile Yeats acquired subsequently as poet and dramatist. While the sheer power of collections like *The Tower* and *The Winding Stair* guaranteed a monumental reputation as poet, the experimental form through which he treated occult themes in a play like *The Herne's Egg* left audiences bewildered. Seen against the backdrop of the O'Casey fallout and the stagnation into which the Abbey Theatre was sinking in the 1930s, it was far easier to receive the experiments of *The Herne's Egg* as the creation of a mind sinking into incoherence than a last vital attack on the contemporary world in the style of Jarry's *Ubu Roi*. Yet the plays written and performed in the 1920s and 1930s developed thematic preoccupations that extended back to the 1890s. If anything, the direction European politics had taken since the outbreak of hostilities in August 1914 reinforced in Yeats's mind the pertinence of those themes already in evidence in plays of the 1900s; spiritual crisis, cultural uniformity and the hypnotic power of an all-encompassing will that was already in evidence in plays of the 1900s.

The manner in which Yeats shaped plays like *The Only Jealousy of Emer*, *The Player Queen* and *The Words Upon the Window-pane* according to his notion of *commedia dell'arte* shared much with Pirandello's experiments, particularly *Six Characters in Search of an Author* of 1921. This derived in significant measure from Yeats's obsession with will in his late work, an obsession springing from a fulsome determination to remake himself artistically as the onslaught of physical decline took hold, and from his acute sensitivity to the all-consuming power of collective will taking form in the Bolshevik Revolution and the creation of the Soviet empire. A consonance with the recurrent themes of Expressionist theatre between the wars was evident here, particularly the plays of Ernst Toller that Yeats read in the 1930s. These points of comparison are evidence of that experimental spirit Yeats brought to his work in the theatre from the 1890s. They illustrate the extent to which the obscure and disturbing occult motifs in much of his later drama gave form to the private trauma his decades-long passion for Maud Gonne had generated, but also show how attentive he was to the shape European politics was taking between the wars. The violent esoteric symbolism of *The Herne's Egg* and *Purgatory* not only resonated with Spengler's idea of the 'Faustian' nature of western culture, characterized by will and force, and now in its final phase. It also gave expression to that idea through the peculiar abstract energy these plays realized in performance. In this way, Yeats made a significant contribution through these plays to European avant-garde theatre of the 1920s and 1930s.

The lack of critical interest in Yeats's drama in recent times and the rarity of performances in Ireland today create the impression that his drama was of minor significance in its time and even less so now. This contrasts sharply with the huge international acclaim the drama of Samuel Beckett continues to enjoy and a recent revival of interest in the drama of Synge with the Druid theatre's extraordinary production of the entire cycle of his plays under the direction of Gary Hynes in 2005, a production that was taken subsequently to Britain, the United States and China. At face value this is hardly surprising. Yeats's plays were written in blank verse, a form virtually obsolete in contemporary theatre; they were steeped in Irish folklore and mythology, for many, outdated subjects for serious Irish theatre today; they were laden with obscure symbols deriving from Yeats's interest in esoteric mysticism of diverse provenance. Sam MacCready's laudable efforts to sustain interest in the plays in Ireland, primarily through annual productions at the International Yeats Summer School in Sligo, have not redressed this to any significant degree. Ulick O'Connor's production of Yeats's version of *Deirdre* in February 2008 at the National Library of Ireland in Dublin alongside his own Noh-style interpretation of the legend achieved a measure of success without generating a new enthusiasm. The unwillingness to recognize Yeats's drama as a unique contribution to the European avant-garde in the early twentieth century has been an unfortunate consequence of this general indifference, particularly the manner through which his experiments with Craig bridged the gap between French Symbolism of the 1890s and German Expressionism in the years of the First World War. The classical, mythological and esoteric aspects of his later drama resonated also with certain works of French Surrealism, particularly Cocteau's *Orpheus*. However much Yeats's drama championed antiquity, mysticism and classicism, his experiments with the medium of theatre were far-reaching in their day, exuding in their best moments a mood of estrangement forbidding in scale and intensity.

NOTES

1. Frank Fay, *Towards a National Theatre: the Dramatic Criticism of Frank J. Fay*, ed. Robert Hogan (Dublin: The Dolmen Press, 1970), p.103.
2. W.B. Yeats, 'Speaking to the Psaltery', in *Essays and Introductions* (London: Macmillan, Press, 1961), pp.14–15.

3. Lionel Pilkington, *Theatre and the State in 20th Century Ireland: Cultivating the People* (London: Routledge, 2001), pp.64–5.

4. Adrian Frazier, *Behind the Scenes: Yeats, Horniman, and the Struggle for the Abbey Theatre* (Berkeley, CA: University of California Press, 1990), pp.217–18.

5. Russell K. Alspach (ed.), *The Variorum Edition of the Plays of W.B. Yeats* (London: Macmillan, 1966), p.315, hereafter referred to in the text as *VP1*.

6. *The Collected Letters of W.B. Yeats*, III, 1901–1904, ed. John Kelly and Ronald Schuchard (Oxford: Clarendon Press, 1994), p.312; hereafter referred to in the text as *CL3*.

7. Richard Ellmann, *Yeats: The Man and the Masks*, 2nd edn (London: Faber, 1961), p.186.

8. Lady Augusta Gregory, *Our Irish Theatre: A Chapter of Autobiography*, 3rd edn (Gerrards Cross: Colin Smythe, 1975), p.20.

9. Terry Eagleton, *Heathcliff and the Great Hunger: Studies in Irish Culture* (London: Verso, 1995), pp.273–319.

10. Lady Augusta Gregory, *Cuchulain of Muirthemne* (London: J. Murray, 1903), pp.106–7.

11. Ludwig Wittgenstein, *Philosophical Investigations*, 3rd edn, trans. G.E.M. Anscombe (Oxford: Basil Blackwell, 1958), pp.47, 81; Ferdinand de Saussure, *Course in General Linguistics*, trans. Roy Harris (London: Duckworth Press, 1983), p.88. Thomas Sturge Moore would point Yeats to Wittgenstein's *Tractactus Logico-Philosophicus* many years after the composition of *Deirdre*, though later admitting his own inability to understand him. See Moore to Yeats, 15 November 1929, in *W. B. Yeats and T. Sturge Moore: Their Correspondence, 1901–1937*, ed. Ursula Bridges (London: Routledge & Kegan Paul, 1953), p.157.

12. James Flannery, 'Yeats, Gordon Craig and the Visual Arts of the Theatre', in *Yeats and the Theatre*, ed. Robert O'Driscoll and Lorna Reynolds (London: Macmillan, 1975), pp.102–3.

13. Edward Gordon Craig, *Rearrangements* (1915), in *Twentieth Century Theatre: A Sourcebook*, ed. Richard Drain (London: Routledge, 1995), p.17.

14. See *The Dome: A Quarterly Containing Examples of all the Arts* (London: The Unicorn Press), Vol.2 (1897), pp.48–9; Vol.3 (1897), p.59; Vol.4 (1898), pp.67, 69; Vol.5 (1898), p.37. See also *The Dome: An Illustrated Magazine and Review of Literature, Music, Architecture and the Graphic Arts*, vol.1 (1898), p.36.

15. Donald Keene, *Noh, The Classical Theatre of Japan* (Tokyo, 1966), p.19. Quoted in Liam Miller, *The Noble Drama of W.B. Yeats* (Dublin: The Dolmen Press, 1977), p.193.

16. Oswald Spengler, *The Decline of the West: Form and Actuality*, 2nd edn, trans. Charles Francis Atkinson (London: George Allen & Unwin, 1926), p.352.

CHAPTER EIGHT

Yeats's Thought

DAVID DWAN

INTRODUCTION

Yeats was not a notably systematic thinker and his writings contain many contradictions. This may have been a point of pride to someone who professed to despise 'logic' and often equated 'reason' with ugliness, but it also makes the substance of his thought hard to grasp.[1] He volunteered opinions on a wide range of thinkers and subjects, but his judgements were often as sweeping as they were idiosyncratic. He insisted, for instance, that Thomas Hobbes (1588–1679) had corrupted political thought; at other points, however, Jean-Jacques Rousseau (1712–78) was the supreme evil genius.[2] However, his understanding of both thinkers appears to have been extremely thin. He professed himself an amateur in philosophy; yet he philosophized copiously nonetheless. The uneven quality of these performances does nothing to detract from his majesty as a poet. On one point Yeats was convinced: 'that whatever of philosophy has been made poetry is alone permanent' (E&I, p.65). Nevertheless, some engagement with his more abstract or philosophical thought is a necessary prerequisite for a full appreciation of his poetry. 'All writers', he claimed, 'in so far as they have been deliberate artists at all have had some philosophy' (p.154), and Yeats was also keen to have his own theoretical system. Works such as *A Vision* are a testimony of this ambition; but their combination of insight and august nonsense reveals the highly unorthodox character of Yeats's 'system'.

Yeats's thought is not reducible to a single or coherent doctrine, but it contains, nevertheless, some overarching preoccupations. For instance, he was strongly committed to the idea of 'Unity of Being'. What he meant by this was not always obvious. He first used the phrase in one of his 'automatic' scripts of 1918, although he was pledged to the idea long before then.[3] He later attributed the phrase to the Florentine poet Dante Alighieri (1265–1321); however, it was also related in his mind to a host of other figures from St Patrick to the poet William Blake (1757–1827).[4] Drawing on Dante, he compared 'Unity of Being' to 'a perfectly proportioned human body', but this was not a particularly developed explanation.[5] It left open the question of how a body should be viewed – as a simple entity or as something composite – and how unity, therefore, should be precisely conceived. Absolute unity, he sometimes suggested, could not have a corporeal form, because a body implied a limit or a division between itself and other entities. Unity eluded definition, but he would search for it for most of his life. Even as he did so, however, he wondered if perfect unity was possible or wholly desirable. There were good philosophical and practical grounds for his misgivings. The structure of these doubts is worth considering, because they reveal core features of his thought.

THE METAPHYSICS OF UNITY

Yeats's search for unity was based upon a strong set of metaphysical assumptions; arguably, it was only on the basis of these assumptions that he could discover so much rupture in the world. The world's 'fall into division' (A, p.502) presupposed a prior integration to which he yearned to return. Here Yeats revealed a distinctly 'Platonic' mindset: in other words, he was committed to an ideal of cosmic unity involving a hierarchical account of being that had been championed in different forms in the West for over 2,000 years. 'Plato thinks all things into Unity', he opined, and Yeats was also inclined to do so (V, pp.262–3). His understanding of Plato (427?–347 BC) was heavily mediated through others – through a Christian tradition of Platonism; through writers such as Shelley (1792–1822), William Blake (1757–1827) and Walter Pater (1839–94); through the rituals of theosophy and the aesthetic practices of Symbolism – but in later life he claimed to be reading Plato on a daily basis.[6] He also immersed himself in one of Plato's most gifted interpreters, the Egyptian philosopher Plotinus (AD 204–70). His friend Stephen MacKenna

(1872–1934), completed a translation of Plotinus's *Enneads* in 1931 and Yeats turned to it repeatedly as a reservoir of metaphor and esoteric wisdom.[7] He was also keen to establish Plotinus's folk credentials: the citizens of Connaught, he insisted, shared views remarkably similar to the ancient Egyptian.[8] In later poems, he set out to 'mock Plotinus' thought / And cry in Plato's teeth' ('The Tower', *VP*, p.415), but he would find it difficult to relinquish his Platonic habits of mind.

What were these habits? Platonism and Neo-Platonism were primarily a useful source of symbols – he was particularly indebted to Plotinus's student Porphyry for images of generation such as water – but they also furnished the poet with basic conceptual frameworks through which sense of cosmic order was conceived. The linchpin of this system was Plato's notion of the 'Good', or what Plotinus called the 'One' – insisting that the 'One' and the 'Good' had an 'identical nature' – or what Christianity would call God.[9] Yeats deployed all of these terms as well as an eclectic mix of others. For Plato, the Good was the source of all reality and it was the point to which all things aspired to return.[10] It gave everything its shape, but it was not subject to the shaping influence of any other thing. If it was so dependent, it would not take its rule from itself; it would be contingent and not absolute or wholly sovereign. For this reason, Plotinus declared the Good to be 'formless', for a form implies a specific determination or limit and there were no limits to the Good; it was the measure of all things, but it was not subject to measurement itself.[11] For this reason, it existed outside time and space and was both everywhere and nowhere. It thus eluded understanding and always exceeded the hard edges of our categories and concepts. On contact with this ultimate reality, as Yeats suggested, 'man is stricken deaf and dumb and blind' ('Dialogue of Self and Soul', *VP*, p.478).

Yeats was greatly attracted to the Neo-Platonic idea of a perfect reality that existed outside 'the deserts of time and space' (*E&I*, p.133). His early works involve a series of imaginative attempts to access this through the limited resources of language. Thus he often moves from description to redescription – 'Red Rose, proud Rose, sad Rose of all my days!' ('To the Rose upon the Rood of Time', *VP*, p.100) – in an ambitious, albeit doomed, attempt to capture the ideal in language. His aim is similar to that of the French poet Stéphane Mallarmé (1842–98) whom he admired: to describe the flower 'that is absent from all bouquets'.[12] Implicit in the search for the supreme flower is a Platonic investment in ideal forms – the eternal, changeless and incorporeal objects behind everyday things. For Plato, all sensible life derived from a super-sensible template; material existence was merely a degraded copy of an ideal order. Yeats remained committed to key features of this world-picture for much of his career. He endorsed Blake's belief in 'the real and eternal world of which this vegetable universe is but a faint shadow' (E&I, p.135). And he was unhappy with those who assumed 'that the external and material are the only fixed things, the only standards of reality'.[13]

This accounts for his lifelong opposition to empiricism – a philosophical tradition which made experience the sole source and test of knowledge. Threading together a disparate set of thinkers he claimed: 'Descartes, Locke, and Newton took away the world and gave us its excrement instead' (Ex, p.325). He liked to suggest that the Irish were constitutionally disposed to resist this form of empiricism – or what he often termed 'materialism'.[14] In his pursuit of a more enlightened idealism, Yeats sometimes presented 'matter' as an inferior reality or as something which had no essential reality at all. For Neo-Platonists such as Plotinus, matter was a form of non-being. This did not mean that matter did not exist as such; but rather that it was something which produced and measured our distance from true being. Matter was thus a form of privation. As the ground and index of the absence of the Good, it was an 'unredeemed evil'.[15] For material creatures like ourselves, this could come as dispiriting news. Carnal man seemed an 'unclean thing': 'flickering hither and thither at the call of objects of sense, deeply infected with the taint of the body'. Our bodily nature was an index of our corruption: 'a Soul becomes ugly', Plotinus opined, 'by sinking itself into the alien, by a fall, a descent into body, into Matter'.[16] Yeats often conceived of 'the soul betrayed into the flesh' as a type of degradation.[17] He hoped at times to escape the corruption of the flesh, 'the impulse of bodily longing and the restraints of bodily reason' (E&I, p.133). Carnal desire was the expression and aggravation of lack. He often cherished, therefore, the 'autumn of the body' (p.191) and frequently longed for its demise.

Here time was also a privation. In the Platonic tradition, only the Good truly *is*; it is absolute and immutable and transcends all past and future.[18] Earthly creatures, however, are finite and subject to change. Human beings can never simply *be*, but shuttle between states of existence which are always to some extent states of non-being; we move from a past that no longer is, towards a future that is not yet. Thus we live in exile from the absolute. For Yeats, therefore, temporality is often a form of alienation. It is akin to crucifixion in 'To the Rose upon the Rood of Time' (*VP*, p.100). The young poet repeatedly aims to escape time's confines and to arrive at some non-contingent state of being – a state where the soul is 'disentangled from unmeaning circumstance and the ebb and flow of the world' (*E&I*, p.95). This desire often expressed itself in fantasies of death. 'He mourns for the change that has come upon him and his Beloved, and longs for the End of the World' (*VP*, p.153) is one such instance; 'He wishes his Beloved were Dead' (pp.175–6) is another. Since the world of time and space are, to a large degree, forms of non-being, the self-annihilation of the mystic-poet or the homicide of his beloved can be seen as a negation of nothingness; such acts are a reassertion of faith in pure being.

The tradition of Neo-Platonism, therefore, furnished Yeats with a formidable theory of integration. The 'One' is an *absolute* unity; it was, as Plotinus suggested, a perfect 'Simplex' and was characterized by 'an utter absence of distinction'.[19] In contrast to this oneness, our world of difference and division seemed to be 'a manifold illusion'. The phenomenal world yielded many kinds of untruth, but the idea of a manifold was arguably the greatest illusion of all. In 'Meru', Yeats speaks of the 'desolation of reality' (*VP*, p.563) where all sense of difference breaks down. This involves a unity so perfect that it is almost akin to nothingness. The One after all is not 'something', for to be a thing is to possess an identity that is bounded and relative to other things; but the One has no limits and has no relation to anything external to itself. As Plotinus put it: 'Generative of all, The Unity is none of all; neither thing nor quantity nor quality nor intellect nor soul; not in motion, not at rest, not in place not in time'.[20] This may seem like an ornate description of nothing, but it is the only thing which truly *is*. This is the metaphysical thesis implicit in the title of one of Yeats's tales of the 1890s: 'Where there is Nothing, there is God'.[21] Our return to God or to the 'One' involves a sense of annihilation that is really a return to absolute being. It is consummated by a perfect form of understanding in which all difference between knower and known is obliterated. In 'Fergus and the Druid', Fergus finds himself 'grown nothing, knowing all' (VP, p.104).

Significantly, however, Fergus still seems a disconsolate figure who finds 'great webs of sorrow' (VP, p.104) in minute things. This may be a reiteration of Platonic verities: seen from the context of the absolute all earthly things are a form of lack. On more than one occasion, Yeats explicitly invoked Plotinus to argue that in human life 'it is not the interior soul and the true man, but the exterior shadow of the man alone, which laments and weeps' (UP II, p.112). But figures like Fergus remain attached to external things and find their abandonment a source of some upset. The attainment of transcendence comes at a price, at least when it was viewed from an earthly position; it demands a turn from the physical world and even the obliteration of the embodied self. Yeats was acutely sensitive to these costs. He craves unity with the absolute in 'To the Rose upon the Rood of Time', but he also retreats from it:

> Come near, come near, come near – Ah, leave me still
> A little space for the rose-breath to fill!
> Lest I no more hear common things that crave; (VP, p.101)

All craving is an expression of lack, but from the earthly position that most of us occupy, it is also the ground of value. In late poems such as 'Vacillation' the soul instructs us to '[s]eek out reality, leave things that seem' (VP, p.502). But Yeats finds such leave-taking quite difficult. In situations such as these, he is often tempted to reject Plato's account of the Good as an implausible and harmful fantasy; it was an incitement to reject our concrete environments in the name of some impossible ideal.

Yeats's encounter with the German philosopher Friedrich Nietzsche (1844–1900), strengthened this impression. He read Nietzsche for the first time on a sustained and serious basis in 1902 and was much impressed by the 'strong enchanter'.[22] Nietzsche was a vociferous critic of Platonism; Plato was the great 'viaduct of corruption'; he was also 'boring'.[23] Nietzsche despised, above all, his 'ideomania' and his 'religious lunacy about forms'.[24] Plato's account of a super-sensible realm that stood over and above the sensible played a role in some aspects of Nietzsche's early thought, but later in his career he dismissed this metaphysical picture outright. Plato's idealism 'reversed the concept of "reality"', and sanctioned an ascetic rejection of the concrete world.[25] According to Nietzsche, this asceticism survived in the Christian tradition. Similarly, Yeats would come to regard Plato as the world's 'first Christian' (V, p.263; see also UP II, p.465). He also criticized the excessively abstract nature of Plato's idealism: 'when he separates the Eternal Ideas from Nature and shows them self-sustained he prepares the Christian desert and the Stoic suicide' (V, p.271).

According to Nietzsche, Plato's account of the sensible and supersensible features of the human personality divided people from themselves and encouraged them to hold their bodies in contempt. Nietzsche's hero, Zarathustra, condemns the 'despisers of the body'; such figures are 'angry with life and with the earth'.[26] In his Platonic moments, Yeats seemed to be one of those despisers. But, partly under the influence of Nietzsche, he began to reconsider his distrust of the bodily and the world of sense. The body eventually became for him a source and criterion of value: 'When the individual life no longer delights in its own energy, when the body is not made strong and beautiful by the activities of daily life, when men have no delight in decorating the body, one may be certain that one lives in a passing order, amid the inventions of a fading vitality' (E&I, pp.302–3). Here he promoted a holistic view of the self and shrank 'from every abstract thing, from all that is of the brain only, from all that is not a fountain jetting from the entire hopes, memories, and sensations of the body' (pp.292–3). He was sceptical, therefore, of abstract contrasts between mind and body, intellect and emotion. His aim was to capture a 'thinking of the body' which integrated all features of the self (p.292). Late in life, he attacked the Catholic Church for its contempt of the body; this, he insisted, was a violation of the Church's own doctrine: as St Thomas Aquinas (1225–74) had taught, 'the soul is wholly present in the whole body and in all its parts' (UP II, p.478). In its distrust of carnal desire, Irish Catholicism owed more to a Byzantine Platonism than it did to Aquinas. His poetic persona, Crazy Jane, would resume these theological issues in her quarrels with the Bishop.

In his reappraisal of the body, Yeats seemed to make his peace with both the material and finite character of the self. Matter was not an unmitigated evil, and time was not simply privation. This is the lesson that one of Yeats's earliest poetic personas, Oisin, seems to be faced with – but does not fully grasp – in his search for eternal life: our sense of value is inextricably linked to our mortal nature; removed from our time-bound condition, life would have no meaning. Yeats was thus already well disposed to appreciate Nietzsche's attack on Platonic 'Being'. For Plato, Being is the true reality; everything else is in a state of becoming and therefore never truly is. But Nietzsche was one of those who often championed becoming over Being. 'I call it evil and misanthropic', Zarathustra declares, 'all this teaching about the one and the perfect and the unmoved and the sufficient and the intransitory.' As far as Zarathustra is concerned, 'the best images and parables should speak of time and becoming: they should be a eulogy and a justification of all transitoriness'.[27] Yeats frequently produced such eulogies. He delighted in the 'living stream' of existence and was suspicious of those who wished to transcend the flux of nature in the name of some fixed and immutable principles ('Easter 1916', VP, p.393). This became a moral and political point for Yeats as much as it was a metaphysical notion. Drawing on Nietzsche as well as the great eighteenth-century Irish statesman Edmund Burke (1729–97), he repeatedly castigated Irish nationalists for their apparent commitment to abstract principles and fixed ideals; these absolutes were at odds with the temporal character of life itself.[28]

He found it difficult, of course, to relinquish fully his own hankering for the eternal. In 'Sailing to Byzantium' he seeks entry to the 'artifice of eternity'; even here, however, he acknowledges that the very concept of the eternal is potentially a fiction (VP, p.408). In his later poetry, Yeats described himself as a Platonist, but this was partly in self-disparagement. He was still haunted by the idea of an absolute unity beyond all difference; yet he also recognized that a metaphysical conception of unity often produced the very ruptures it sought to overcome. It led to a schism between the eternal and temporal, super-sensible and sensible worlds. Even though one of these worlds was supposed to originate from and, as Plato would have it, participate in, the other, there was no adequate ontological bridge between them. This rupture led in turn to the self-division of man and to an interminable quarrel between body and soul. Yeats, as we have seen, engaged in these quarrels, but he also searched for a more holistic conception of human beings and of their world. Here Yeats arguably remained pledged to a concept of unity, but he refused to conceive of it in Platonic terms. At other times, he seemed to subscribe to Platonic dualisms – or what he often called antinomies – but delighted in the rupture they seemed to constitute. Here he perceived the world as a 'continual conflict' and regarded discord as a condition of life (V, p.72). He sometimes implied that this conflict was oriented towards 'Unity of Being'; at other points, however, such prospects of integration were not to be found.[29] His uncertainty on this score had much to do with very concrete forms of discord in Ireland.

THE POLITICS OF UNITY

Yeats's metaphysical commitments had a sharp bearing on his politics; the reverse was also true. In 'If I were Four and Twenty' (1919), he appeared to recommend 'Unity of Being' as a national programme:

> When Dr. Hyde delivered in 1894 his lecture on the necessity of 'the de-anglicisation of Ireland', to a society that was a youthful indiscretion of my own, I heard an enthusiastic hearer say: 'This lecture begins a new epoch in Ireland'. It did that, and if I were not four-and-fifty, with no settled habit but the writing of verse, rheumatic, indolent, discouraged, and about to move to the Far East, I would begin another epoch by recommending to the Nation a new doctrine, that of unity of being. (Ex, p.280)

Here his endorsement of 'unity of being' was only hypothetical and was laced with bitter ironies. But it had been a serious practical ambition of his youth; it had shaped his sense of patriotism and gave to his art a broader social vocation. 'I always rouse myself to work', he wrote in 1909, 'by imagining an Ireland as much a unity in thought and feeling as ancient Greece and Rome and Egypt' (Mem, p.251). These societies had exhibited their sense of integration through their collective pursuit of cultural excellence, and he had hoped that modern Ireland would pursue a similar goal. He believed that the Young Ireland movement of the 1840s had shown – with the aid of some dubious poetry and bellicose journalism – that Irish citizens could unite under a common set of ideals. Yeats aimed for a similar kind of unity, but one organized around a richer model of art and a more complex understanding of the Good. His search for this solidarity made him a strong critic of 'individualism' – a broad ethical disposition which he traced back to the Renaissance.[30] His opposition to individualism was in part a logical extension of his metaphysical convictions. Viewed from Neo-Platonic heights, individuality was a distortion of true being, a form of alienation from the Good; it needed to be transcended if true unity were to be enjoyed.[31] This is one reason why we often find in his early poetry an overburdened subjectivity seeking to transcend itself through a set of liminal experiences – sleep, sex or death. But there were also more prosaic or concrete causes of alienation: the alienated self, after all, was both the symptom and source of a fragmented social order.

Yeats was convinced that the modern world 'was now but a bundle of fragments' (A, p.189). Deprived of shared frameworks of meaning, human beings necessarily fell back on their own resources for a sense of orientation in life; on the other hand, this turn to the self exacerbated the divisions to which it was a response. Individualism culminated in a collective alienation that was often misrepresented as freedom. He believed that freedom was a desirable good, but he also seemed to think that it was necessarily subordinate to a higher end. In one of his more authoritarian moments, he recommended 'not the widening of liberty, but a recovery from its errors'.[32] The political and moral consequences of individualism were regrettable, but it had also made dangerous inroads into art. It led to an aesthetic cult of personal idiosyncrasy and originality which disavowed in advance any shared understanding of life. 'Talk to me of originality', he declared in old age, 'and I will turn upon you with rage' (E&I, p.522). Art had a more important vocation than individual self-expression or personal satisfaction. Its role was to expound 'the ideal hope not of individual life, but of the race, its vision of itself made perfect' (UP II, p.200).

This search for a unified culture strained against some of the basic features of modern social organization. Modern life was a complex affair; its organizational logic was built around the 'division of labour' – a subdivision of economic practices and social roles that made for a more productive social system. Here efficiency and specialization went hand in hand. Like his early mentor, William Morris (1834–96), Yeats worried about the social costs of the division of labour and believed that the dominance of 'specialists' led to the demise of culture (Ex, p.432). Civilization seemed to replicate itself 'by division like certain low forms of life'; in doing so it eroded its conditions for social unity and deprived individuals of an integrated understanding of their world (A, p.194). The division of labour, he believed, destroyed human character; the pursuit of a highly restricted set of skills connived against a more integrated form of personal development in which all talents found full expression. Yeats craved this wholeness and hoped to resurrect 'the normal, passionate, reasoning self, the personality as a whole' (E&I, p.272). His father, however, remained deeply sceptical of these plans: 'You are haunted by the idea ... that man can be a complete man. It is a chimera – a man can only be a specialist.'[33]

Yeats dreamed that art would redeem human beings from an over specialized world, but he also worried that art would fall prey to the same specialization. His own career often epitomized the problem: for all his commendation of 'popular poetry', he sometimes celebrated – and arguably produced – extremely esoteric forms of art. He would always be drawn to the arcane wisdom and social exclusiveness of clubs and cults, but he also felt that art would suffer if it became a rarefied conversation between experts. He insisted, therefore, that 'it is needful that the populace and the poets shall have one heart – that there shall be no literary class with its own way of seeing things and its own conventions'.[34] This art would be both the condition and expression of social unity: under its aegis the whole nation, 'artist and poet, craftsman and poet and day-labourer would accept a common design' (A, p.194). But his plan for a unified culture often seemed to presuppose the social unity that it set out to install. Moreover, it also ran counter to some of the basic mechanisms of modern social development. For this reason, Yeats's search for 'Unity of Being' assumed a self-consciously primitive dimension.

Yeats drew on contemporary sociology to support his impression of Ireland's primitive virtue. In 1886 he invoked the famous sociologist Herbert Spencer to defend the 'barbarous truth' of Irish art (UP I, p.87). For Spencer, 'the law of all progress' dictated a move from simplicity to complexity, 'from the homogeneous to the heterogeneous'.[35] Yeats also believed in the same 'law of division and sub-division and of ever increasing complexity', but he came to very different conclusions about the virtues of this process (UP I, p.272). Once again his metaphysical commitments shaped his sociological perspective: the Good, it seemed, was simple and multiplicity was error. He railed against 'all that sterile modern complication', and believed that the task of 'all culture is certainly a labour to bring again the simplicity of the first ages' (A, p.152; E&I, p.167). Spencer promoted the division of labour as the engine of civilization, but Yeats believed that it had destroyed Unity of Being: 'Man is like a musical instrument of many strings, of which only a few are sounded by the narrow interests of his daily life; and the others, for want of use, are continually becoming tuneless and forgotten' (UP I, p.84).

Primitive – or 'heroic' – art redeemed us from this dissonance. 'Heroic poetry', he explained, 'is a phantom finger swept over all the strings, arousing from man's whole nature a song of answering harmony' (UP I, p.84). The very form of heroic poetry ('thought woven with thought – each line the sustainer of his fellow') embodied the unity of its world (p.92). Such art was truly popular art and was distinct from modern verse, which was largely 'written by students, for students'. Heroic poetry had a universal appeal; 'for it has gone deeper than knowledge or fancy, deeper than the intelligence which knows of difference – of the good and the evil, of the foolish and the wise, of this one and of that' (p.101). Here Yeats returned to his fantasy of an absolute unity that existed beyond or prior to all difference. By returning to this primordial state, he hoped to flee the 'leprosy of the modern – tepid emotions and many aims' (p.104).[36]

For the early Yeats, therefore, history was a form of degeneration; its move from simplicity to complexity was a fall from true being. By taking Ireland as its object, however, an exhausted modernity could restore itself to its initial purity. In Ireland, after all, there were people 'who still remember the dawn of the world' (UP II, p.196). Ireland's messianic vocation remained an extraordinarily obdurate fantasy for Yeats. It was a dominant motif in as late a poem as 'The Statues' (1939). Here Ireland is still potentially poised to restore balance to a degenerate modernity. But its ability to execute this task is far from obvious: Ireland too has been cast on the 'filthy modern tide / And by its formless spawning fury wrecked' (VP, p.611).

Despite moments of wishful thinking, Yeats generally recognized that Ireland was not going to stand as a glorious exception to modern laws of social development. In a series of disillusioned poems – particularly in the *Green Helmet* collection (1910) and *Responsibilities* (1914) – he insisted that Ireland had succumbed to the grasping materialism that typified, for him, modern life in general (a fact confirmed for him by the Dublin Corporation's refusal in 1911 to finance Hugh Lane's plans for a new art gallery on the Liffey) ('September 1913', *VP*, pp.289–90). 'Romantic Ireland was dead and gone', assuming it had ever existed (pp.289–90). Ireland, he now believed, lacked the social preconditions for even Young Ireland's version of patriotism. This was because modern nations were not communities of sentiment or belief. They lacked 'a definite table of values understood by all' which smaller groups such as a monastic order enjoyed; nor did they possess a collective mode of 'feeling and thought' that characterized, he believed, traditional peasant societies (*Mem*, p.251).

In this context, a 'Unity of Being', organized around some shared set of principles was impossible. Nor was it even desirable. Modern states were too large, too populous and too complicated to allow for anything more than the most basic agreement on what should operate as a common table of values. To insist upon a more developed model of the good life in this setting was either naive or authoritarian, or both; it either ignored or overruled the plural nature of modern social life. The patriotism of Young Ireland, for instance, was a 'conscious simplification' and could 'only perish or create a tyranny' (*Mem*, pp.250–1). Yeats was not necessarily opposed to tyrannical solutions to modern problems, as his later interest in fascism suggests, but in the face of other people's authoritarianism he was inclined to adopt a more liberal position.[37] Young Ireland's ideal of a harmonious community, he therefore insisted, was an outdated and illiberal dream: it purchased social unity at the expense of personal freedom and individual difference. It resulted in 'a mob held together not by what is interior, delicate and haughty, but by law and force which they obey because they must' (*Mem*, p.251).

In the face of this coercive synthesis, Yeats dwelt less on 'Unity of Being' than on the virtues of conflict. He now professed to delight in controversy and promoted his theatre as 'a wise disturber of the peace' (*CL3*, p.118). Discord, he insisted, was the sign of a nation's good health:

England sometimes taunts us with our divisions, divisions that she has done her best to foment; as if she herself was ever united, as it was natural for any country to be united. No land lives out a wholesome life, full of ideas and vitality that is not fighting out great issues within its own borders. It is part of the sacrifice we have had to make for our national existence that from time to time the whole of Ireland has to be gathered into one great party. But let us not forget the sacrifice. When all Ireland was so marshalled, we had no individuality of thought.[38]

This emphasis on 'individuality of thought' marked another volte-face. He had repeatedly condemned individualism in the name of an expansive patriotism, but his practical encounters with Irish nationalism left him deeply disillusioned.

Since the fall of the Protestant aristocrat Charles Stewart Parnell (1846–91), a Catholic middle class was increasingly dominant in Irish politics. In Yeats's eyes, this class combined dogmatic religious views with a zealous philistinism. Against the ignorance and intolerance of mainstream public opinion, Yeats struck an aggressively individualistic attitude. In his various defences of J.M. Synge (1871–1909) – who had attracted nationalist opprobrium since the first performance of the *Shadow of the Glen* in 1903 – he condemned coercive forms of public solidarity in the name of 'an always individualising' life. The genuine artist had no need for the comforts of the herd. He was a radical iconoclast, eternally at war with the false idols of public opinion: 'He swings his silver hammer and the keepers of the temple cry out, prophesying evil, but he must not mind their cries and their prophecies, but break the wooden necks in two and throw down the wooden bodies' (Ex, p.120). This was a Nietzschean celebration of artistic power, but Yeats's criticisms of idolatry had also a theological resonance that was bound to upset some Catholics in Ireland.[39]

Yeats's sense of his own Protestantism would increase as his enthusiasm for Irish nationalism diminished. He also championed an aristocratic conception of culture that was inaccessible to the ill-bred many. As he put it in 1910, 'ideas and images which have to be understood and loved by large numbers of people must appeal to no rich experience, no patience of study, no delicacy of sense' (E&I, p.313). His conception of art as the basis and expression of national solidarity was now abandoned for a more exclusive form of culture. 'Unity of Being', conceived as nation-wide project, was no longer feasible.

CONCLUSION

Yeats may have relinquished his project to install 'Unity of Being' on a practical basis, but it would remain a core concept in much of his subsequent thought. And despite repeated misgivings, he would still choose Plato 'for a friend' ('The Tower', VP, p.409). Plato's account of a unified reality which inclined towards the Good was, after all, a cosmic ratification of Yeats's own need for order; it provided him with a rich account of universal connectedness while preserving a firm sense of a hierarchical order. Broadly conceived, Yeats's politics for most of his life were distinctly Platonic: here the role of a community was not to secure peace, or security or material well-being for its members, but to pursue the supreme Good. It was precisely for this reason that Yeats tended to regard democracy as a corrupt form of government: it conflated the Good with the popular will and the latter was often as foolish as it was intolerant. He professed to 'hate democracy' and stressed the moral and practical significance of elite leadership in all walks of life: every society needed its 'prophet, priest and king'.[40] Such leaders should impose unity on the multitude even if this meant trampling on the 'decomposing body of liberty' (UP II, p.434) – to invoke the phrase of Mussolini that he was so wont to quote. His search for a metaphysical, moral and social coherence developed, therefore, a strong authoritarian dimension. But in other settings, Yeats shrank from this authoritarianism, and defended the principle of individual liberty and difference. This involved an entirely different cosmology which privileged conflict, chaos and an 'always individualising' life (Ex, p.120). The most interesting features of Yeats's thought express, therefore, a fundamental tension between an exacting demand for order and a delight in the irreducible plurality of existence.

NOTES

1. In 'Tom O'Roughley' he regretted the fact that 'logic-choppers rule the town'. Peter Allt and Russell K. Alspach (eds), *The Variorum Edition of the Poems of W. B. Yeats* (New York: Macmillan, 1957), p.337, hereafter referred to in the text as VP. He believed – attributing the same conviction to William Blake – that 'Reason not only created

Ugliness, but all other evils'. W.B. Yeats, *Essays and Introductions* (London: Macmillan, 1961), p.68, hereafter referred to in the text as *E&I*.

2. 'After the individualist, demagogic movement founded by Hobbes and popularized by the Encylopaedists and the French Revolution', he declared, 'we have a soil so exhausted that it cannot grow that crop again for centuries'. Allt and Alspach (eds), *The Variorum Edition of the Poems*, 828. For his critical remarks on Rousseau, see W.B. Yeats, *Explorations* (London: Macmillan, 1962), pp.275, 314, 350, hereafter referred to in the text as *Ex*. See also W.B. Yeats, *Memoirs*, ed. and transcribed by Denis Donoghue (London: Macmillan, 1972), p.170, hereafter referred to in the text as *Mem*.

3. George Mills Harper, *The Making of Yeats's 'A Vision': A Study of the Automatic Script*, 2 vols. (Basingstoke: Macmillan, 1987), Vol. 2, p.78. He admitted that his commitment to 'Unity of Being' long preceded his use of the phrase. See W.B. Yeats, *Autobiographies* (London: Macmillan, 1955), p.246, hereafter referred to in the text as *A*.

4. See Yeats, *Explorations*, p.250; Yeats, *Autobiographies*, pp.245, 295; W.B. Yeats, *A Vision* (London: Macmillan, 1937), pp.82, 258, hereafter referred to in the text as *V*; Yeats, *Essays and Introductions*, p.518.

5. Here he claimed to be quoting Dante's *Convivio*, but, according to George Bornstein, he conflated different parts of Dante's treatise. See George Bornstein, 'Yeats's Romantic Dante', *Colby Library Quarterly*, 15 (1979), pp.93–133 (p.107).

6. Ursula Bridges (ed.), *W.B. Yeats and T. Sturge Moore: Their Correspondence, 1901–1937* (London: Routledge & Kegan Paul, 1953), p.83.

7. 'I read all MacKenna's incomparable translation of Plotinus, some of it several times', he declared (*V*, p.20).

8. See R.F. Foster, *W.B. Yeats: A Life*, II: *The Arch-Poet, 1915–1939* (Oxford: Oxford University Press, 2003), p.326.

9. See Plotinus, *The Enneads*, trans. Stephen MacKenna (London: Penguin, 1991), p.108.

10. According to Plato, 'the things which are known say not only that their being known comes from the good, but also that they get their existence and their being from it as well – though the good is not being, but something far surpassing being in rank and power'. Plato, *The Republic*, ed. G.R.F. Ferrari, trans. Tom Griffith (Cambridge: Cambridge University Press, 2000), p.215.

11. See Plotinus, *The Enneads*, p.539.

12. Stéphane Mallarmé, 'Crise de vers', in *Oeuvres complètes*, ed. Henri Mondor and G. Jean-Aubry (Paris: Gallimard, 1945), pp.360–8, (p.368 [my translation]). Yeats had gained an understanding of Mallarmé's work through Arthur Symons and attempted to call on the French poet during his visit to Paris in 1894. See W.B. Yeats, *The Collected Letters of W.B. Yeats. Volume 1: 1865-1895*, ed. John Kelly, associate ed. Eric Domville (Oxford: Clarendon Press, 1986), p.381.

13. John P. Frayne and Colton Johnson (eds), *Uncollected Prose by W.B. Yeats*, II: *1897–1939* (London: Macmillan, 1975), p.45, hereafter referred to in the text as *UP II*.

14. The Celt's attachment to the ideal, according to Matthew Arnold (1822–88), made

him deplore 'the despotism of fact'. Matthew Arnold, *The Study of Celtic Literature* (London: David Nutt, 1910), p.84. Yeats propounded a similar view throughout his career; for his use and endorsement of Arnold's remark, see Yeats, *Essays and Introductions*, p.173. In later life, he championed the philosophy of George Berkeley (1685–1753) as an exemplary instance of Irish idealism. He was also keen to point out that Berkeley 'kept his Plato by his Bible' (UP II, p.462).

15. Plotinus, *Enneads*, p.107.

16. Ibid., p.51.

17. This is from a draft of 'Among School Children'. See Thomas Parkinson, *W.B. Yeats: The Later Poetry* (Berkeley and Los Angeles, CA: University of California Press, 1966), p.97.

18. According to Plato's *Timaeus*, we should only use the word 'is' in relation to Eternal Being or the Good, 'reserving *was* and *shall be* for the process of change in time: for both are motions, but that which is eternally the same and unmoved can neither be becoming older or younger owing to the lapse of time, nor can it ever become so; neither can it now have *become* nor can it come to *be* in the future; nor in general can any of the attributes which becoming attached to sensible and changing things belong to it, for they are all forms of time which in its measurable cycles imitates eternity'. Plato, *Timaeus and Critias*, trans. Desmond Lee (London: Penguin, 1965), pp.51–2.

19. Plotinus, *Enneads*, p.458.

20. Ibid., p.539.

21. W.B. Yeats, *Mythologies* (London: Macmillan, 1959), pp.184–90.

22. W.B. Yeats, *The Collected Letters of W. B. Yeats. Volume 3: 1901-1904*, ed. John Kelly and Ronald Schuchard (Oxford: Oxford University Press, 1994), p.284, hereafter referred to in the text as CL3.

23. Friedrich Nietzsche, *The Will to Power*, ed. Walter Kaufmann (New York: Vintage, 1968), p.118; Friedrich Nietzsche, *The Anti-Christ, Ecce Homo, Twilight of the Idols*, ed. Aaron Ridley and Judith Norman, trans. Judith Norman (Cambridge: Cambridge University Press, 2005), p.225.

24. Friedrich Nietzsche, *The Gay Science*, ed. Bernard Williams, trans. Josefine Nauckhoff and Adrian Del Caro (Cambridge: Cambridge University Press, 2001), p.217.

25. Nietzsche, *The Will to Power*, p.308.

26. Friedrich Nietzsche, *Thus Spake Zarathustra*, trans. R.J. Hollingdale (London: Penguin, 1961), p.61.

27. Ibid., pp.110–11.

28. For a fuller account of this rhetoric, see David Dwan, *The Great Community: Culture and Nationalism in Ireland* (Dublin: Field Day, 2008), pp.111–37.

29. In a *Vision*, for instance, he identified 'consciousness with conflict', but suggested that this discord was ultimately oriented towards harmony (V, p.214).

30. He was convinced that the 'resolution to stand alone, to owe nothing to the past, when it is not mere sense of property, the greed and pride of the counting-house,

is the result of that individualism of the Renaissance which had done its work when it gave us personal freedom' (E&I, p.353).

31. In a postscript to an essay he wrote for the Golden Dawn, Yeats insisted that 'individuality is not as important as our age has imagined'. He added that, 'it becomes an evil when it conflicts with some larger communion'. See George Mills Harper, *Yeats's Golden Dawn: The Influence of the Hermetic Order of the Golden Dawn on the Life and Art of W.B. Yeats* (Wellingborough: Aquarian, 1974), pp.270–1.

32. 'A Victor at Last', *Irish Independent*, 4 August 1924.

33. J.B. Yeats, *Letters to his Son W.B. Yeats and Others 1869–1922*, ed. with a memoir by Joseph Hone (London: Faber & Faber, 1944), p.97.

34. W.B. Yeats, *Uncollected Prose. Volume 1: 1886–1896*, ed. John P. Frayne (London: Macmillan, 1970), p.147, hereafter referred to in the text as UP I.

35. Herbert Spencer, *Essays: Scientific, Political, and Speculative*, 2 vols (London and Edinburgh: Williams & Norgate, 1883), Vol. 1, p.3.

36. For an account of Yeats's conception of the primitive past as conflict rather than as unity, see Sinéad Garrigan, *Primitivism, Science, and the Irish Revival* (Oxford: Oxford University Press, 2004), pp.57–8.

37. For a discussion of Yeats's fascist views, see Conor Cruise O'Brien, 'Passion and Cunning: An Essay on the Politics of W.B. Yeats', in *Excited Reverie: A Centenary Tribute to William Butler Yeats 1865–1939*, ed. A. Norman Jeffares and K.G.W. Cross (London: Macmillan, 1965), pp.207–78; Elizabeth Cullingford, *Yeats, Ireland and Fascism* (London: Macmillan, 1981); Paul Scott Stanfield, *Yeats and Politics in the 1930s* (London: Macmillan, 1988); Foster, *Yeats, A Life II*, particularly, pp.466–83; W.J. McCormack, *Blood Kindred. W.B. Yeats: the Life, the Death, the Politics* (London: Pimlico, 2005).

38. W.B. Yeats, 'Four Lectures by W.B. Yeats', ed. Richard Londraville, in *Yeats Annual No. 8*, ed. Warwick Gould (1991), pp.78–122 (p.105).

39. In this context, Yeats was Zarathustra's disciple: 'he who has to be a creator in good and evil, truly, has first to be a destroyer and break values'. See Nietzsche, *Thus Spake Zarathustra*, p.138.

40. W.B. Yeats, *The Letters of W.B. Yeats*, ed. Alan Wade (London: Rupert Hart-Davis, 1954), p.813; E&I, pp.261–4.

CHAPTER NINE

Yeats and Women, or, Yeats and Woman: An Introduction, and Some Conclusions

ANNE MARGARET DANIEL

Yeats and women. It sounds like a punchline. Think of the phrase, and what springs to mind? Yeats the dreamer, his love for his muse Maud Gonne unreciprocated, a young and ageing man with his greatest earthly desire unconsummated. Yeats the *cavalier servente* to the great lady of Coole, her Renaissance court poet, admirer of the legends she assembled, cofounder with her and Synge of the Abbey. Yeats the striver, sexually inexperienced or inept, memorably mocked by Florence Farr, and nearly entrapped by Mabel Dickinson. Yeats the old husband of a young woman, seduced by her automatic writing as not by her body, engendering his family at spirit commands. Yeats and the rank and file of late ladies: Dorothy Wellesley, Edith Heald, Margot Ruddock, company in many ways but, with the possible exception of Wellesley, no true companions. Yeats the poet of youth, scared of anything more than synecdoche, in love with long heavy hair and a silken dress, who gave us noble mythic women of Ireland and of Troy. Yeats the poet of age, the wild old wicked man, full of straining thighs and rods butting heads, who gave us Crazy Jane and the girl of 'Politics'.

It is hard, and always feels artificial, to separate the women of Yeats's writing from those in his life. Of course, it is critically correct to do so, but with Yeats, whose dreams are ever more real than so-called realities, the constructions of women in his work are shaped by, enhanced by, and sometimes dictated by the women he knew. The Countess Cathleen would not have been what she is without Augusta Gregory's artistic hand; fine Yeats scholars say matter-of-factly that 'No Second Troy' is about Maud Gonne; the women in A Vision, including Leda, owe an immense debt to George Yeats and what she could, in her mind's eye, see.

Much has been written on Yeats and women, and more is to come – where the women regarded as most important in his life are concerned: George Yeats, Augusta Gregory and Maud Gonne. Richard Ellmann's lyrical and enduring Yeats: The Man and the Masks was written with the approval of and assistance from George Yeats, and bears corresponding marks;[1] Brenda Maddox has, more recently, written extensively about Yeats and his wife in George's Ghosts.[2] James Pethica's forthcoming book about Yeats's collaboration with Lady Gregory will define for years to come this important woman in Yeats's life and art. Gonne wrote an autobiography, A Servant of the Queen, and is the subject of a clutch of biographies all dealing with her status as inspiration and complication for Yeats. Together, this earthly, spiritual, though not particularly holy, trinity of women have been given their due by Yeats scholars and biographers since his death.

One woman is missing from the lists: Olivia Shakespear. She is the principal subject of the memoir Yeats did not publish during his lifetime. She was his first lover, for many years his best friend, his theatre companion, his first reader for many poems, his sounding-board and adviser. She introduced him to Ezra Pound, who married her daughter and took his make-it-new hammer to Yeats's increasingly Modern poetry. Though her life touched and concerned those of Yeats's other women – she introduced Yeats to George, ended her affair with him upon realizing he still loved Maud, and had little if anything to do with Gregory, by choice I believe – she refused to participate in sharings or parallels or triangles with the others. Like Bartleby, she simply preferred not to, and Yeats, who loved forging and reshaping women he knew – or had encountered in books and then re-imagined for himself – in his writings, could or did not force her. This makes Shakespear unique and tremendously important in Yeats's life and work: keen on balances and oppositions, points and counterpoints, comparisons and contrasts as he was, he found in Olivia someone who refused to do anything but stand alone and be constant in this, always reliable and steadfast. Biographers, particularly Roy Foster, have more recently begun to give Shakespear the place of prominence she deserves in Yeats's feminography. John Harwood, in the only biography of Shakespear to date (and still a biography principally in terms of Yeats and their connection), has carefully amassed the few surviving letters and documents of her life, written on her nearly-forgotten novels, and done justice to her influence on, particularly, the poems of *The Wind Among the Reeds* and *The Shadowy Waters*.

However, Shakespear still remains too much an afterthought when one says 'Yeats and women'. I believe that Yeats's conception of women in his writing was shaped by Shakespear more than by any other woman in his artistic life, including Gonne. In as close a look as we are able to take at their relationship (her letters to him are gone, or have largely not come to light, and she evidently returned his to her when he asked for them), it is notable and remarkable to find such companionship, honesty, and – that cipher of a word – normality between Yeats and a woman.

For forty years, from the end of their first affair until her death, only shortly before his, in October 1938, Olivia Shakespear was the one soul who made no intense demands upon Yeats, expected nothing in particular of him after the end of their first affair, shared with him the grace of her company, conversation and her London homes – which were as important to Yeats, the long-time Londoner, in some practical and necessary ways as Coole Park ever was. Shakespear was the one person upon whom Yeats could rely to give him her honest opinions on nearly all matters without intrusions of self-interest, business, politics and the personal agendas that marked and marred Yeats's relationships with all other women, and with most men. Such friends, indeed: in Yeats's own chronicling of friends, there's only one who is almost too precious for public view in his poems and other writings, except for the memoir that did not appear until 1972. Olivia is not left out because she didn't matter, but because she mattered too much.

Olivia Shakespear first began to write fiction just before she and Yeats met, in the early 1890s, when she was 30 and in a dispassionate marriage (since 1885) to Henry Hope Shakespear, a London solicitor fourteen years her senior. Of an upper-middle-class family whose men had served in Queen Victoria's Little Wars, most notably in India, Shakespear was also the cousin of Yeats's good friend and fellow poet Lionel Johnson. She was an extremely beautiful and intelligent woman; as Roy Foster puts it, her marriage to the plain, cold Shakespear is, simply, 'hard to explain'.[3]

Olivia Tucker was born on St Patrick's Day, 1863, in a handsome house on the Isle of Wight that has since fallen down, together with the crumbling chalk cliffs upon which it once stood. She was a middle child; her sister Florence was seven years older, and their brother, who rejoiced in the name Henry Tudor (and was mercifully called Harry), was three years her junior. She was close to both parents; her father, a retired officer, wrote letters to his young daughter showing an intimate relationship of equals. Tucker muses upon politics ('that poor Jew Dizzy') with Olivia, tells her secrets that he says he keeps from her mother Harriet, and in one lovely passage recounts his amusement at the engagement in 1881 of a wealthy family friend, Caroline Tremenheere, to a poor Irishman:

> he is quite divine – Mother T. doats [sic] on him simply, & Caroline's love surpasses the love of ordinary women – he is so charming that when he departed for the East not only Mrs Trem & Cunningham & C. herself but even the foolish fat cook & house-maid all wept so they reported at least & Mama says that they were quite in earnest & serious & the drawback to all these charms of manner & character is that there are no Brass Farthings worth speaking of – & Carry is in consequence learning to stitch & sew & cook – Yes! Really – you may not believe it, but so her mother said – but only fancy – poor incapable Carry & she nursed in the lap of luxury ease idleness & oh! if he shd. turn out to be a Fenian in disguise or even a Land Leaguer & being Irish its quite impossible to know beforehand.[4]

When Olivia married, it was in her late twenties, and to a man far from being a Fenian or Land Leaguer – though he had travelled to Sligo, among many other places, to pursue his hobby as a landscape painter. Hope Shakespear, London lawyer, had enough of the touch of the artist to convince this beautiful woman to marry him. There is no evidence, though, that he was a sensitive and artistic soul. The honeymoon swiftly disabused Olivia of such notion, and any romance ended at, or swiftly after, the altar, if we can believe Yeats's *Memoirs*, quoting Olivia, on the point: '[Hope] ceased to pay court to me from the day of our marriage', she had said.'⁵ Whatever the facts, one is unavoidable: nine months and some weeks after the wedding, Dorothy was born. The future Mrs Ezra Pound was the couple's only child.

Unhappily, but comfortably, married, for a time Olivia contented herself with her daughter, an active London social life, writing – and writers. Her beloved cousin Lionel Johnson introduced her to his friends, and, when the circle had arisen, to The Rhymers, that group of young men including Ernest Dowson, Richard LeGallienne, Aubrey Beardsley, Arthur Symons and Yeats. Richard Ellmann describes them beautifully as 'futile, convinced young men' but had to admit that 'The Rhymers furnished much of the talent for the *fin de siècle* reviews, the Yellow Book and the Savoy.' They loved Pater's prose, the Pre-Raphaelite artists' painting and poetry, and as Yeats was immersed in his chief project of the early 1890s, his and Edwin Ellis's edition of William Blake, he felt and showed the influence of this company. Johnson, already drinking in the manner that would kill him young, 'made Yeats conscious of his own ignorance, telling him, "I need ten years in the wilderness, you need ten years in a library", and in 1893 presented him with a copy of the works of Plato and made him read it'.⁶ It's nice to know that we can thank Olivia Shakespear's cousin for Yeats's manifold shadows on the cave walls – his increasing neo-Platonic insistence, couched first in Celtic myths and then in other world legends and religions, that illusions and their lush counterparts, dreams, were more real than 'reality'.

In June of 1894 – after Yeats had finished his Plato – Shakespear's first novel, *Love on a Mortal Lease*, was published. It is nearly impossible to find Shakespear's novels in libraries or through book-dealers; when one can, the inexpensive paper they're printed on flakes beneath one's fingers. The plot of *Love on a Mortal Lease* is not unlike those Shakespear would use later, nor unlike those of commonplace Victorian works. The heroine, Rachel Gwynne, has dead parents, as is the case from *Oliver Twist* through hundreds of other ensuing tripledeckers. Rachel is a novelist; most of Shakespear's heroines would be writers. And she is in love with a military man many years her senior. After he refuses to marry her because he fears mamma will dislike Rachel and therefore disinherit him, Rachel becomes his mistress. Once the snobby old mother meets Rachel by happenstance in London they immediately adore each other, and the Colonel may now marry Rachel though she doesn't love him any more and he seems none too fond of her. They muddle along in unhappy matrimony until Rachel conveniently discovers (as we've known for a while) that the Colonel has had another long-time mistress, a stupid society girl, throughout the course of their marriage and even during their preceding affair. When the Colonel even more conveniently falls on his head and dies, Rachel is made a wealthy widow in her mid-twenties, free to marry a nice young writer who knows about, but forgives her, her former relationship. It's a fine, fun read, happily wish-fulfilling perhaps for a young woman writer in a bad marriage, and Rachel has some interesting ideas about her profession: speaking of clever girls who scribble, she hopes for the day that 'the cleverness and the scribbling ... fall from her, like a disguise, and she stands revealed in her true form – then she may never write another word, or she may write something immortal'.[7]

Shakespear had finished her draft and had a publisher, Osgood and McIlvaine, lined up when Lionel Johnson invited her to a writers' event that April. The party was for the original fin-de-siècle little magazine, The Yellow Book; the place, Hotel d'Italia, in Old Compton Street. Willie Yeats was at the supper-party, and it was here that he and Shakespear first met. Arthur Waugh, Evelyn's father, went there with him on public transportation, as he wrote the next day in a letter to Edmund Gosse: 'at Baker Street we were joined by W.B. Yeats. Have you met him? A tall, sallow, black haired youth with the jaw of a monk, & a sort of catch in his voice – rather an interesting personality, tho he would talk about the theory of poetry inside a bus, which seriously alarmed two homely old ladies and scandalized a City man.'[8] And here is the tall, sallow, black-haired youth's own account of their first meeting in his own words, from those memoirs Yeats chose not to publish during his lifetime:

> At a literary dinner where there were some fifty or sixty guests I noticed opposite me, between celebrated novelists, a woman of great beauty. Her face had a perfectly Greek regularity, though her skin was a little darker than a Greek's would have been and her hair

was very dark. She was exquisitely dressed with what seemed to me very old lace over her breast, and had the same sensitive look of distinction I had admired in Eva Gore-Booth. She was, it seemed, about my own age, but suggested to me an incomparable distinction. I was not introduced to her, but found that she was related to a member of the Rhymers' Club and had asked my name. (*Mem*, p.72)

The passage needs no parsing. Nor does Shakespear's reaction to him. She was beautiful when they met – what did Yeats look like? There is the cynic's view, as voiced by Waugh, and by Violet Martin to Edith Somerville: 'He is thinner than a lath – wears little paltry clothes wisped around his bones, and the prodigious and affected greenish tie. He is a little affected and knows it – He has a sense of humour and is a gentleman – hardly by birth I fancy – but by genius.'[9] Martin, and Somerville, might not be the best judges of male attractiveness. We have, after all, the photographs of that iconic 1890s face, the dark flowing hair, the deep eyes, the Byronic collars. And we also have the way George Moore described his friend in *Evelyn Innes* in a book published a few years later. Yeats wrote, rather proudly in the moment, to Augusta Gregory on 1 June 1898, getting the name of his character not quite right and with advice designed to cut into Moore's sales: 'Get Moores [*sic*] Evelyn Innes from the library. I am "Ulric Dean", the musician.' Two weeks later, he reported to Gregory that he was reading *Evelyn Innes* aloud to Maud Gonne.[10] And no wonder; here is Yeats as Ulick Dean:

> He had one of those long Irish faces, all in a straight line, with flat, slightly hollow cheeks, and a long chin. It was clean shaven, and a heavy lock of black hair was always falling over his eyes. It was his eyes that gave its sombre ecstatic character to his face. They were large, dark, deeply set, singularly shaped, and they seemed to smoulder like fires in caves, leaping and sinking out of the darkness. He was a tall, thin young man, and he wore a black jacket and a large, blue necktie, tied with the ends hanging loose over his coat … Ulick's teeth were almost the most beautiful she had ever seen, and […] they shone like snow in his dark face.[11]

Olivia immediately asked her cousin to arrange a proper introduction to

this handsome young man. She added a p.s. to the letter Johnson wrote
to his friend, inviting Yeats to an afternoon at the comfortable, indeed
elegant, Shakespear home in Porchester Square, in mid-May: 'I shall be
so glad to see you'.[12] Yeats remembered that meeting down to her
words:

> Presently the member of the Rhymers' Club introduced me to the
> lady I had seen between the two famous novelists, and a friendship
> I hope to keep till death began. In this book I cannot give her her
> real name – Diana Vernon sounds pleasantly in my ears and will
> suit her as well as any other. When I went to see her she said, 'So-
> and-so seemed disinclined to introduce us; after I saw your play
> [The Land of Heart's Desire] I made up my mind to write to you if [I]
> could not meet you otherwise.' She had a profound culture, a
> knowledge of French, English, and Italian literature, and seemed
> always at leisure. Her nature was gentle and contemplative, and she
> was content, it seems, to have no more of life than leisure and the
> talk of her friends. Her husband, whom I saw but once, was much
> older and seemed a little heavy, a little without life. As yet I did not
> know how utterly estranged they were. I told her of my love sor-
> row, indeed it was my obsession, never leaving by day or night.
> (Mem, p.74)

Though Shakespear remained 'Diana Vernon' in The Man and the Masks (as
Ellmann did not wish to make any more trouble for Dorothy Shakespear
Pound, dealing at the time with her husband's treason charges), there is
no evidence that Yeats ever called her this to her face – like Swift, Yeats
was always a great renamer of his women, giving them mythical aliases
or the names of Sir Walter Scott's heroines, referring to them by Golden
Dawn initials, and turning feminine Georgies into masculine Georges.
However, Shakespear had a name, and names, Yeats loved: the surname
of his best beloved English playwright-poet, and the Christian name of
one of Shakespeare's loveliest romantic heroines. It is perhaps inevitable
that Yeats should have told Olivia, finding her beautiful and open-minded,
and a woman of leisure – a word that for Yeats has always the ring of
liberty and grace to it – about his love sorrow and obsession. Not for
nothing did George Yeats dub her husband 'William Tell'[13] – he was a

gut-spiller from early youth. Shakespear knew about Maud Gonne from the start – and much to her credit, and to the continuing power of her friendship with Yeats, Shakespear never pretended not to have.

On 30 January 1889, Gonne had arrived at the Yeatses' door on Bedford Road for political discussion and, in the opinion of Lolly Yeats, something else. Lolly wrote in her diary that evening:

> Miss Gonne, the Dublin beauty (who is marching on to glory over the hearts of the Dublin youths), called today on Willie, of course, but also apparently on Papa. She is immensely tall and very stylish and well dressed in a careless way. She came in a hansom all the way from Belgravia and kept the hansom waiting while she was here. Lily noticed that she was in her slippers. She has a rich complexion and hazel eyes and is, I think, decidedly handsome. I could not see her well as her face was turned from me.

– and toward Lolly's 23-year-old brother. Lolly recorded dryly the following day, 'Willie dined at Miss Gonne's tonight.'[14] The first time that Yeats wrote Maud Gonne's name, in a letter to John O'Leary some days later, he prophetically spelled it with one n.[15]

That afternoon at his father's house was the day, Yeats famously wrote, when 'the troubling of my life began' (Mem, p.40). Both honest and foolish enough to pour out the story of his 'love sorrow' to Shakespear in their first conversation, Yeats may be commended, if we trust this account of his, and there is little reason not to, for never keeping the truth of his feelings for Gonne from Olivia.

Despite William Tell's somewhat self-indulgent honesty, Yeats and Shakespear to began to write each other, to see each other at the Shakespears' home in the company of Johnson and others, and – most importantly – to share their work. The first surviving letter of their correspondence is her postscript to him on Johnson's letter – his first to her is a long letter, dated 6 August 1894, about her novella Beauty's Hour. The letter is noted as property of Michael Yeats, as are nearly every one of Yeat's letters to her. One cannot doubt from this evidence that Olivia returned Yeats's letters to him when he asked her to, for to have done so was according to her nature. Shakespear didn't secrete a few to hand along later to Ezra Pound, and she didn't publish during their lifetimes as Katharine Tynan did. Unfortunately, Olivia's correspondence for the years of their affair and its aftermath, 1895–99, appears not to have survived. Of all her letters to Yeats, only a handful have been found and published – and we can tell from his replies to her that there were many more.

In this letter of August 1894, Yeats's language, as in so many other missives to her, is, for him, court-paying and even flirtatious. The words he uses are intense and desiring, as he writes to criticize Shakespear's hero, Gerald, as too undefined. Gerald is going to lose the girl, Yeats warns, exactly because he is not like Yeats: Gerald is 'one of those vigerous [sic] fair haired boating or cricket playing young men, who are very positive, & what is called manly', but who are incapable of understanding a woman's character, heart and soul. Men need, Yeats reminds Olivia, 'protection & care in those deeper things where [a woman is strong]'. He speaks of longing to hear her read aloud, and Yeats refers to his letter, which he asked to be forwarded to Shakespear – she and her husband were on holiday – as doing what he is also doing, 'pursuing you', and adds a teaser at the end 'I have much to say' that he must perforce leave unsaid, as he must relinquish this manuscript now so as to be sure to catch the post. He makes her think, and keeps her wondering. Of course, he also praises her: Florence Farr, who would soon be Olivia's collaborator in The Bride of Hathor and The Golden Hawk, is 'very delighted with you' – and Yeats is downright blissful that Shakespear likes his own stories; her liking of his stories is to him 'a very great pleasure & the best of pleasures' (CL1, pp.396–7).

Olivia shared, to some degree, Yeats's interest in visions and in the occult – interests that increased after her recognition that Yeats was so keen. He used Romantic with a capital 'R', Platonic language to explain that fiction should not be 'mere phantasies but the signatures – to use a medieval term – of things invisable & ideal', and told her how much he liked her subject matter and her literary style: 'I no more complain of your writing of love, than I would complain of a portrait painter keeping to portraits ... I have never come upon any new work so full of a kind of tremulous delicasy [sic], so full of a kind of fragile beauty as these books of yours however' (CL1, p.397). As Roy Foster notes, he's engaging in 'calculated flattery'[16] here, for clear reason – but Yeats is right about both her genuine and graceful treatment of love as a theme, and the fragile beauty of her work.

Shakespear and Yeats began planning an affair by mid-1895, if not before. They were serious about each other to the point of eloping – with Olivia leaving behind husband and child for him, as she would have had to under law at the time, and following Yeats into a life of financial insecurity and societal disapprobation which she was evidently quite willing to do, like the heroine of 'Gypsy Davy' and other ancient ballads. However, when Yeats had returned from Sligo that May, he was quickly caught up both in the furore of the Oscar Wilde trials, and planning the *Savoy*, two not entirely unrelated matters (Symons chose the title for the magazine as homage to the hotel where Wilde shared rooms with Alfred Douglas, and to which rent boys came). It was also a dreadful time for Yeats at home, where he lived still: his mother remained in bed, his aunt in an asylum, Jack was married and gone, his father depressed and unable to paint.[17]

And then Yeats moved into Fountain Court with Symons, where they sublet a suite of rooms from Havelock Ellis; one truly wishes those walls could speak. Their top-floor rooms looked upon the fountain, and away from the bustle and noise of London. Today the courtyards of the Temple remain like those of an ancient college, calm and carless, with the Thames silently backgrounding the space.

Space, and place, always mattered immensely to Yeats, more than for any other Modern writer. Hemingway loved his Paris cafés, Spanish mountains, and great lakes for inspiration, but he could write about them anywhere. Joyce wrote constantly of Dublin, but he did it all over Europe, and under every conceivable circumstance of poverty, and of variable employment, instead of in Dublin. Yeats is more, literally, grounded. Every so often Yeats needed to *be* where his mental landscape was; like Antaeus, he needed to touch the earth, to hold in his hand, or feel under his feet, the sod of a place he loved. Felicitously, though, Yeats had just finished his and Ellis's edition of William Blake in 1893, and was, when Shakespear met him and on through the mid-1890s, still hard at work with it, promoting it and trying to make it sell. Though an illustrator of the mind and particularly of the spirit, both in words and with his brushes, Blake *was* London to Yeats at this time. And of vital importance, Blake was proof that a life lived in the big city – and not in a more remote, rural place – could be that of an artist, an artist's life undestroyed by urban horror and violence. Blake had, moreover, spent the end of his life at 3 Fountain Court, where he could see the Thames 'like a bar of gold' and said, while listening to the children playing in the courtyard, 'This is heaven.'[18] The power of living where Blake had lived, as well as where many of Yeats's contemporary writers, like Ernest Dowson and George Moore, were Yeats's neighbours must have inspired the young Yeats immensely.[19]

Blake was not all delight and ease for Yeats, though, and he forced Yeats into his avowedly least favourite genre: Yeats complained to Douglas Hyde in August 1889 about 'William Blake – on whose Mystic System myself & a friend are … making a big book – the devil take all this prose' (CL1, p.183). Devil take prose, yet Yeats loved prose. He devoured novels, when his eyes would permit him. When doctors told him he couldn't write poetry in the late 1930s, as it might be too exciting, Yeats occupied himself with westerns, thrillers and detective novels.[20] By 1891 he was a published writer of prose himself, something it's too easy to forget in light of his rush of poetry of the middle and later 1890s, and something else that he and Shakespear had in common. *John Sherman* particularly influenced the first writing she did after meeting and falling in love with Yeats, her novella *Beauty's Hour*. *John Sherman* is a novel of humour, even elegance, and Yeats's depiction of Sligo – renamed Ballah – is very moving, and telling. Just as he was (no matter how he tried to deny or scoff at it) a born businessman, Yeats was also a born editor. His suggestions, some made in that first letter to Shakespear, colour the characters of *Beauty's Hour*, their relationships, their interests; and *John Sherman* is clearly not only a book Shakespear has read, but studied. Its autobiographical nature must have made it fascinating to a woman falling in love with Yeats. She not only quotes directly from the novel in the climactic, concluding scene as Mary Hatherley and Gerald are parting for the last time, but uses Yeats's bluff sporting William Howard in Gerald, the flirtatious and spoiled Margaret Leland in both Bella Wilfer and Mary Hatherley, and – chiefly – the calm, steady Mary Carton in Mary Gower. Sherman himself, the Yeats character, is the only one Shakespear doesn't touch.

Their initial connection as writers of fiction had given them an intellectual and artistic link, and now, living out of his family home in his own rooms, Yeats had a place to be alone in private with Shakespear. However, he was not quite alone there – Arthur Symons was often at home working feverishly on plans for *The Savoy*, writing, or keeping Yeats awake at night with stories of the latest dancer or snake-charmer or little Lolita who had caught his eye. And, with the idea of Maud Gonne still powerfully in his head and heart, Yeats could not commit to Olivia. He is so plainspoken about this in his *Memoirs*, in patches brutally so, as to seem entirely honest: Shakespear's

> beauty, dark and still, had the nobility of defeated things, and how could it help but wring my heart? I took a fortnight to decide what I should do. I was poor and it would be a hard struggle if I asked her [to] come away, and perhaps after all I would but add my tragedy to hers, for she might return to that evil life. But, after all, if I could not get the woman I loved, it would be a comfort even but for a little while to devote myself to another. No doubt my excited senses had their share in the argument, but it was an unconscious one. At the end of the fortnight I asked her to leave home with me. She became very gay and joyous and a few days later praised me [for] what she thought my beautiful tact in giving at the moment but a brother's kiss. Doubtless at the moment I was exalted above the senses, and yet I do not [think] I knew any better way of kissing, for when on our first railway journey together – we were to spend the day at Kew – she gave me the long passionate kiss of love I was startled and a little shocked (*Mem*, pp.85–6).

Still more time had to pass. In order for the couple to meet 'officially' at Fountain Court, Yeats arranged for Symons to be invited to the Shakespears', and then Symons invited Olivia and Valentine Fox, her 'sponsor' or chaperone for their affair – imagine a world in which affairs needed chaperones – to tea at Fountain Court in autumn of 1895. Symons then discreetly absented himself, leaving the moment to Shakespear, Yeats – and Fox. Yeats, with his mind on Maud, proceeded to go out and buy cake for tea and forgot his latchkey. Tea was delayed while a man more agile than Yeats 'climbed along the roof and in at an attic window'. After the ladies left, Yeats talked for three hours that night to an exhausted Symons, who had stayed out until midnight to give Yeats some space, not about Olivia and the afternoon, but about Maud (Mem, pp.86–7).

Almost immediately thereafter, as if she knew what was transpiring in London, Gonne began writing to Yeats more frequently than she had in months. No longer in France, where she and Lucien Millevoye had lost a son and separated for a time, Gonne had retreated to Dublin – and, back in Ireland, her mind turned to Yeats. In the Maples Hotel, Kildare Street, in November 1896, she wondered if he was thinking of her. Was he dreaming of her, she asked? For she was dreaming of him. And Maud, like young Laura Armstrong before her but far more surely, knew exactly what Yeats wanted to hear: just before midnight, Gonne has had a vision of him with her on Howth, that untamed headland surveying the entrance to Dublin port, every bit as magical to Yeats as to Joyce. 'I saw you again and together we went down to the cliffs at Howth, but the sea birds were all asleep & it was dark & so cold, & the wind blew so horribly. I came back & quite woke up, but I knew you were still not far off.'[21]

Gonne came to London to find him soon after, and following dinner wrote to Yeats from the Charing Cross Hotel a letter she timed at 'one o'clock morning' on 14 November:

> I was very glad to see you, but very sorry to see that you were still troubled & worried. All I would say is go on with the great work you are doing for Ireland by raising our literature. For the honour of our country, the world must recognise you one of the Great Poets of the century. Be true to yourself & let nothing interfere with your literary work. This is surely your first duty. Do not let your life be tied down by other lesser ones. (GYL, p.55)

Gonne's insistence that Yeats work for Ireland, Irish literature and his own poetry – and that it is his duty to do so, ending with that terse directive on the prospect of his life being tied down by lesser things – really makes it sound as if Yeats must have told Maud about Olivia, exactly as he had told Olivia about Maud. I fully expect he did, and fully expect she didn't like it. Gonne might not have wanted Yeats herself, but never wanted anyone else to have him, either. Yeats took her advice seriously, as invariably he did for decades, and he very nearly followed Gonne to France when she left. He would of course continue for many years to visit to her there, during which he was both dissuaded and encouraged – first by Gonne, and then by her daughter Iseult.

To make matters even worse at this particular moment, Shakespear's 'sponsor' Valentine Fox advised that they not seek a divorce for Olivia, and marriage. An unnamed friend of Yeats's advised the same: as Yeats remembered, 'both, people of the world, advised us to live together without more ado' (*Mem*, p.87). This neither Shakespear nor Yeats, nice middle-class folk, were willing to do. Shakespear did ask her husband for a separation, however, at this point – at which, Yeats recalled, Hope Shakespear 'was deeply distressed and became ill, and she gave up the project and said to me, "It will be kinder to deceive him". Our senses were engaged now, and though we spoke of parting it was but to declare it impossible' (*Mem*, p.88).

Roy Foster makes the point that Shakespear's '(and literary London's) claims on [Yeats] were reinforced by the great event of 11 January 1896, when the first number of The Savoy was published in London'.[22] It is absolutely true that for forty years London and Shakespear, and to a more immediate degree in 1896, The Savoy and Shakespear, were always linked for Yeats.

The two poems by Yeats, and the short story, in that first number of The Savoy are about love of women and its difficulties – a theme he would never have to seek for, or contrive, throughout his long life. 'The Shadowy Horses' (later 'He bids his Beloved be at Peace') and 'The Travail of Passion' (yes, sometimes it is work) are both quite Shakespearean, in the sense of Olivia. It's true that Maud Gonne also had long waving masses of hair, but hers was red; Trinity don Louis Purser provided such a memorable contemporary description of Gonne as 'a great red-haired yahoo of a woman'.[23] These are poems for, and of, Olivia: 'Beloved, let your eyes half close, and your heart beat / Over my heart, and your hair fall about my breast / Drowning Love's lonely hour in deep twilight of rest / And hide their tossing manes and their tumultuous feet.' 'We will bend down and loosen our hair over you, / That it may drop faint perfume and be heavy with dew ...'[24]

The story in the January number of The Savoy is 'The Binding of the

Hair', starring Aodh and Dectira, who will serve again, later and with slight name changes, as avatars for Yeats and Shakespear. She is the beautiful young wife of an old, foolish man, and he the travelling bard, singer of songs, visiting her husband's great hall. Aodh dies in battle; his head, hanging from a bush by its own dark hair, sings a song to the queen about her long tumbling dark tresses (the poem 'He gives his Beloved certain Rhymes'). His Orphic song is cut short when 'a troop of crows, heavy like fragments of that sleep older than the world, swept out of the darkness, and, as they passed, smote those ecstatic lips with the points of their wings, and the head fell from the bush and rolled over at the feet of the queen'.[25] The singer of songs has literally lost his head over cascades of long dim hair.

There was another great event for Yeats in early 1896, a very simple one that made loving a woman not a spiritual epic, but a physical possibility. He got a room of his own. To consummate an affair was, for two polite and discreet people, amazingly difficult even in the decadent decade dubbed the fin de siècle, even with a room-mate as laissez-faire as Arthur Symons. There was no going to hotels; there were servants round and about in every home and country house; and London was a remarkably small town. On the technical front, as John Harwood matter-of-factly and also humorously reminds us, women's clothing took forever to remove and to put on, and condoms were woeful: 'Oisin had never been required to unlace a corset in near-freezing temperatures, or wrestle with a nineteenth-century condom, and Yeats's knowledge of these subjects was much the same as Oisin's'.[26] Yeats sadly remembered their being constrained to meet for more than a year 'at Dulwich Picture Gallery and in railway trains' when he and Shakespear wanted to be alone (Mem, p.89). So, finally, when he could almost afford to, Yeats moved in February 1896 from his shared rooms in Fountain Court into No.18 Woburn Buildings, his London address for years to come. At the time, it was a nasty street; when John Masefield went there in 1900 he found 'a kind of blackguard beauty about Woburn Buildings at night' and heard that 'Yeats was known as "the toff what lives in the Buildings". He was said to be the only man in the street who ever received letters.'[27]

Yeats furnished the rooms with bits and pieces bought and borrowed from Arthur Symons, including a table, a bolster, '7 pieces of tapestry

canvas' '2 pieces of plushette' '2 blankets' and a fender and fire-irons –
total value of everything, approximately three pounds.[28] Augusta
Gregory stopped by while his father was sketching Yeats in December
1897, 'not very successfully – probably knows his face too well', to
measure the window for a curtain. She found the 'sitting room ... very
nice – large & low – looking on a raised flagged pavement where no
traffic can come', but Yeats's bedroom, in the back, 'very small &
draughty looks out on St Pancras Church with its caryatides & trees – ...
I wish poor W. cd be a little better waited on – his room had not yet been
done up.' Gregory was mistaken; the room had been done up as well as it
was going to be, for Yeats had occupied it a year by the time she visited.
Gregory was particularly bothered by the 'remains of breakfast (cooked by
himself) still there' – in the bedroom, that is; Yeats had no kitchen.[29]

The set-piece saga of Yeats and Shakespear shopping for the bed they
would share is well known to Yeats scholars and fans, but the story as he
tells it is kind and sad and moving and, in the end, full of pain and also
of beauty:

> I took my present rooms at Woburn Buildings and furnished them
> very meagrely with such cheap furniture as I could throw away
> without regret as I became more prosperous. She came with me to
> make every purchase, and I remember an embarrassed conversa-
> tion in the presence of some Tottenham Court [Road] shop man
> upon the width of the bed – every inch increased the expense.
>
> At last she came to me in I think January of my thirtieth [thirty-
> first, actually] year, and I was impotent from nervous excitement.
> The next day we met at the British Museum – we were studying
> together – and I wondered that there seemed no change in me or
> in her. A week later she came to me again, and my nervous excite-
> ment was so painful that it seemed best but to sit over our tea and
> talk. I do not think we kissed each other except at the moment of
> her leaving. She understood instead of, as another would, changing
> liking for dislike – was only troubled by my trouble. My nervous-
> ness did not return again and we had many days of happiness. It
> will always be a grief to me that I could not give the love that was
> her beauty's right, but she was too near my soul, too salutary and
> wholesome to my inmost being. (*Mem*, p.88)

Friday was their usual meeting day, that late winter and early spring (CL2, p.34 n.1). But Maud was firmly back in the picture – if ever she was gone – even as Yeats's affair with Shakespear began. That January she was, though not directly and couching it in terms of poetic and national duty, inviting him to join her in expatriation, and intimating that it was his own idea to do so: 'Your idea of working in France is very good for an Irish Poet it would not be good to live always in London' (GYL, p.58). When word clearly reached her in Dublin of someone new in Yeats's life, Maud's letter to him is a masterpiece of manipulation and careful, allusive craftsmanship. In May 1896, as he was preparing to leave for Ireland for the summer, Maud reported as the latest local gossip

> an interesting piece of news going about Dublin, taken I believe from some London papers ... that you have lately married a widow! At first I thought this could not be as having seen you in London [that spring past, as she was en route from Paris to Dublin] I thought we were sufficiently friends for you to have told me, but on reflection this is absurd as marriage after all is only a little detail in life (a foolish one generally I think, as one would have to spend so much energy & time in loosening a chain one had forged) So it is quite possible you are married & didn't think it important enough to talk to me about. Well if you are, I won't congratulate you, or even condole, as I hope it will make no difference in your life or work or character. (GYL, p.60)

Yeats swiftly sent Maud *The Savoy* – not the January number, with those poems and that story, and not the August and September issues, containing 'Beauty's Hour', but the July issue, with his first Blake article and the poem 'O'Sullivan Rua to Mary Lavell'. Gonne replied from Dublin to Yeats in Sligo, late in the summer, to compliment him on the Blake article without mentioning the love poem, but to say, specifically, that she wanted to see the earlier numbers of *The Savoy*: I 'look forward greatly to reading your wild dreamy stories. I would like much to see you & have some long talks on many subjects, but I cannot come to the west ... I would have loved to have spent a week in Sligo while you were there we would have tried if the fairies would have been good to us' – and oh yes, one more thing: 'I shall hope to see you in Paris in the winter' (GYL, p.62). Before Christmas 1896, go to Paris he did indeed, in his own words following 'the old lure' (*Mem*, p.104), because Maud had called. From springtime until the end of 1896, Yeats and Shakespear had scarcely seen each other. Olivia had been writing; her novel *The False Laurel* was published in June of 1896. It's dedicated to Lionel Johnson, and is the story of a girl who wants to be a writer. However, she has the misfortune to marry an intense young poet who proves to be the real literary genius, and so she goes mad, destroys her own writings, and commits suicide. The young poet survives all with flying colours and finds a nice girl in the end. Here's his concluding moment – just listen to Olivia's language, Yeats-laden and longing: the young poet has reached 'not perhaps the land of his heart's desire, for which he had once set sail so confidently; but some island in still waters, where it was enough that the sun shone, and there was peace'.[30]

Well, Yeats had headed off to his island in still waters, though with debatable sunshine, by the time *The False Laurel* appeared. Only a few months after he and Shakespear had begun making love in his rooms at the start of the year, Yeats left for Ireland with Symons for the summer, and ended up staying for the rest of 1896. Yeats met Augusta Gregory that summer – having been invited, he told John O'Leary proudly in June 1897, to stay at 'Coombe, Galway' (CL2, p.108) – and began a very different sort of relationship with her. Symons liked Gregory at first, and was flattered by her 'kind invitation' to come to Coole during the summer of 1899 with Yeats; he turned it down because his proofs for *The Symbolist Movement in Literature* had just arrived in London.[31] Only after his breakdown did Symons find he couldn't stand Gregory – by 1912, according to John Butler Yeats, he had dubbed her *La Strega*, the witch, 'and moans at the mention of her'.[32] Other friends of Yeats's agreed about Gregory, and earlier on. Robert Bridges wrote in a letter of 1898, 'Yeats will go to the bad I am afraid. With his old woman who lives on the bog near Tuam' (CL2, p.83n). Yeats's old woman was 44 when they met; we have a strange idea of Lady Gregory as perpetually 60-something and overly regal, a sort of budget Queen Victoria, but perhaps this is because Yeats has handed her to us this way.

Their meeting, while not nearly as devastating to Yeats's relationship with Shakespear as his connection to Gonne, certainly did not help.

Gregory occupied his time and, from the beginning, he was enchanted by her house. Richard Ellmann's laconic comment, containing multitudes, upon Yeats's immediate enthusiasm that summer for Gregory and her work collecting local legends sums up much: 'Never had Yeats been a more enthusiastic supporter of the peasantry.'[33]

When Yeats finally returned to London and to Shakespear in January 1897, having scarcely seen her since May of 1896, Gonne kept him on the line from Paris, writing to him immediately and often, flatteringly, persuasively, with promise. '[Maud] certainly had no idea of the mischief she was doing' (Mem, p.89) to his relationship with Shakespear, Yeats stated later with amazing obtuseness, or calculated ignorance. As was characteristic for him, Yeats was commendably honest with Olivia, and let her know where his affections lay straightaway. He couldn't daub it further: when Shakespear came to his rooms early in 1897, 'instead of reading much love poetry, as was my way to bring the right mood round, I wrote letters. My friend found my mood did not answer hers and burst into tears. "There is someone else in your heart", she said. It was the breaking between us for many years' (Mem, p.89).

This is how Yeats recalled the end of the affair in his Memoirs. There is also the retrospective of his poetry, stranger and truer always for Yeats than those shifty, self-creating, often self-justifying, and sometimes revisionist Memoirs and Autobiographies.[34] 'Aodh to Dectora', also called 'The Lover Mourns for the Loss of Love', first published in May of 1898 and collected in The Wind Among the Reeds, is an intensely autobiographical poem of Olivia and Willie – and the addressee is Maud.

> Pale brow, still hands, dim hair,
> I had a beautiful friend,
> And dreamed that the old despair
> Might fade in love in the end:
> She looked in my heart one day,
> And saw your image was there,
> She has gone weeping away.

Olivia's pale brow, leisurely hands, and long dim hair make her beautiful, but the most important word is friend. In his heart she has seen not Maud, but the image Yeats recognizes he has set up there. As to how far away Shakespear went, how long her weeping lasted, and what constitutes many years: I suspect Yeats of self-indulgent drama on this part, and believe that she recovered fairly quickly from the end of their affair, perhaps engaging in another, and restored their friendship sooner than has been believed through her own choice. Ellmann, who clearly appreciated the 'Diana Vernon' he came to know through George Yeats and the papers he was allowed to examine, is not kind to Yeats on the course of his first love affair, but he is not as unkind as Yeats, rueful and regretting, is to himself:

> So much a part of him did his theories of unsuccessful action and unsatisfied love become that in 1895 and 1896, when a beautiful married woman fell in love with him, he spent the first year in idealized chastity, meeting her only in museums and railway carriages; and then, when they finally went to bed together, he kept expecting love to end until finally it did, and he returned to his former hopeless adoration of Maud Gonne and to his twilit state between chastity and unchastity. He was too ardent, underneath all his theorizing and idealizing, to be happy in this state, and so his poems are full of vague sorrow.[35]

There's nothing vague about the sorrow in 'The Lover Mourns for the Loss of Love'.

Yeats was a reactive person. It seems very probable to me that he turned back to Olivia's calm, attractive company after hearing from Maud, in December 1898, about her life and children with Millevoye. Olivia had not been weeping over him, or at least not only weeping over him, in 1897 and 1898; she had been working on a new novel, *Rupert Armstrong*. Published in January of 1899, and dedicated to her 'chaperon' Valentine Fox, it is – finally – not a story about writers. It is, however, about artists. The patriarch and title character of the novel is a famous painter whom Deirdre Toomey has argued, gracefully and most convincingly, to be based upon John Millais – and the novel in places certainly tracks the story of Effie Ruskin, later Millais. That Rupert is also a portrait painter may have a touch of John Butler Yeats, too. Yet again, the heroine of the novel is a lovely young woman thwarted in her creative capacities by marriage to an old man; yet again, she is freed from this match and rewarded with a handsome, young kindred spirit. Art does not always imitate life; often, it improves upon life. What didn't happen for Shakespear in her life could happen for her heroines in her novels.

While Shakespear was writing this book, Yeats was grappling with his play that is in many ways a tale of his time with Shakespear, *The Shadowy Waters*, and completing his collection of poems, *The Wind Among the Reeds*, reflecting the best of the 1890s for him, namely Sligo and Shakespear. Though critics agree about the presence of Shakespear in these two volumes, biographers are variable as to just when Shakespear and Yeats reconnected as friends, and when, or even if, the two ever resumed a physical connection. Does the latter matter? Perhaps not, but it is more dreamy, and also more realistic, to believe that they did than that they didn't. Richard Ellmann, far closer to the time and to still-living people like George who would have known, speaks without doubt: Olivia broke off the affair in 1897 when she realized Yeats was still obsessed with Maud, but they 'resumed it later, more casually, and remained good friends for life'.[36] Roy Foster is not so sure: 'Sundered as lovers, it is possible that a sexual relationship had been restored at some point; in any case, they were [by 1910] firmly reunited as friends.'[37]

Yeats and Shakespear were far more in touch, and more intimately, from much sooner than anyone has quite been willing to say. In 1901 he was in torment over his autobiographical novel *The Speckled Bird*, with its heroine originally named Olive; Yeats referred to the time from April 1900 to February 1901 as 'worst part of life. Both in regard to [women] matters & other things.'[38] When he sat down at Coole Park in 1910 to do horoscopes and astrological calculations, Deirdre Toomey has shown us that Yeats devoted an immense amount of time and energy to details from Olivia's life.[39] But 1910 is far, far too late. As soon as June 1897, bare months after their breakup, Yeats was already back in touch with Olivia, signing for her, on what was to be Bloomsday, a copy of *The Tables of the Law and The Adoration of the Magi*. (When this book sold in 1940 at Parke Bernet, in New York, its pages were uncut.)[40] Warwick Gould once mourned the absence of any signed copy of *The Wind Among Reeds* or *The Shadowy Waters*, 'absences surely due to the estrangement of Yeats from Olivia Shakespear, and to the presence in both texts of an "Olivia Shakespear" figure'.[41] On 19 December 1900, Yeats did indeed inscribe a copy of *The Shadowy Waters*, in intimate words unique for him to use and absent his usual signing of his name, to 'Olivia Shakespear from the writer'. It is in private hands in New York.[42]

By 1900, I believe that Yeats and Shakespear were in regular communication, seeing each other among friends, and sharing theatre evenings. When Shakespear's mother died in May, only months after Susan Yeats's death, Yeats wrote movingly and from his heart to Olivia:

> My dear Friend: I need not tell you how profoundly I sympathize with you in your sorrow. At such times there is little more that one can say, for those great sorrows are beyond any comfort that is in words. Of one thing and only one can I think be sure. It is very well with the dead & better than with the living ... The Irish poor hardly think of a mothers [sic] death as dividing her very far from her children & I have heard them say that when a mother dies all things go better with her children for she has gone where she can serve them better than she can here. That may endeed [sic] be the very truth. (CL2, pp.529–30)

Olivia kept working, and soon began to write book reviews for a little monthly called the *Kensington*. Here's what she had to say, tartly and alliteratively, about a tome entitled *The Love Letters of an Englishwoman*, in early 1901: 'The author of these letters is a sentimentalist and a prig; her effusions lack distinction, both of matter and of manner, they are pretentious, precious and prolix and at their best remind one of Mrs Browning at her worst.' It is quite convivial and friendly that by the June issue of the *Kensington* we find a nice little contribution on a Celtic topic near to his heart, 'The Fool of Faery', by one W.B. Yeats.[43]

Their circles kept crossing, or more aptly their gyres kept running on, intersecting. Shakespear wrote two plays, *The Beloved of Hathor* and *The Shrine of the Golden Hawk*, with Florence Farr, and they were put on in London in 1902. Yeats went, and commented a little too circumspectly to Frank Fay only on their 'decorative scenery' and their being 'fairly well written'. Well written indeed: well written enough for *The Shrine of the Golden Hawk* to be selected as the preview for *The Shadowy Waters* when it was produced in 1905 – and the *Sunday Times* reviewer, thinking the authoress of the former play must be Irish, commended 'O. Shakespear' as 'a sort of present-day Swan of the Liffey'. The reviewer also complained that *The Shadowy Waters* was 'rather monotonous', and claimed that 'only by a [mostly] heroic effort did I prevent myself from falling into as sublime a slumber as that which he dreamed for a blessing to the race'.[44]

Olivia moved on to complete, in 1904, *The Devotees*, a rather creepy novel quite similar to that creepiest of Victorian novels, W.M. Thackeray's *Henry Esmond* (1852). The object of the central character Tony Atherton's devotion is his mother, the lovely, light-headed, loose Louise. Louise sleeps with many men while Tony goes to Oxford and ends up marrying one of his mother's former lover's daughters. Mamma ends up a cocaine addict, a pothead and an abuser of morphine, but this does not stop her from marrying a nice young man her son's age. Reviewers were uniformly horrified and took moral offence. Ezra Pound liked it and recommended it to friends, though with the caveat that the novel 'is not nearly so enjoyable as she is'.[45]

Yeats loved *The Devotees*, and found it, somewhat remarkably, based upon reality. He wrote warmly, passionately, to Shakespear from Coole that summer:

> My dear ... the novel is a delight. I am only about two thirds through – I have got to Tonys [sic] discovery of his mothers [sic] drug taking – I cannot go quicker as my eyes are very bad indeed. It is much the best thing you have done. I know all the people intimately and I find all true & not the less charming & that is a rare thing ... I wonder at the skill with which you make one feal [sic] the passage of Time & at the same time make the change gradual like time itself ... You must have been a young man & gone to school in Babylon or Alexandria. Perhaps you played with a peg-top somewhere in the hanging gardens.

Upon finishing the book he found that the 'whole book had a beautiful wisdom & sanity & gentleness', much like its author. Yeats also remarked how much he would be looking forward to Shakespear reading aloud her new work to him when he returned to London.[46]

An account of an American interview with Yeats in 1904 – after he and Olivia were certainly friends once more – has, perhaps, the loveliest and most secret moment he recalled about her from their renewed relationship.

'Dim hair' – as we saw already in 'Aodh to Dectira' – is throughout *The Wind Among the Reeds*, Yeats's Sligo-and-Shakespear volume. The 'long dim hair' of Bridget the bride, spliced in with the 'passion-dimmed eyes and long heavy hair / That was shaken out over my breast' – the 'dim heavy hair' of – very appropriately – 'The Lover Asks Forgiveness because of his Many Moods' – all refer to Olivia. Perhaps the only word in *The Wind Among the Reeds* Yeats uses as often as 'hair' is 'dim'. Here's what the American interviewer, Ashton Stevens, asked him in 1904: Stevens wanted to know if Yeats was a decadent, and Yeats refused the category 'good-humoredly'. Then Stevens said, 'One of your critics ascribes your decadence to your insistence on the hair in describing women – 'dim heavy hair' and such phrases.' 'I think I know the one you mean', Yeats smiled. 'And he did describe a mood in my work that is passed, whether for good or evil – I sometimes think for evil; for I can no longer produce in myself that mood of pure contemplation of beauty…'[47] Yeats was smiling, remembering whose beauty he'd been contemplating during the writing of those particular poems in *The Wind Among The Reeds*, and wishing, as he repeatedly does when speaking of Shakespear in his *Memoirs*, that the mood had not passed.

From 1903, Maud Gonne had removed herself from all sorts of possibility, permanently as far as Yeats knew, by marrying, disastrously, Major John MacBride and promptly becoming pregnant with his child. A second affair that began, according to George Yeats, in 1903 or even before, ended, I believe, when two things came to pass: Dorothy left her home to marry the poet she loved, Ezra Pound, in 1914; and Maud Gonne was freed from the fact of John MacBride by MacBride's execution in 1916.

Critics and biographers of Yeats have tended to skip over Shakespear from early 1897 until 1910 or so, when she and Yeats were both in their fifties, and they had clearly, and publicly, re-established a connection as friends. Even then, the focus of attention is not on Shakespear, but on Pound. A closer look shows that the focus of attention of both poets, during this later time, should be upon Shakespear. She shaped the lives of both Yeats and Pound in profound ways. Among the people Yeats met at Olivia's home, still in Kensington but now in Brunswick Gardens, and where he went regularly by 1910 when he wasn't out at the theatre or at museums with her, were Pound, a 25-year-old American poet bent on making his acquaintance; Olivia's new sister-in-law, Nelly Hyde-Lees; and Nelly's two children from her first marriage, Harold, 20, and Georgie, 18.⁴⁸ Dorothy Shakespear and Georgie Hyde-Lees were best friends, and they would both marry the poets into whose company Olivia brought them.

Shakespear had a dramatic effect upon Pound; on meeting her in early 1909 he reported to his mother that 'a certain Mrs. Shakespeare ... is undoubtedly the most charming woman in London'.⁴⁹ However, Olivia and Hope both disapproved of Ezra's courtship of Dorothy, and she told him in the summer of 1910 that he was no longer welcome in their home – after Dorothy was already in love with him, and after he had already established his relationship with Yeats. Olivia relented, but slowly: the reasons why are speculative, apart from Pound's sad financial state, but I wonder if, even subconsciously, Olivia resented her daughter's offer of marriage from her poet, when from Yeats she herself never had one.

At first Pound and Yeats settled comfortably for each other's company instead – they lived together intermittently in Sussex, at Stone Cottage, during the winters of 1913 to 1915, with Pound famously, or perhaps infamously, serving as Yeats's secretary and editor. Yeats took Shakespear, whose brother had a cottage close by at Coleman's Hatch,⁵⁰ with him to check out the cottage before renting it.⁵¹ Interestingly, Shakespear offered to Pound, after he and Dorothy were finally engaged in early 1914, a flat at 5 Holland Place Chambers, not far – but far enough – from the Shakespears' home, with a great main room shaped like a pentagram. Olivia's name was on the lease as its legal tenant, and when she had initially taken the space, and how long she had maintained it, are not certain. Apparently, she continued to pay the rent on these rooms of her own while Pound languished there and waited to marry her daughter.⁵²

When Pound and Dorothy married, after their up-and-down, hot-and-cold six-year courtship, in April 1914 they spent their honeymoon at Stone Cottage (Yeats wasn't there), and then returned to live with Yeats for parts of the next two winters. Yeats wrote to Mabel Beardsley: 'Pound has a charming young wife who looks as if her face was made out of Dresden china. I look at her in perpetual wonder. It is so hard to beleive

[sic] she is real; & yet she spends all her daylight hours drawing the most monstrous cubist pictures.'[53] Soon Olivia was raising her grandson Omar Pound, a rather ironic turn: having stayed with Hope Shakespear chiefly to maintain her place as Dorothy's mother, Olivia watched as Dorothy got to marry her poet – and as Georgie Hyde-Lees married hers, too – while Olivia remained friend to all, and in loco parentis to small Omar, whose stories of her, many decades later, were told with immense love and admiration.[54]

What had become of Maud Gonne, while Yeats and Shakespear and, increasingly, the new additions to the Shakespear family, the Hyde-Lees children, spent much time together in 1914 and 1915? Married to MacBride in 1903, mother of his son in 1904, Maud had divorced him in 1905, but neither she nor Yeats regarded her as a single woman thereafter until she was widowed in 1916. After MacBride was executed, Yeats went swiftly to France to console Maud, where he proposed yet again to her – and then became increasingly obsessed with Iseult. After this came to pass, it's an unprovable, but most likely, supposition that Olivia ended her second affair with Yeats, and saw him more or less safely to Georgie. The last moving moment together between them, apart from the letters that continue until her death, was at the end of 1914, and occurred in the same manner and sort of space as their initial meetings at the Dulwich Picture Gallery. Yeats wrote in his diary in December about a trip he and Olivia took to the Sussex coast together:

> at Rottingdean two days ago Olivia & I were looking at the Burne Jones Window. She was gazing at the Raphael window on the right. Presently she said 'Don't think me a fool. It is the colour. It is like a sword. It has carried me back twenty years.' When I looked at her she was in tears.[55]

* * *

His marriage and the writing of *A Vision* intervened for a time. However, from the late 1920s until her death Shakespear was Yeats's most important, most casual and most intimate correspondent. These things rarely coincide. To read Yeats writing to her, and very occasionally a surviving letter of hers in reply, is to see a side of Yeats that, both literally and literarily, no one else did. A drawing he finds at Coole Park in 1926, of 'two charming young persons in the full stream of their Saphoistic enthusiasm', got into Yeats's dreams 'and made a great racket there', he tells Olivia eagerly. Come and live in Rapallo, he encourages her late in 1928: 'if one had not to take exercise life would be perfect'. He is anxious about having James Joyce in the house: 'If he comes I shall have to use the utmost ingenuity to hide the fact that I have never finished Ulysses' (L, pp.715, 748, 698). He always sent her drafts of poems – after she received 'Leda and the Swan', which Yeats referred to as a lullaby, Olivia shot back: 'My dear Willy, your lullaby, though very beautiful, is extremely unsuitable for the young! Leda seems to have a peculiar charm for you – personally, I'm so terrified of swans that the idea horrifies me.'[56]

He begged for her advice and approval on the Crazy Jane poems, both of which she honestly granted. He hand-delivered copies of his books to her in 1933: 'My copies only came on Monday. I decided to bring you your copy out of sheer laziness.' In April 1936 he insisted that illness had at last made him 'comparatively thin and elegant' once more, a reminder of his look in 1896. He asked his sister Lily to help out in embroidering presents for her: 'I want to give Mrs. Shakespear a present of a table centre and I have asked Sturge Moore to design it.' He didn't want tulips on it, as tulips have been 'spoilt for us by Liberty'. She returns from a vacation to the country in 1917, and he thinks about her skin: 'I wonder if you are sunburned.' Since he was a little boy Yeats had loved creatures: he kept beetles in his pockets, one of his earliest letters features a rather good sketch of a newt; he treated his cats like friends. When Olivia sent him in 1921 a nest of singing canaries, he was delighted with them. He wrote to her from Thoor Ballylee for appropriate nesting material, which she shipped from London. In no time there were four nests of canaries to go along with the 'stares in a hole over my bedroom window' … 'I have suggested a pie but George won't hear of it' (L, pp. 818, 854, 603–4, 628, 681). As he wrote 'Sailing to Byzantium' and 'Byzantium', the thought of those tiny, happy yellow birds from Olivia was in his mind.

Upon learning of her sudden death of a heart attack, in October 1938, Yeats reacted strongly and with great sorrow:

For more than forty years she has been the centre of my life in London and during all that time we have never had a quarrel, sadness sometimes but never a difference. When I first met her she was in her late twenties but in looks a lovely young girl. When she died she was a lovely old woman ... She was not more lovely than distinguished – no matter what happened she never lost her solitude. She was Lionel Johnson's cousin and felt and thought as he did. For the moment I cannot bear the thought of London. I will find her memory everywhere. (L, p.916)

Solitude is a strange word to use as a compliment – but remember Yeats writing decades before to Katharine Tynan about how he best loved to be alone: 'Solitude having no tongue in her head is never a bore. She never demands of us sympathies we have not. She never makes the near war on the distant.'[57] To be with Olivia became for Yeats to be, very literally, by himself. Four months after her funeral, Yeats died, far from London as the crow flies, but perhaps not so far from London in his mind.

* * *

In his *Dramatis Personae* 1896–1902, Yeats says of himself, 'A romantic, when romanticism was in its final extravagance, I thought one woman, whether wife, mistress, or incitement to platonic love, enough for a life-time ...'[58]

Disingenuous, as much of the *Autobiography* and indeed most autobiographies are, but true, too. Only one woman filled all three of the roles Yeats lists here, and for most of his lifetime. Never his wife, she filled many practical obligations of a wife from shopping for him to tending to him to encouraging him in his work and life. Olivia helped him choose his wife and was the first woman he slept with. She managed remarkably to combine the spiritual and the physical for Yeats's downright Keatsian imagination in a way that made him, to hazard the word, more normal. The best friend from whom he held nothing back, not qualifying his letters to her as he did to Gregory or Gonne, not creating a particular persona beyond what he was, an ageing and ardent man with feelings and regrets, Shakespear was the recipient of his finest and most engaging late letters. When one thinks of Yeats and women, one does not think of him saying, of any woman, 'she was too near my soul, too salutary and wholesome to my inmost being'. Perhaps, for a better understanding of Yeats and the woman who chiefly shaped his view of women for most of his writing life, we should.

NOTES

1. Richard Ellmann, *Yeats: The Man and The Masks* (1948; New York: Norton, 1978).
2. Brenda Maddox, *George's Ghosts: A New Life of W.B. Yeats* (London: Picador, 2000).
3. R.F. Foster, *W.B. Yeats: A Life,* I: *The Apprentice Mage* 1865–1914 (Oxford: Oxford University Press, 1997), p.153.
4. John Harwood, *Olivia Shakespear and W.B Yeats: After Long Silence* (Basingstoke: Macmillan, 1989), pp.5; 9–10. The principal biographical details of Shakespear's life, unless otherwise noted, perforce come from Harwood's careful book about her and about Yeats.
5. W.B. Yeats, *Memoirs,* transcribed and ed. Denis Donoghue (London: Macmillan, 1972), pp.87–8, hereafter referred to in the text as *Mem.*
6. Ellmann, *Yeats: The Man and The Masks,* pp.144, 143.
7. Olivia Shakespear, *Love on a Mortal Lease* (London: Osgood & McIlvaine, 1894), pp.28–9.
8. Arthur Waugh to Edmund Gosse, 17 April 1894, in Ann Thwaite, *Edmund Gosse: a Literary Landscape, 1849–1928* (Chicago, IL: Chicago University Press, 1984), p.355; see Harwood, *Olivia Shakespear and W.B Yeats,* p.31.
9. Foster, *W.B. Yeats,* I, p.167.
10. *The Collected Letters of W.B. Yeats,* II, 1896–1900, ed. Warwick Gould, John Kelly and Deirdre Toomey (Oxford: Oxford University Press, 1997), pp.232, 238, hereafter referred to in the text as *CL2.*
11. George Moore, *Evelyn Innes* (New York: D. Appleton, 1906 [1898]), pp.162–4.
12. Letter, Lionel Johnson and Olivia Shakespear to WBY, 8 May 1894 (MBY); quoted in Harwood, *Olivia Shakespear and W.B Yeats,* p.37.
13. Ellmann, *Yeats: Man and Masks,* p.168.
14. See ibid., p.104.
15. *The Collected Letters of W.B. Yeats,* I, 1865–1895, ed. John Kelly, assoc. ed. Eric Domville (Oxford: Clarendon Press, 1986), pp.136–7, hereafter referred to in the text as *CL1.*
16. Foster, *W.B. Yeats* I, p.153.
17. Ibid., p.155.
18. Peter Ackroyd, *Blake* (London: Sinclair-Stevenson 1995), p.337; for a fine overview of Yeats and Blake see Harold Bloom, *Yeats* (New York: Oxford University Press, 1970), pp.64–82.
19. See, for example, Foster, *W.B. Yeats,* I, pp.156–7.
20. W.B. Yeats, *The Letters of W.B. Yeats,* ed. Allan Wade (London: Rupert Hart-Davis, 1954), p.832, hereafter referred to in the text as *L.*
21. Anna MacBride White and A. Norman Jeffares (eds), *The Gonne–Yeats Letters 1893–1938*

(New York: Norton, 1992), p.53, hereafter referred to in the text as *GYL*.

22. Foster, *W.B. Yeats* I, p.157.

23. Ibid., p.91.

24. *The Savoy*, January 1896, p.83.

25. Ibid., p.138.

26. Harwood, *Olivia Shakespear and W.B Yeats*, p.55.

27. John Masefield, in E.H. Mikhail (ed.), *W.B. Yeats: Interviews and Recollections*, 2 vols., (London: Macmillan, 1977), I, p.47; quoted in part in Harwood, *Olivia Shakespear and W.B Yeats*, p.54.

28. CL2, p.7 n.3, quoting letter from Symons to Yeats, 26 September 1899, reminding Yeats that he still hadn't paid Symons for these items.

29. James Pethica (ed.), *Lady Gregory's Diaries 1892–1902* (Gerrards Cross: Colin Smythe, 1996), p.160.

30. Olivia Shakespear, *The False Laurel* (London: Osgood, 1896), p.246.

31. Arthur Symons, *Selected Letters 1880–1935*, ed. Karl Beckson and John M. Munro (London: Macmillan, 1989), p.131.

32. J.B. Yeats, *Letters to his Son W.B. Yeats and Others, 1869–1922*, ed. Joseph Hone (London: Faber & Faber, 1944), pp.151–2; see also Joseph Hone, *W.B. Yeats 1865–1939* (New York: St Martin's, 1962), p.131.

33. Ellmann, *Yeats: Man and Masks*, p.150.

34. Remember Ellmann's cleanly put insight that 'Because he was a myth-maker his autobiography was never pure', *Yeats: Man and Masks*, p.3.

35. Ibid., p.85.

36. Ibid., p.xxiv.

37. Foster, *W.B. Yeats*, I, p.437.

38. George Mills Harper, *Yeats's Golden Dawn: The Influence of the Hermetic Order of the Golden Dawn on the Life and Art of W.B. Yeats* (Basingstoke: Macmillan, 1974), pp.27, 105.

39. Deirdre Toomey, '"Worst Part of Life": Yeats's Horoscopes for Olivia Shakespear', in *Yeats Annual No. 6*, ed. Warwick Gould (London: Macmillan, 1988), pp.223–4; see also Harwood, *Olivia Shakespear and W.B Yeats*, pp.91–3.

40. Harwood, *Olivia Shakespear and W.B Yeats*, p.90.

41. Warwick Gould, 'Books by Yeats in Olivia Shakespear's Library', in *Yeats Annual No. 9*, ed. Deirdre Toomey (Basingstoke: Macmillan, 1992), p.301.

42. Conversation with the collector/owner, and viewing of scanned book and inscription, New York, July 2008.

43. Harwood, *Olivia Shakespear and W.B Yeats*, p.109.

44. Ibid., p.111.

45. Humphrey Carpenter, *A Serious Character: The Life of Ezra Pound* (New York: Delta, 1988), p.105.

46. *The Collected Letters of W.B. Yeats*, III, 1901–1904, ed. John Kelly and Ron Schuchard (Oxford: Clarendon Press, 1994), pp.628, 633.

47. Foster, *W.B. Yeats* I, pp.533–7, (p.536 [appendix]).

48. Ibid., p.437.

49. Carpenter, *A Serious Character*, p.103.

50. Ibid., p.221.

51. Foster, *W.B. Yeats*, I, p.504.

52. Carpenter, *A Serious Character*, p.236.

53. WBY to Mabel Beardsley, c. 7 January, 1915, Beardsley Collection, Princeton University Libraries; quoted in part in Roy Foster, *W.B. Yeats: A Life*, II: *The Arch-Poet* (Oxford: Oxford University Press, 2003), p.6.

54. Omar Pound, many conversations at lunchtime in the Annex Restaurant, Princeton, New Jersey, 1993–94.

55. W.B. Yeats, Diary, December 1914, ms (National Library of Ireland, Michael B. Yeats), quoted in Harwood, *Olivia Shakespear and W.B Yeats*, p.101.

56. John Harwood (ed.), 'Olivia Shakespear: Letters to W.B. Yeats', in *Yeats Annual* No. 6, ed. Warwick Gould (1988), pp.59–107 (p.71).

57. W.B. Yeats, *Letters to Katharine Tynan*, ed. Roger McHugh (Dublin: Clonmore & Reynolds, 1953), p.26.

58. W.B. Yeats, *The Autobiography of W.B. Yeats* [1938] (New York: Collier Macmillan 1965), p.289.

CHAPTER TEN

Yeats's Influence

STEVEN MATTHEWS

It can sometimes seem as if Yeats's influence is all-pervasive in subsequent Irish poetry. Mention in a poem of any of the stock of images he gave distinctive power to – for instance, images of swans, 'Big Houses', roses or towers – can *seem* immediately to evoke Yeats as the presiding presence over that poem. Seamus Heaney's sonnet 'Postscript' – just one of many places where he seems engaged with Yeats's 'spirit' – is a case in point.[1] Describing the sight of 'the earthed lightening of a flock of swans' as its speaker drives on the coastline of County Clare, the poem remarks upon the impossibility of truly capturing this sight, on the necessity merely to glimpse it before moving on. But the swans have disoriented this speaker:

> You are neither here nor there,
> A hurry through which known and strange things pass
> As big soft buffetings come at the car sideways
> And catch the heart off guard and blow it open.[2]

Heaney's poem might *seem* to be capturing something of the mid-life uncertainties about the future, and about the continuation of potency and poetic power, which Yeats had given classic formulation to in 'The Wild Swans at Coole'. Yeats's final lines, after all, bring an anxious questioning ('Among what rushes will they build, / By what lake's edge or pool / Delight men's eyes') when the swans have deserted the poet left at Coole.[3] To that extent, Heaney's decision in his poem to stay 'on the move', not to be preoccupied by anxieties about his craft here, seems a lesson consciously learnt from Yeats's experience.

But this is not to suggest that Heaney's poem is any the less unsettled because of this 'Yeatsian' understanding. The final line of 'Postscript', 'And catch the heart off guard and blow it open' might seem a further reference to Yeats, and the famous conclusion to 'The Circus Animals' Desertion', with its resolve, now that the poet's key myths and images have left him, to return to poetry's 'start' 'In the foul rag-and-bone shop of the heart' (p.348). Like Yeats, Heaney's notion in this poem that poetry itself might be inadequate to the task of rendering heightened moments of perception leaves him, his heart, the more vulnerable. 'Postscript', after all, is an additional note 'added to' the first collection published after Heaney had received what Yeats called 'the bounty of Sweden', the Nobel Prize for Literature.

'Postscript' in all of these ways *seems*, therefore, to be a conscious engagement by the later poet, at a certain moment in the trajectory of his own career, with major themes, and ideas of development across a poetic life, as formulated by Yeats. And yet. The extent to which Heaney would want to seem to be establishing a *conscious* dialogue with the spirit of Yeats here is uncertain. His poetic form, for instance, in its lack of rhyme, would seem to want to avoid the sonorous declarations of the Yeats 'models' mentioned. Further, the relation of the speaker in Heaney's poem to the experience described in it is ambiguous. In 'The Wild Swans at Coole' and 'The Circus Animals' Desertion', as in all of his more reflective lyrics, Yeats establishes the speaker of the poetry firmly at the centre of its perspectives and concerns. This is an 'I' firmly aware of where he is in place and time, even ludicrously so: 'The nineteenth autumn has come upon me / Since first I made my count', as he says of his swans here.

Heaney's speaker, however, is more obliquely related to the experience contained in 'Postscript'. His poem opens with the line 'And some time make the time to drive out west ...' The word-play in the opening clauses makes the temporal location of this utterance uncertain. Has the poet in fact 'made the time'? Is he talking to himself or to someone else here (who is the 'you' later mentioned in the poem)? The poem forms an injunction to action by the poet, one which might be set alongside earlier famous self-injunctions by Heaney, such as the 'Some day I will go to Aarhus' of 'The Tolland Man'.[4] It locates the experience and reflection upon it which form the substance of the poem in some undefined future, a space in which these insights *might* bear fruit, but might not.

Heaney is not openly stating anything about the situation described in the poem, as the deliberately mealy-mouthed opening ('some time make the time'), or the vulnerable 'And' as his opening word signals. Unlike Yeats, Heaney is not telling himself, or his auditor, anything direct and definable, and that is the subtle brilliance of his treatment in his sonnet of what the elder poet called 'vision'.

If we are to see the issues in 'Postscript' as referring back to Yeats, therefore, as the imagery of the poem suggests we might, we can only do so in a qualified and unratifiable way. As far back as a lecture given in 1978, when he considered the issue of Yeats's impact upon contemporary Irish poets (a lecture in which he acknowledged that Yeats is 'the ideal example for a poet approaching middle age'), Heaney notably added a question-mark around the matter. The English poet W.H. Auden's 1940 essay 'Yeats as an Example' became, in Heaney's revision, 'Yeats as an Example?'.[5] I take that question-mark as emblematic, in this chapter, when considering Yeats's importance for subsequent Irish poetry. Yeats's work is *inevitably* diffused across that writing, either directly through quotation or, as in the Heaney case in point, through Yeats's having established a whole panoply of poetic 'furniture' which gets taken up by later writers. That 'furniture' includes a range of imagery; symbol; methods for poetry's engagement with politics, with history, with spiritual and religious matters. It includes also the major love poetry, which echoes in more recent poems by such as John Montague. Yeats is an example *to be negotiated with*; not one to be accepted in inevitably positive terms, but, nonetheless, to be recognized as having established an *agenda* for Irish poetry which was unavoidable. As this chapter will particularly seek to dramatize, what is striking about this process of negotiation with Yeats's ghost in subsequent Irish poetry is that it involves a series of revisitings, and re-encounters, in which Yeats's presence is almost personally evoked. This happens through real or imagined meetings with the man, or through trips taken to his major sites of writing, Coole and Ballylee. What is involved here is a literal negotiation, then, over places which, due to Yeats's writing, have obtained a symbolic power, and which are almost obsessively reconsidered and reworked in later Irish poetry.

Or, perhaps it is better to say that Yeats's poetry established *a set of* agendas for later poets. It is perhaps the variety and multiplicity of Yeats's own poetry, the rapid shifts of style and preoccupation across Yeats's own career, which makes him a particularly potent example. To begin with one such shift of emphasis in his work which resonates within later poetry: certainly, the issue of Yeats being a figure to be negotiated with (positively and negatively) partly derives from the fact that, from the time of the multiple disillusionments of *Michael Robartes and the Dancer* (1921) onwards, Yeats sought more concertedly to foreground the virtues, as he framed them, of his family traditions and of his Protestant inheritance. This had, clearly, a difficult impact (to say the least) upon those poets who had known and admired Yeats's nationalism hitherto. Austin Clarke, for instance, in his 'A Centenary Tribute' from the tellingly titled collection *The Echo at Coole* (1968), recalls walking past the aged Yeats's house in Riversdale. But Clarke here notably perceives his former self as a kind of 'hedge-walking tramp with empty wallet' – the sort of figure celebrated by Yeats in his later poetry (Crazy Jane, Tom at Cruahane) – rather than as a figure of the poet like Yeats himself, who Clarke remembers having been 'chary' of visiting.

Yet Clarke, in this same retrospective book of poems, brings out his own uncertainty over his negotiation with the figure of Yeats, and what he later came to represent. Another poem in *The Echo at Coole*, 'The House-Breakers', which recalls a lunch Clarke had with Yeats, seems to strike a more lamenting and satiric note about the felling of trees at the Coole Park estate – and, by inference, at the loss of a heritage:

> Woods, that had scattered leaves, Protestant tracts,
> Cut down, big house thrown out on the roadside.
> Hatred's, that well-known Irish firm of Contractors,
> Counted the lumbering lorries with their load.[6]

This latter, more complex, attitude to Yeats and to his programmes, seems closely attuned to the opinions which Clarke had expressed in the later 1930s about the senior poet, and especially in two articles produced at the time of Yeats's death in 1939 – an obituary essay 'W.B. Yeats', and 'Poet and Artist'. In both of these pieces, Clarke emphasized the 'paradoxical' nature of Yeats's poetry, 'the shifting background of his literary life,' as the obituary article has it. Clarke admits that 'Yeats's attitude to home rule in Irish letters in his later years is somewhat of a mystery.' But, in both pieces, and despite proclaiming Yeats's central significance within poetry in English, Clarke is concerned to distance Yeats from England itself: rather, for him, Yeats displays an 'individual Anglo-Irish note', which is not at all 'representative of English genius'. Primarily, though, Clarke (as all later poets do) praises the 'unique and self-sustained' qualities of the Yeatsian poetic line; Yeats's 'remembering ... that the poet's real vocation is to sing'.[7] When faced, in other words, with his uncertain feelings about the Yeatsian inheritance, Clarke extricates the *poetic* merit from the political and cultural issues which cause potential difficulty.

Clarke's view might be taken as typical of those older poets flourishing around the middle of the twentieth century who wanted to separate Yeats from English or modernist appropriations of him, but who also wanted to extricate Yeats's troubled and troubling version of Anglo-Irish nationalism from his qualities as a supreme writer. Patrick Kavanagh, for instance, was notably dismissive of Yeats's adherence to that 'weary, parochial thing, Irish nationalism'. Yet Kavanagh also suggested that a simple re-routing of the direction of Yeats's creative brilliance might have achieved his broader political ambitions by default:

> Yeats was the god, the authority, the Mother Mind to whom all things could be referred. Any person possessing this myth-making quality can transform a commonplace society into an Olympian one.[8]

In Kavanagh's own case, this strategy of negotiation with Yeats's work might be taken as one which enables Kavanagh successfully to defuse the potent reference of this 'Mother Mind': his own poetry runs almost in a deliberate counter-direction to Yeats's, eschewing 'Olympian' perspectives for grounded, parochial and vernacular ones.[9]

For the Planter poet John Hewitt, however, such counter-moves were culturally impossible. Yet, like Kavanagh, Hewitt remained anxious to defend Yeats as a craftsman against interpretations of him which suggested that the poetry had broader mystical or political significance. In his essay deriving its title from Yeats's self-elegy 'Under Ben Bulben', 'Irish Poets Learn Your Trade', Hewitt also typically demonstrated his unease with those Olympian qualities (symbols, images, masks) of Yeats's poetry which Kavanagh had found so impressive, if unrepeatable. Instead, for

Hewitt, Yeats 'was tremendously skilled and versatile, with an expert ear for the renewal of neglected and forgotten forms'.[10] Yeats, in this reading, acts primarily as a conservator of the *poetic* tradition, keeping it alive for later poets to inherit, but also revivifying parts of the tradition which have become neglected.

It is in what Hewitt conceived of as a trilogy of poems, written in the decade after Yeats's death, that he negotiated most intensely with both the technical and the *thematic* implications of this version of Yeats's inheritance. In *Conacre* (1943), 'Freehold' (1939–46) and 'Homestead' (1949), Hewitt reviews most intently his own situation as a Northern Protestant with long roots in Ireland, as an 'insider' through family inheritance who is also an 'outsider' to Ireland's myths and traditions. In this trilogy, Hewitt negotiates these tensions partly through an implicit, and occasionally allusive, discussion with Yeats.

In *Conacre*, Hewitt celebrates a version of pastoral, of the land and landscape, which is distinctly unYeatsian. It is more Hardyesque, in fact, in its urging the notion that 'in the landscape loved / the hedge and copse the use of man has proved'. The ambulatory nature of Hewitt's couplets seems temporally set to what he calls here 'the comfortable pace / of safe tradition'. Yet, in subsequent passages, we find Hewitt meditating upon the limitation of this point of view. He notes the Blakean range that poetry is supposed to achieve, in contrast to his own narrow focus. He reminds himself that poetry should display 'a cosmos weighed within a human hand'. It is as though thinking of Blake instantly recalls Yeats, promoter of the Romantic poet in various essays and in his own poetic choices. Hewitt's speaker here draws himself up short, pointing out that there lies 'this way madness or a cynic mind / that in Yeats' ditch hears blind man thumping blind'. As 'a happy man who seldom sees / the emptiness behind the images', Hewitt's speaker must reconcile himself to the 'sufficient joy from being here alive'.[11] Hewitt's socialism makes him wary of the frenzy which seems echoed in the view of life promoted in Yeats's 'A Dialogue of Self and Soul', the source of Hewitt's image about the 'blind man thumping blind'. But he also wishes to avoid the note of 'tragic joy' which characterizes late poems by Yeats such as 'Lapis Lazuli'. He has not had the doubt about his creativity that Yeats had over his 'images' in such work as 'The Circus Animals' Desertion'.

Hewitt's linked poem to *Conacre*, 'Homestead', however, complicates this picture of wary rejection of Yeats. Here, we find Hewitt seeking to embrace Irish mythology through the figure of Oisin, in order to find himself more local mythic literary forebears. In this sense, Yeats again plays an equivocal part:

> Yeats was Oisin.
> The dinted symbols rust in the crumbling tower
> but Oisin is not there now. I saw Yeats carried
> to the wailing of bagpipes through the wind-washed town
> and watched Oisin elbow back through the holiday crowd,
> going the opposite way as we followed the hearse ...[12]

Hewitt offers a very explicit figure here of the equivocal presence which Yeats offers subsequent poets, one free of the wariness, of the need to sustain a steady rhythm and perspective, which had marked *Conacre*. In 'Homestead', Yeats is presented as himself a mythic figure, curiously removed by his human death from those very 'images' which he had made for himself – including the 'crumbling tower'. Yet, at the same time, the legendary figure survives the actual funeral, is potently out there to be appropriated (as Hewitt does in his poem) by later writing, which seeks to draw upon an Irish myth-kitty in order to establish its own credentials separate from England.

Similar equivocations, about the persistence of Yeats's key innovative strategies regarding the establishment of a cultural Irishness within a commanding poetic authority, play around the attitude to Yeats manifested in the essays and poetry of Louis MacNeice. His war-time critical book, *The Poetry of W.B. Yeats*, was written, MacNeice affirms, to explore 'why Yeats appealed to me so much', and also in the hope of presenting Yeats's work 'sympathetically to others'. MacNeice notes Yeats's affinities to the Irish landscape in Sligo and Galway, and the fact that his 'orientation towards Ireland' was what saved Yeats from the late nineteenth-century aestheticism of Walter Pater which mars, in MacNeice's view, the early work. But, ultimately, MacNeice focuses his sense of the impact of Yeats upon form, upon the way in which, unlike Eliot and Pound, Yeats used traditional forms to 'select and systematize' the chaotic modern world:

> Treatment of form and subject here went hand in hand. Yeats's

formalizing activity began when he thought about the world; as he thought it into a regular pattern, he naturally cast his thought in regular patterns also.[13]

This is the inheritance which, MacNeice feels, Yeats passed forward to the poets who began to be noticed in the 1930s in Britain and Ireland, such as himself, W.H. Auden and Stephen Spender. Although T.S. Eliot provided these poets with much of their modern rhetoric and urban subject-matter, it was Yeats who dictated their attitude as poets towards the experience to be rendered in their poetry, which retained for the most part tight formal and traditional structures.

In his 1948 collection *Holes in the Sky*, MacNeice reveals an affinity with the western littoral and landscape correlative to what he describes as Yeats's. But, already, MacNeice sets that affinity at a remove, as part of family history, but not of his own particularly. So, for him, the West has come to seem a dreamed place. In 'The Strand', for example, MacNeice recalls himself following his father's footsteps to 'the western sea' which his father 'so loved'. But the poet's is a tourist's perspective, as a 'visitor' whose presence in the landscape will soon be 'blotted' by the sea's 'foam'. In 'Carrick Revisited', MacNeice openly parades his distance from the origins of his family history ('the pre-natal mountain is far away'), in a manner which suggests his own inability, whatever his poetic ambition, to re-establish a link to the past:

> Torn before birth from where my fathers dwelt,
> Schooled from the age of ten to a foreign voice,
> Yet neither western Ireland nor southern England
> Cancels this interlude; what chance misspelt
> May never now be righted by my choice.[14]

Having seemingly signalled his own distance, in 'voice' and in locale, from the grounding he felt underpinned Yeats's poetry, then, the impact of Yeats's poetry can perhaps best be seen in MacNeice's sensing of the formal example which it provided to his generation of writers. MacNeice would seem to have shared with Yeats a strong feeling of the 'chaotic' nature of the modern world; for what, in his most famous poem 'Snow', he called the 'incorrigibly plural' nature of things. But he also revealed a countering sense that the formal coherence of poetry was the means by which to capture and address that bewildering complexity. 'Snow' itself, which appeared in MacNeice's first book, *Poems* (1935), reveals a firm use of form to control the topsy-turviness of the world described, through its three quatrains in which lines 2 and 4 rhyme. Looking at a vase of pink roses in a bay-window, outside of which snow falls, the poem concludes ruminatively:

> ... world
> Is more spiteful and gay than one supposes –
> On the tongue on the eyes on the ears in the palms of one's hands –
> There is more than glass between the snow and the huge roses.[15]

The effect of the variousness of the world upon the poem's sentences is caught in the tumbling third line quoted. But the strict barriers and borders between kinds of perception, as between all the different kinds of human activity and its politics, is firmly reasserted in the rhymed last line. What seems permeable and transparent between states of mind, as between the things in the world, is not so, and the form of the poem mimics this delimitation.

Essentially what MacNeice's *The Poetry of W.B. Yeats* and his own poetic practice after Yeats mount, then, is a defence of poetry which is open to local (Irish) inflections, but a poetry which primarily resists, according to a Yeatsian model, the formal experimentation of modernist poetry by such as Pound, Eliot and their followers. Similar tensions to these, but from the opposite point of view, complicate the story of Yeats's influence upon Irish poetry in the 1950s, with the emergence of a poetic generation, including Padraic Fallon, Thomas Kinsella and John Montague, who were much more sympathetic to, and excited by, the ambition of modernist poetry, and who sought to translate some of its features into Ireland. In a series of poems from the 1950s through the 1960s, Fallon re-encountered the Yeatsian symbols, particularly those relating to the tower and Coole. In the first of these, 'Yeats's Tower at Ballylee', the poet recalls a visit he paid in 1950, at the height of the Korean War, when Yeats's example, especially his 'Meditations in Time of Civil War', seems to offer lessons and method to a later poet having to write about conflict. Yet, the visit achieves the opposite, as it confirms the emptiness of Yeats's symbols now that time has passed:

This tower where the poet thought to play
Out some old romance to the end caught up
The dream and the dreamer in its brutal way
And the dream dies here upon the crumbling top.
I know the terror of his vision now:
A poet dies in every poem, even
As blossom dies when fruit comes on the bough,
And world is endless time in which things happen
In endless repetition ...[16]

Fallon, like Hewitt, seems alert to Yeats's vision of life founded upon eternal struggle, promoted for example in 'A Dialogue of Self and Soul'. His image for the 'mass' of humanity on this torn earth is, like Yeats's of the 'blind man's ditch', 'frogspawn' (p.236). What Fallon's poetic visit to the Tower mainly confirms, however, is the transience of images, however masterful. The poignant picture of the empty tower renders Yeats's example here other than what might have been expected; in a modernist manoeuvre which would have been alien to Yeats himself, the vision of the tower succeeds in confirming the fruitless repetition of the world and of its violence, rather than providing symbols adequate to this modern predicament.

Such a view would seem to be confirmed in Fallon's work by the later poem 'Yeats at Athenry Perhaps', a fantasy about Yeats arriving in Fallon's home place. Athenry is somewhere Yeats would have stopped at on his way to Gort, but it is a ragged set of buildings, which has 'Exhausted history'. Fallon doubts that Yeats would have 'bothered with us', since the older poet had 'his sight turned in'. As a visionary, 'he wouldn't have dared a town / Where every peeling window was an eye'. Yet Fallon's poem seems caught also in its own sense of opposite potentials, yielding at the end to a rehearsal of Yeats's aristocratic imagery: Coole House, the swans, Juno's peacock. It is as though, however void such imagery might have become, the insufficiencies of the poet's own situation can offer little itself by way of poetic inspiration, and hence displays awe at Yeats's dominance. As the further poem on this subject, 'On the Tower Stairs' puts it, 'What does it matter now? / Who can question the work done?' by Yeats.[17] Yeats's influence establishes an impasse within Fallon's work from which his modernist influencers (primarily Pound) cannot entirely redeem him.

In this regard, Thomas Kinsella's project is the more salutary. Coming out of what Kinsella calls a 'dual tradition' in Irish poetry which combines Gaelic and English writing, his career offers a more aggressive, if also admiring, 'take' on Yeats's work from the outset. For Kinsella, 'Yeats is in the tradition of Irish literature: he gives it body and, in many ways, meaning for the twentieth century. But he is isolated in the tradition.' Kinsella therefore sees Yeats's whole career as a dramatization of this 'predicament', that, 'remembering the past persecutions of the Irish people under English colonization', Yeats's love/hate relationship with England and with English literature becomes the crux upon which his work is renewed. Kinsella, like the previous poets reviewed so far in this chapter, is anxious to see Yeats, the 'great artist' (and particularly the later Yeats who, in Kinsella's view, had eschewed nationalism), as separate from political dynamics, which had become successfully 'absorbed' in his poetry, through its increasing resort to images of violence. But this does not remove the fact that, for Kinsella, Yeats, in his Coole poems specifically, takes 'the colonial view' of the Irish land: 'it is property, and the undisturbed possession of it, that is at the root of this idea'.[18]

'Magnanimity', a poem dedicated to Austin Clarke on his seventieth birthday, finds Kinsella intriguingly in the process of negotiating these issues literally. Recounting a visit to Coole Park, Kinsella is able to define his distance from the resonances and echoes there. Clarke had suggested on the visit that 'Coole might be built again as a place for poets', as Kinsella reports in his poem. But this suggestion receives his own counter-assertion that 'I am sure that there are no places for poets, / Only changing habitations for verse to outlast.' Kinsella is anxious to break the already forming tradition that Irish poetry derives from a set of symbolic Yeatsian places: for him rather, each poem forms a 'habitation' for the poet's spirit in itself. He is willing to take on what had seemed such a difficulty for an earlier writer like Clarke himself, as also for Fallon – the sense that the modern world has sunk into a poor banality with few fit symbols, when compared to what Yeats could make out of Coole, with its tree carved-into by poets: 'Houses shall pass away, and all give place / To signposts and chicken-wire.'[19] In this instance, Kinsella's eye seems drawn to the compensatory potential within nature, which similarly 'outlasts' human symbols. 'Pale cress persists', as the poem's last line reminds us. But this is not a recourse which Kinsella's writing, firmly rooted in Dublin and environs ('centre city' as he calls it), can often take advantage of.

The long poem 'Nightwalker', which appeared in 1968, remains Kinsella's most direct engagement with Yeats in these circumstances. The poem takes its title from Yeats's 'Byzantium': 'The Emperor's drunken soldiery are abed; / Night resonance recedes, night-walkers' song' (p.248). The removal of day's 'unpurged images' in Yeats's poem allows space to open for the images of the mind to enter. Kinsella's meditation on a night-time ramble around Dublin and Howth does not operate in territory remote from this. Part 4 of the poem, for instance, finds in the moon, 'Virgin most pure', apt counter-mask to 'my dismay', 'it was a terrible time'. But where Kinsella's poem *ends up* is a place more like Eliot's *The Waste Land*, than amongst the 'fresh images' of later Yeats. Whilst he derives something of his openness and honesty from the declaration of Yeats's prescription in 'A Coat' ('there's more enterprise / In walking naked' (p.127)), Kinsella's speaker comes to 'A true desert, / Sterile and odourless. Naked to every peril.' In other words, Kinsella ultimately turns inward, to an arid but haunted sphere of images ('If I stoop down and touch the dust / It has a human taste').[20] In the sequence's final section, he evokes 'love' as a salvation from this. But, in contrast to Yeats's major poems on the theme, Kinsella's *credo* is hesitant and unconvinced:

> I believe now that love is half persistence,
> A medium in which from change to change
> Understanding may be gathered.[21]

Kinsella invokes the Yeats word 'change' in a countervailing manner to Yeats's use: 'change' is not something which, as in 'Easter 1916', can occur absolutely, once in history, but rather, a metamorphic process in which 'understanding' – perhaps here echoing 'Leda and the Swan's' word 'knowledge' – *may* occur.

Against the philosophic rigours of Kinsella's approach, and with no condescension, John Montague's long-term and continuing engagement with Yeats offers a more relaxed and genial approach. In recent work, such as the mini-sequence from *Smashing the Piano*, 'Prayers for my Daughters', the stock of Yeatsian imagery seems to be underlying the poetry in an enabling way. 'The Sick Bird' of this sequence, for instance, a parable of nurture and recovery for the poem's addressees, takes a seemingly surprising but otherwise entirely acceptable turn in its final stanza:

> Now it rests on the unlit stove
> in a cushioned box, beside where I write,
> inspected, every so often, by tiptoeing children.
> Its heart is still furiously beating;
> when will it take flight?[22]

In returning us to the final stanza of 'The Wild Swans at Coole', Montague sets the process of eventual departure, as continuous with, and necessary to, the strong continuation of life. As with the Yeats original, the bird serves to sponsor the poem ('besides where I write'); unlike the Yeats, the eventual disappearance of the bird does not seem cause for anxiety, but rather for celebration of difficult times which have been survived.

In this recent work by John Montague, therefore, little of that uncertainty or even equivocation about Yeats's influence, which has marked many of the instances cited in this chapter, remains. There is also a surprising ease with regard to that influence to be perceived elsewhere in recent Irish work. Eavan Boland's prose collection, *Object Lessons*, for example, is notable in many ways, but not least for the way in which it promotes Yeats. It does so, if not for the formal and rhetorical model he offers, but for the notion he evolved of the political poet writing in a time of violence. Making a sharp distinction between her own earlier output, which she feels had too readily accepted the re-eruption of the Troubles in Ireland as the 'news' which poetry had to deal with, Boland shows herself to have revised her view to centre her notion of the political in poetry rather upon what she calls the 'intensity of a private world' which 'destabilizes' any poem's view of the ongoing civil war:

> I do not believe the political poem can be written with truth and effect unless the self who writes that poem – a self in which sexuality must be a factor – is seen to be in radical relation to the ratio of power to powerlessness with which the political poem is so concerned.[23]

Despite the emphasis upon sexuality and gender in this discussion by Boland, an emphasis which culminates with her proposing the importance of a female *erotics* to be explored in poetry, she cites Yeats's 'Meditations in Time of Civil War' as her 'beautiful example' of the kind of political poetry she wishes to write. Yeats's determination to focus, from his Tower, his response to the violence through his own experience enables Boland to free herself of the 'ratio of power' in poetry which she had particularly felt pressing upon her as a woman poet. As her *ars poetica*, the title poem of her sequence 'Outside History', has it:

> I have chosen:
>
> out of myth into history I move to be
> part of that ordeal
> whose darkness is
>
> only now reaching me ...[24]

Part of the lesson here from Yeats would seem to be that poetry in this mode can be more overtly declarative about its own procedures; that it must be, in these circumstances where roads are 'clotted as / firmaments with the dead'. By placing what she calls the 'difficult "I"' as both the subject of the poem, and as its object of perception, Boland feels that she has partly followed Yeats's example in showing a responsibility to the history of her times. A similar level of self-consciousness about the role of the poet in relation to history is evident in the work of Paul Muldoon, particularly in the monumental sequence of works deploying the *ottava rima* form which has stretched now from his collection *The Annals of Chile* (1994) through to *Horse Latitudes* (2006).

Yeats had become interested in Byron's version of the eight-line stanza form in the mid-1920s, and deployed it in several of his key later reflections upon the situation of the poet, and of the visionary imagination, within and against the pressures of history – including 'Among School Children', 'The Statues', 'The Gyres' and 'The Circus Animals' Desertion'. In Muldoon's hands, with the improvisational feel brought to the form by the use of variable line lengths, the form becomes a space and place in which the conglomeration of moments in history – whether as mediated through family, or more broadly – is reproduced in appropriately dizzying turmoil. As an example of this, we can see in the culminating sequence of *Moy Sand and Gravel* (2002), 'At the Sign of the Black Horse, September 1999', a process whereby the minutiae of everyday life both expand into, and resist, the telling of the appalling events of twentieth-century and earlier diasporic histories. The sequence as a whole is punctuated by the written-out slogans from road signs in the district around the Muldoon family house in America, a house which had been constructed by exiled Irish navvies escaping depredations in the previous century:

> The red stain on the lint
> that covered whatever it was in the autoclave brought
>   back an afternoon in Poland
> when the smoke would flail and fling itself, Maximum
>   Headroom,
> from a crematorium
> at Auschwitz. It was not without some
> trepidation, so, that I trained my camcorder
> on this group of creel carters
> bearing clay, hay, hair (at shoulder height, or above)
>   through the awesome
>
> morning after Hurricane Floyd ... [25]

The ironic 'it was not without some / trepidation' displays the speaker's wry awe before the implications of his raising such subject-matter. Training his camcorder on the ghosts of the navvies bringing the materials to build his house, Muldoon is in the position of surveillance as Yeats is in his tower, recalling the history of violence which it arose from (p.202). Muldoon's is a situation in which nature – the Hurricane – symbolizes in its violence the events of the past few centuries, including the Holocaust which blighted his wife's family. As such, therefore, as for Yeats, the poetic form is made to constrain a panoply of personal and historical forces which, whilst in themselves seemingly chaotic, are also consonant with the situation in which the poet finds himself.

Muldoon's recent work mounts a continuing tribute, then, to the significance of Yeats's presence over and within Irish poetry, a significance which ranges more broadly than the limits of this chapter allow. Many other Irish poets, including Derek Mahon, Michael Longley and Medbh McGuckian, have variously manifested the example of Yeats in their work, as something to be negotiated with in deriving their own poetic stance. This chapter has striven merely to outline some of the formal, political and historical facets of this ongoing process of negotiation.

NOTES

1. The poem 'Where does spirit live?' ('Squarings' xxii), from *Seeing Things* (London: Faber, 1991), p.78 is Heaney's most overt engagement with some of the issues discussed below regarding 'Postscript'.
2. Seamus Heaney, *The Spirit Level* (London: Faber, 1996), p.70.
3. Richard J. Finneran (ed.), *The Collected Poems of W.B. Yeats: A New Edition*, (Basingstoke: Macmillan, 1991), p. 132. All subsequent references to Yeats's poetry are from this edition, with page numbers provided in the text.
4. Seamus Heaney, *Wintering Out* (London: Faber, 1972), p.47.
5. Seamus Heaney, *Finders Keepers: Selected Prose 1971–2001* (London: Faber, 2002), p.107.
6. Austin Clarke, *Collected Poems*, ed. R. Dardis Clarke (Manchester: Carcanet, 2008), pp.395, 411.
7. *Reviews and Essays of Austin Clarke*, ed. Gregroy A. Schirmer (Gerrard's Cross: Colin Smythe, 1995), pp.10–11, 14.
8. Patrick Kavanagh, *Collected Prose* (London: MacGibbon & Kee, 1967), pp.251, 255.
9. Antoinette Quinn has identified 'Come Dance With Kitty Stobling', from the 1960 collection of that name, as a rare moment in which Kavanagh receives Yeats's inheritance positively. See *Patrick Kavanagh: Born Again Romantic* (Dublin: Gill & Macmillan, 1991), pp.414–16.
10. *Ancestral Voices: The Selected Prose of John Hewitt*, ed. Tom Clyde (Belfast: Blackstaff Press, 1987), p.79.
11. *The Collected Poems of John Hewitt*, ed. Frank Ormsby (Belfast: Blackstaff Press, 1991), pp.8–9.
12. Ibid., p.70.
13. Louis MacNeice, *The Poetry of W.B. Yeats* (London: Faber, 1967 [1940]), pp.17, 50, 156.
14. Louis MacNeice, *Collected Poems*, ed. Peter McDonald (London: Faber, 2007), pp.264, 262.
15. Ibid., p.24.
16. Padraic Fallon, *Collected Poems* (Loughcrew: Gallery Press, 1990), p.44.
17. Ibid., pp.112–13, 118.
18. Thomas Kinsella, *The Dual Tradition: An Essay on Poetry and Politics in Ireland* (Manchester: Carcanet, 1995), pp.66, 89–90.
19. Thomas Kinsella, *Collected Poems* (Manchester: Carcanet, 2001), pp.72–3.

20. Andrew Fitzsimmons, in his discussion of the sequence, points to an unpublished note of Kinsella's on Yeats, which emphasizes the power of the 'private philosophic structure' behind Yeats's work. See *The Sea of Disappointment: Thomas Kinsella's Pursuit of the Real* (Dublin: UCD Press, 2008), p.108.

21. Kinsella, *Collected Poems*, p.84.

22. John Montague, *Smashing the Piano* (Loughcrew: Gallery Press, 1999), p.26.

23. Eavan Boland, *Object Lessons: The Life of the Woman and the Poet in Our Time* (Manchester: Carcanet, 1995), pp.189, 185.

24. Eavan Boland, *New Collected Poems* (Manchester: Carcanet, 2005), p.188.

25. Paul Muldoon, *Moy Sand and Gravel* (London: Faber, 2002), p.82.

Select Bibliography

Any abbreviation used in the text is noted here in brackets following the full reference.

WORKS BY W.B. YEATS

Poems and Plays

Allt, Peter and Russell K. Alspach (eds), *The Variorum Edition of the Poems of W.B. Yeats* (New York: Macmillan, 1957). (*VP*)

Alspach, Russell K. (ed.), *The Variorum Edition of the Plays of W.B. Yeats* (London: Macmillan, 1966).

Albright, Daniel (ed.) *W.B. Yeats: The Poems* (London: J.M. Dent, 1990).

Finneran, Richard J., (ed.), *The Collected Poems of W.B. Yeats: A New Edition* (Basingstoke: Macmillan, 1991).

Jeffares, A.Norman, *Yeats's Poems*, with an appendix by Warwick Gould (Basingstoke: Macmillan, 1991).

Holdsworth, Carolyn (ed.), *W.B. Yeats: The Wind Among the Reeds: Manuscript Materials*, (Ithaca, NY: Cornell University Press, 1993).

Finneran, Richard J. (ed.), *The Collected Works of W.B. Yeats*, I, *The Poems*, 2nd edn (New York: Scribners, 1997). (*CW* I)

Larrissy, Edward (ed.), *W.B. Yeats*, Oxford Authors (Oxford: Oxford University Press, 1997). Second edition published as *W.B. Yeats: The Major Works* (World's Classics), ed. Edward Larrissy (Oxford: Oxford University Press, 2001).

Clark, David R. and Rosalind E. Clark (eds), *The Collected Works of W.B. Yeats*, III, *The Plays* (New York: Scribners, 2001).

Prose

A Vision (London: Macmillan, 1937). (*V*)

Autobiographies (London: Macmillan, 1955). (*A*)

Mythologies (London: Macmillan, 1959).

Essays and Introductions (London: Macmillan, 1961; New York: Collier, 1968). (*E&I*)

Explorations (London: Macmillan, 1962). (Ex)

The Autobiography of W.B. Yeats (New York: Collier Macmillan, 1965 [1938]).

Memoirs, ed. and transcribed by Denis Donoghue (London: Macmillan, 1972). (Mem)

Frayne, John P. (ed.), *Uncollected Prose by W.B. Yeats, I: First Reviews and Articles, 1886–1896* (London: Macmillan, 1970). (UP I)

Frayne, John P. and Colton Johnson (eds), *Uncollected Prose by W.B. Yeats, II: 1897–1939,* (London: Macmillan, 1975). (UP II)

Adams, Stephen L. and George Mills Harper (eds), 'The Manuscript of Leo Africanus', *Yeats Annual*, No. 1, ed. Richard J. Finneran (1982), pp.3–47.

Yeats, W.B. and Lady Gregory, *A Treasury of Irish Myth, Legend, and Folklore* (New York: Gramercy Books, 1986).

Yeats, W.B., 'Four Lectures by W.B. Yeats', ed. Richard Londraville, in *Yeats Annual No. 8*, ed. Warwick Gould (1991), pp.78–122.

O'Donnell, William H. and Douglas N. Archibald, *The Collected Works of Yeats, W.B., III, Autobiographies* (New York: Scribners, 1999).

Paul, Catherine E. and Margaret Mills Harper (eds), *The Collected Works of W.B. Yeats: XIII: A Vision: The Original 1925 Version* (New York: Scribners, 2008).

Letters

Kelly, John and associate ed. Eric Domville (eds), *The Collected Letters of W.B. Yeats*, I, 1865–1895 (Oxford: Clarendon Press, 1986). (CL1)

Gould, Warwick, John Kelly and Deirdre Toomey (eds), *The Collected Letters of W.B. Yeats*, II, 1896–1900 (Oxford: Oxford University Press, 1997). (CL2)

Kelly, John and Ronald Schuchard (eds), *The Collected Letters of W.B. Yeats*, III, 1901–1904 (Oxford: Clarendon Press, 1994). (CL3)

Wade, Alan (ed.), *The Letters of W.B. Yeats* (London: Rupert Hart-Davis, 1954). (L)

Bridges, Ursula (ed.), *W.B. Yeats and T. Sturge Moore: Their Correspondence, 1901–1937,* (London: Routledge & Kegan Paul, 1953).

Yeats, W.B., *Letters to Katharine Tynan*, ed. Roger McHugh (Dublin: Clonmore & Reynolds, 1953)

MacBride White, Anna and A. Norman Jeffares (eds), *The Gonne–Yeats Letters 1893–1938* (New York: Norton, 1992). (GYL)

Harwood, John (ed.), 'Olivia Shakespear: Letters to W.B. Yeats,' in *Yeats Annual No. 6*, ed. Warwick Gould (1988), pp.59–107.

BIOGRAPHY

Brown, Terence, *The Life of W.B. Yeats: A Critical Biography*, 2nd edn (Oxford: Blackwell, 2001).

Ellmann, Richard, *Yeats: The Man and the Masks*, 2nd edn (London: Faber, 1961).

Foster, R.F., *W.B. Yeats: A Life*, I: *The Apprentice Mage 1865–1914* (Oxford: Oxford University Press, 1997).

Foster, R.F., *W.B. Yeats: A Life*, II: *The Arch-Poet* (Oxford: Oxford University Press, 2003)

Hone, Joseph, *W.B. Yeats 1865–1939* (New York: St Martin's Press, 1962).

McCormack, W.J., *Blood Kindred. W.B. Yeats: the Life, the Death, the Politics* (London: Pimlico, 2005).

SELECTED WORKS ON W.B. YEATS

Adams, Hazard, *The Book of Yeats's Poems* (Gainesville, FL: University of Florida Press, 1989).

Allison, Jonathan, 'Yeats and Politics', in *The Cambridge Companion to W.B. Yeats*, ed. Marjorie Howes and John Kelly (Cambridge: Cambridge University Press, 2006), pp.185–205.

Bell, Vereen M., *Yeats and the Logic of Formalism* (Columbia, MO: University of Missouri Press, 2006).

Bloom, Harold, *Yeats* (London: Oxford University Press, 1972).

Bornstein, George, *Yeats and Shelley* (Ithaca, NY: Cornell University Press, 1970).

Bornstein, George, 'Yeats's Romantic Dante', *Colby Library Quarterly*, 15 (1979), pp.93–133.

Bornstein, George, *Transformations of Romanticism in Yeats, Eliot, and Stevens* (Chicago, IL: University of Chicago Press, 1984).

Bornstein, George, 'Yeats and Romanticism', in *The Cambridge Companion to W.B. Yeats*, ed. Marjorie Howes and John Kelly (Cambridge: Cambridge University Press, 2006), pp.19–35.

Brearton, Fran, *The Great War in Irish Poetry* (Oxford: Oxford University Press, 2000).

Cairns, David and Shaun Richards, *Writing Ireland: Colonialism, Nationalism and Culture* (Manchester: Manchester University Press, 1988).

Chaudhry, Yug Mohit, *Yeats, the Irish Literary Revival and the Politics of Print* (Cork: Cork University Press, 2001).

Craig, Edward Gordon, 'The Actor and the Über-marionette', in On the Art of the Theatre (London: Heinemann, 1911), pp.54–94.

Craig, Edward Gordon, Rearrangements (1915), in Twentieth Century Theatre: A Sourcebook, ed. Richard Drain (London: Routledge, 1995), pp.17–22.

Cullingford, Elizabeth, Yeats, Ireland and Fascism (London: Macmillan, 1981).

Cullingford, Elizabeth, Gender and History in Yeats's Love Poetry (Cambridge: Cambridge University Press, 1993).

Dougherty, Adelyn, A Study of Rhythmic Structure in the Verse of William Butler Yeats (The Hague: Mouton, 1973).

Dwan, David, The Great Community: Culture and Nationalism in Ireland (Dublin: Field Day, 2008).

Eagleton, Terry, 'Politics and Sexuality in W.B. Yeats', Crane Bag, 9, 2 (1985), 138–42.

Eagleton, Terry, Heathcliff and the Great Hunger: Studies in Irish Culture (London: Verso, 1995).

Eagleton, Terry, 'Yeats and Poetic Form', in Crazy John and the Bishop and Other Essays on Irish Culture (Cork: Cork University Press, 1998), pp.273–95.

Eglinton, John, Irish Literary Portraits (London: Macmillan, 1935).

Eliot, T.S., 'The Poetry of W.B. Yeats', in The Permanence of Yeats, ed. James Hall and Martin Steinmann (New York: Collier Books, 1961), pp.331–43.

Ellmann, Richard, Eminent Domain: Yeats among Wilde, Joyce, Pound, Eliot, and Auden (New York: Oxford University Press, 1967).

Flannery, James, 'Yeats, Gordon Craig and the Visual Arts of the Theatre', in Yeats and the Theatre, ed. Robert O'Driscoll and Lorna Reynolds (London: Macmillan, 1975), pp.82–108.

Foster, R.F., 'Protestant Magic: W.B. Yeats and the Spell of Irish History', Proceedings of the British Academy, 75 (1989), pp.243–66. Revised version in Paddy and Mr Punch: Connections in Irish and English History (London: Allen Lane, 1993), pp.212–32.

Frazier, Adrian, Behind the Scenes: Yeats, Horniman, and the Struggle for the Abbey Theatre (Berkeley, CA: University of California Press, 1990).

Garrigan, Sinéad, Primitivism, Science, and the Irish Revival (Oxford: Oxford University Press, 2004).

Gould, Warwick, 'Books by Yeats in Olivia Shakespear's Library' in Yeats Annual No. 9, ed. Deirdre Toomey (1992), p.301.

Grene, Nicholas, Yeats's Poetic Codes (Oxford: Oxford University Press, 2008).

Gregory, Lady Augusta, *Cuchulain of Muirthemne* (London: J. Murray, 1903).

Hall, James and Martin Steinmann (eds), *The Permanence of Yeats* (New York: Collier Books, 1961).

Harper, George Mills, *The Making of Yeats's 'A Vision': A Study of the Automatic Script*, 2 vols (Basingstoke: Macmillan, 1987).

Harper, George Mills, *Yeats's Golden Dawn: The Influence of the Hermetic Order of the Golden Dawn on the Life and Art of W.B. Yeats* (Basingstoke: Macmillan, 1974).

Harper, Margaret Mills, *Wisdom of Two: The Spiritual and Literary Collaboration of George and W.B. Yeats* (Oxford: Oxford University Press, 2006).

Harwood, John, *Olivia Shakespear and W.B Yeats: After Long Silence* (Basingstoke: Macmillan, 1989).

Hogan, Robert (ed.), *Towards a National Theatre: the Dramatic Criticism of Frank J. Fay* (Dublin: The Dolmen Press, 1970).

Howes, Marjorie, *Yeats's Nations: Gender, Class and Irishness* (Cambridge: Cambridge University Press, 1996).

Howes, Marjorie, 'Introduction', in *The Cambridge Companion to W.B. Yeats*, ed. Marjorie Howes and John Kelly (Cambridge: Cambridge University Press, 2006), pp.1–18.

Innes, C.L., *Woman and Nation in Irish Society 1880–1935* (Hemel Hempstead: Harvester Wheatsheaf, 1993).

Jeffares, A. Norman (ed.), *W.B. Yeats: The Critical Heritage* (London and Boston, MA: Routledge & Kegan Paul, 1977).

Kiberd, Declan, *Inventing Ireland: The Literature of the Modern Nation* (London: Jonathan Cape, 1995).

Kline, Gloria, *The Last Courtly Lover: Yeats and the Idea of Woman* (Ann Arbor, MI: UMI Research Press, 1983).

Larrissy, Edward, *Yeats the Poet: The Measures of Difference* (Hemel Hempstead: Harvester, 1994).

Larrissy, Edward, *Blake and Modern Literature* (Basingstoke: Palgrave Macmillan, 2006).

Lennon, Joseph, *Irish Orientalism: A Literary and Intellectual History* (Syracuse, NY: Syracuse University Press, 2004).

Lloyd, David, *Anomalous States: Irish Writing and the Post-Colonial Moment* (Durham, NC: Duke University Press, 1993).

Mahaffey, Vicki, *States of Desire: Wilde, Yeats, Joyce and the Irish Experiment* (New York: Oxford University Press, 1999).

Matthews, Steven, *Yeats as Precursor: Readings in Irish, British and American Poetry* (Basingstoke: Palgrave Macmillan, 2000).

McAteer, Michael, *Standish O'Grady, AE and Yeats: History, Politics, Culture*

(Dublin: Irish Academic Press, 2002).

McDonald, Peter, *Serious Poetry: Form and Authority from Yeats to Hill* (Oxford: Oxford University Press, 2002).

MacNeice, Louis, *The Poetry of W.B. Yeats* (London: Oxford University Press, 1941).

Mikhail, E.H. (ed.), *W.B. Yeats: Interviews and Recollections*, 2 vols (London: Macmillan, 1977).

Miller, Liam, *The Noble Drama of W.B. Yeats* (Dublin: the Dolmen Press, 1977).

O'Brien, Conor Cruise, 'Passion and Cunning: An Essay on the Politics of W.B. Yeats', in *In Excited Reverie: A Centenary Tribute to William Butler Yeats*, ed. A. Norman Jeffares and K.G.W. Cross (London: Macmillan, 1965), pp.207–78.

O'Neill, Michael, *The Poems of W.B. Yeats* (London: Routledge, 2004).

O'Neill, Michael, *The All-Sustaining Air: Romantic Legacies and Renewals in British, American, and Irish Poetry since 1900* (Oxford: Oxford University Press, 2007).

Parkinson, Thomas, *W.B. Yeats: The Later Poetry* (Berkeley and Los Angeles, CA: University of California Press, 1966).

Perloff, Marjorie, *Rhyme and Meaning in the Poetry of Yeats* (The Hague: Mouton, 1970).

Pethica, James (ed.), *Lady Gregory's Diaries 1892–1902* (Gerrards Cross: Colin Smythe, 1996).

Pierce, David, *Yeats's Worlds: Ireland, England and the Poetic Imagination* (New Haven, CT: Yale University Press, 1995).

Pilkington, Lionel, *Theatre and the State in 20th Century Ireland: Cultivating the People* (London: Routledge, 2001).

Regan, Stephen, 'Poetry and Nation: W.B. Yeats', in *Literature and Nation: Britain and India 1800–1990*, ed. Richard Allen and Harish Trivedi (London: Routledge, 2001), pp.78–94.

Regan, Stephen, 'Yeats and the *fin de siècle*', in *Yeats in Context*, ed. David Holderman and Ben Levitas (Cambridge: Cambridge University Press, 2010), forthcoming.

Ronsley, Joseph, 'Yeats's Lecture Notes for "Friends of My Youth"', in *Yeats and the Theatre*, ed. Robert O'Driscoll and Lorna Reynolds (Basingstoke: Macmillan, 1975), pp.60–81.

Saddlemyer, Ann, 'Poetry and Possession: Yeats and Crazy Jane', in *Yeats: An Annual of Critical and Textual Studies*, No. 9, ed. Richard J. Finneran and Mary Fitzgerald (1991), pp.136–58.

Saddlemyer, Ann, *Becoming George: The Life of Mrs W.B. Yeats* (Oxford: Oxford

University Press, 2002).

Said, Edward, 'Yeats and Decolonization', in *Culture and Imperialism* (New York: Alfred A. Knopf, 1993), pp.220–38.

Smith, Stan, *The Origins of Modernism: Eliot, Pound, Yeats and the Rhetorics of Renewal* (Hemel Hempstead: Harvester Wheatsheaf, 1994).

Stanfield, Paul Scott, *Yeats and Politics in the 1930s* (Basingstoke: Macmillan, 1988).

Surette, Leon, *The Birth of Modernism: Ezra Pound, T.S. Eliot, W.B. Yeats and the Occult* (Montreal: McGill-Queen's University Press, 1993).

Toomey, Deirdre, '"Worst Part of Life": Yeats's Horoscopes for Olivia Shakespear', *Yeats Annual* No. 6, ed. Warwick Gould (1988), pp.223–4.

Vendler, Helen, *Our Secret Discipline: Yeats and Lyric Form* (Oxford: Oxford University Press, 2007).

Vlasopolos, Anca, 'Gender-Political Aesthetics and the Early and Later Yeats', in *Yeats: An Annual of Critical and Textual Studies, 8: Yeats from a Comparatist Perspective*, ed. Richard J. Finneran and Edward Engelberg (1990), pp.113–25.

Yeats, J.B., *Letters to his Son W.B. Yeats and Others 1869–1922*, ed. with a memoir by Joseph Hone (London: Faber & Faber, 1944).

Index

A

Abbey Theatre, 14, 26, 54, 56, 93, 96, 99, 121, 127
  Edward Gordon Craig and, 98, 102
  nationalism and, 96, 97, 98–9
  The Playboy of the Western World riots, 26–7, 57, 62, 64, 97
  rejection of *The Silver Tassie*, 105–6
Adams, Hazard, *The Book of Yeats's Poems*, 2
Æ (George Russell), 10, 100
Africa, 1, 80
  aisling poems, 7
Albright, Daniel, 80, 87
alchemy, 17
alienation, 113, 118
Allison, Jonathan, 82
Anglo-Irish Ascendancy, 3, 22–3, 28, 54–5, 96, 163
  gothic tradition, 8, 25
  nationalism and, 4–5, 8, 23, 24–7, 78, 162, 163
anti-theatre, 104
Archer, William, 102
aristocracy, 5, 11, 54–5, 56, 70–1, 73, 83, 88, 122
Armstrong, Laura, 140
Arnold, Matthew, 5, 21, 40, 79
Ascendancy, Anglo-Irish *see* Anglo-Irish Ascendancy
astrology, 64, 148
Auden, W.H., 19, 42–3, 44, 161, 166
automatic writing, 7, 18, 67, 71, 105, 110, 127
avant-garde, European, 21, 100, 107

B

Barrell, John, 9
Bartók, Béla, 22
Beardsley, Aubrey, 131
Beardsley, Mabel, 153
Beckett, Samuel, 107
Bedouin tribes, 9
Bell, Vereen M., *Yeats and the Logic of Formalism*, 2

Berkeley, George, 18
Black and Tan atrocities, 71
Blake, William, 11, 31, 38, 87, 95, 99, 110, 112, 137–8
Blakean contraries, 2, 33, 35, 36, 46
  Yeats as editor/student of, 17, 33, 45, 46, 131, 137–8, 144, 164
Blavatsky, Madame, 16
Bloom, Harold, 31, 44, 45, 89
Blueshirt movement, 28, 81–2
Boland, Eavan, 171–2
Boru, Brian, 60
Boucicault, Dion, 95
Boyle, William, 97
Brancusi, Constantin, 19
Braque, Georges, 105
Brearton, Fran, *The Great War and Irish Poetry*, 10–11
Bridges, Robert, 145
British imperialism, 3, 5–6, 10, 50, 51, 169
Brown, Terence, 3
Browning, Robert, 15, 94
Buddhism, 9, 89
Burke, Edmund, 116
Butt, Isaac, 23
Byron, Lord, 172

C

Cairns, David, *Writing Ireland: Colonialism, Nationalism and Culture*, 5, 25
Campbell, Mrs. Patrick, 93, 96–7
Carroll, Lewis, 64
Catholicism, 4, 6, 8, 9, 23, 26, 28, 115, 122
Celticism, 3, 8, 9, 20–2, 26, 38, 100
Celtic Twilight, 17, 21, 38, 48
Celts as 'feminine race', 5–6, 7, 21
censorship, 10, 28
Chatterjee, Mohini, Brahmin, 10, 80
Chaudhry, Yug Mohit, 2–3
Cheshire Cheese tavern (London), 59, 64
chess, 100–1
China, 85
Civil War, Irish, 28, 76, 82

Clarke, Austin, 162–3, 169
Clontarf, Battle of, 60
Cocteau, Jean, *Orpheus*, 107
Coleridge, Samuel Taylor, 39, 45
Colum, Padraic, 93
Commedia dell'Arte, 106
commercialism, 81, 90
Comtean positivism, 15
Coole Park, 54–5, 84, 86, 129, 145–6, 148,
    154, 161, 169
  neglect/decline of, 79, 162
  symbols and imagery, 167, 168
Craig, Edith, 101–2
Craig, Edward Gordon, 93, 98, 101–2, 103,
    105, 107
Cuala Press, 81
Cubism, 105
Cuchulain (Hound of Ulster), 20, 35–6, 50,
    51–3, 59–60, 63, 90, 99, 103
  as laughing hero, 49, 53, 55, 56
Cullingford, Elizabeth, 6, 10
cultural nationalism, 22, 23, 34, 46,
    117–18, 165
  Ascendancy caste and, 23, 24–7, 78, 162,
    163
Lane collection and, 27, 57, 62, 121
mythology and, 8, 22, 44
Yeats's alienation from, 26–7, 122–3, 169

D

Dante Alighieri, 31, 39, 68, 110
Darwin, Charles, 16
De Quincey, Thomas, 9
decadence, 40, 89, 151
democracy, 10, 11, 28, 52–3, 81, 89, 123
Descartes, René, 112
Dickinson, Mabel, 127
division of labour, 118–19, 120
divorce laws, 10
Dolmetsch, Arnold, 96
The Dome (periodical), 102–3
Dougherty, Adelyn, 1
Dowson, Ernest, 38, 59, 131, 138
Druid theatre (Galway), 107
Druidism, 8, 9
Drumcliff churchyard, 4
Dublin and the Lane collection, 27, 57, 62,
    121
Dublin lock-out, 27, 57
Dublin Theosophical Society, 10
Dwan, David, 10

E

Eagleton, Terry, 1, 5, 100

Easter Rising (1916), 23, 27–8, 67, 72–3,
    76, 78, 82, 90
execution of MacBride, 151, 153
Edward VII, King, death of, 97
Eliot, T.S., 1, 20, 29, 66, 75, 87, 165, 166,
    167
  ancient sources/primitive rituals and, 9,
    90, 105
  on Yeats, 15, 29
  The Waste Land, 16, 170
elitism, 28–9, 52, 122–3
Ellis, Edwin J., 33, 131, 137
Ellis, Havelock, 137
Ellmann, Richard, 99, 131, 146, 147, 148
  Eminent Domain, 43, 44
  Yeats: The Man and the Masks, 128, 134
empiricism, 39, 112
Enlightenment thought, 22
eroticism, 6, 81, 82, 87
esotericism, 8, 23, 25, 26, 66–7, 104, 105,
    106, 107
eugenics, 28, 81, 87–8, 89
Expressionist theatre, 106, 107

F

Fallon, Padraic, 167–8, 169
famine, 95
Farr, Florence, 93, 96, 127–8, 136, 149
fascism, 10, 28, 29, 81–2, 89, 121
Fay, Frank, 95, 96, 149
Fay, Willie, 96
Fenellosa, Ernesto, 'Noh' or *Accomplishment*,
    102
Fenianism, 23–4, 26
Ferguson, Samuel, 100
Floyd, Hurricane, 173
Foster, R.F., 4, 8, 41, 89, 129, 130, 136–7,
    141, 148
Fountain Court (London), 137, 138,
    139–40
Fox, Valentine, 139, 141, 147
Frazer, Adrian, 97
Frazer, J.G., *The Golden Bough*, 82, 105
Freemasonry, 8

G

gender and sexuality, 5–7, 29, 39, 72–3, 82,
    112, 115, 127, 142, 147, 171–2
  Celts as 'feminine race', 5–6, 7, 21
  eroticism, 6, 81, 82, 87
  female sexuality, 6, 7, 81, 172
  feminine 'wisdom', 7, 71–2
  occultism and, 8, 9, 68
  see also women and Yeats

Gonne, Iseult, 141, 153
Gonne, Maud
    correspondence with Yeats, 140, 144–5, 146,
        156
    first meeting with Yeats, 24, 94, 135
    in France, 141, 144, 145, 146, 153
    marriage to MacBride, 151, 153
    physical appearance, 135, 141
    politics and, 7, 24, 78
    as Yeats's inspiration/muse, 24, 127, 128
    Yeats's obsession with, 24, 63, 106, 127,
        128, 134–5, 139, 140–1, 145, 147, 148
    Yeats's poetry and, 43–4, 53, 60, 63, 64,
        78, 86, 128, 146
    Yeats's proposals of marriage, 153
    A Servant of the Queen (autobiography), 128
Gore-Booth, Eva, 77–8, 133Gosse, Edmund,
    132
Gothic, Anglo-Irish, 8, 25
Gould, Warwick, 148–9
Great War, 10–11, 67, 69, 70–1, 105, 107
Gregory, Lady Augusta, 14, 27, 84, 97, 127,
    128, 133, 143, 145–6
    Abbey Theatre and, 14, 93, 99, 127
    Ascendancy and, 24, 54–5
    Coole Park and, 54–5, 79, 145–6
    The Countess Cathleen and, 128
    first meeting with Yeats, 145–6
    prose version of Deirdre story, 100, 101
    Yeats's poetry and, 54–5, 61, 69, 70,
        78–9, 86
    Cathleen ni Houlihan (co-authored with
        Yeats), 94, 95, 96, 97
    Cuchulain of Muirthemne, 49, 51
    Gods and Fighting Men, 59
    Spreading the News, 93
    The Unicorn from the Stars, 95
Gregory, Major Robert, 70–1, 77, 86
Grene, Nicholas, Yeats's Poetic Codes, 2

H

Harper, Margaret Mills, 8
Harwood, John, 129, 142
Hawk dance, 105
Heald, Edith, 127
Heaney, Seamus, 159–61
Hemingway, Ernest, 137
Henderson, W.J., 93
Henley, W.E., 3
Hermeticism, 16, 33–4, 40
heroic ideal, 36, 49–53, 56, 59–60, 73, 99,
    120
Hewitt, John, 163–5
Hinduism, 18
Hiroshige, Utagawa, 103

historians, 'revisionist', 4
Hobbes, Thomas, 109
Hokusai, Katsushika, 103
the Holocaust, 173
Homer, 20, 79, 96
Horniman, Annie, 93, 96, 97
Howes, Marjorie, 5–6, 81
Hugo, Victor, 26
humanism, Romantic, 35
hunger strikes, 98
Huxley, Thomas, 15, 16
Hyde, Douglas, 117, 138
Hyde-Lees, Georgie see Yeats, George (née
    Hyde-Lees, wife)
Hyde-Lees, Nelly, 152
Hynes, Gary, 107

I

Ibsen, Henrik, The Vikings of Helgeland, 102
imagery and symbols see symbols and
    imagery
India, 1, 9–10, 80
individualism, 118, 122
industrial revolution, 4, 43
Innes, C.L., 6
International Yeats Summer School (Sligo),
    107
Ireland
    British imperialism in, 3, 5–6, 50, 51, 169
    Celts as 'feminine race', 5–6, 7, 21
    Civil War, 28, 76, 82
    English/Anglo-Norman settlement, 3, 4
    Free State, 6, 28
    'messianic vocation', 120–1
    partition, 4, 28
    'primitive virtue' of, 119–20
    Romanticism and, 121
    War of Independence, 28, 71, 76
Irish Ireland movement, 26
Irish Literary Revival, 75, 76
Irish Literary Theatre, 25, 26, 93–4, 95, 96,
    99–100, 121
Irish mythology, 8, 20–2, 64, 131, 165
    Yeats's drama and, 49–53, 58, 99, 100–1,
        103, 104, 107
    Yeats's poetry and, 35–6, 38–9, 40, 41,
        42, 44, 59–60, 127
Irish National Theatre Society, 93, 98
Irish Parliamentary Party (IPP), 24, 94
Irish Republican Brotherhood (IRB), 23
Irish Studies, 24–5
Islam, 9
Ito, Michio, 105

J

Japanese art, 102–5, 107
Jarry, Alfred, 100, 105, 106
Jeffares, A. Norman, 33–4
Johnson, Lionel, 130, 131, 132, 134, 135, 145, 155
journals, 2, 3, 102–3, 131, 132, 149
   the Savoy, 131, 137, 139, 141, 142, 144–5
Joyce, James, 20, 21, 57, 82, 137, 154
Jung, Carl, 18, 35

K

Kaballism, 16–17
Kavanagh, Patrick, 163
Keats, John, 19, 38, 85, 155
Keene, Donald, 103
the Kensington (magazine), 149
Khoung-Fou-Tseu (Confucius), 59
Kiberd, Declan, Inventing Ireland, 7
Kinsella, Thomas, 167, 169–70
Kline, Gloria, 6

L

Lane, Sir Hugh, 27, 57, 62, 121
Lang, Andrew, 105
language, 2, 5, 6, 22, 26, 44–5, 101
Larrissy, Edward, 8, 9, 44, 85
Lavery, John, 86
LeGallienne, Richard, 131
Lennon, Joseph, 9, 10
Leo Africanus, 17, 19
Lewis, Wyndham, 19, 29
Lissadell country house, 72, 78
Lloyd, David, Anomalous States: Irish Writing and the Post-Colonial Moment, 5
Local Government (Ireland) Act (1898), 24
Locke, John, 112
London, 16, 129, 135, 137–8, 139–40, 141, 142–4, 146
Longley, Michael, 174

M

MacBride, Major John, 151, 153
MacCready, Sam, 107
MacKenna, Stephen, 110
MacNeice, Louis, 81, 165–7
MacSwiney, Terence, 98–9
Maddox, Brenda, George's Ghosts, 128
Maeterlinck, Maurice, 94, 102, 105
   the Magi, 9, 57, 64–5
magic and supernatural beliefs see occultism and magic
Mahaffey, Vicki, States of Desire, 8
Mahon, Derek, 174

Mallarmé, Stéphane, 39, 111
Mangan, James Clarence, 'Dark Rosaleen', 34
Markievicz, Constance, 7, 72–3, 77–8
Martin, Henri, 21
Martin, Violet, 133
Masefield, John, 142
The Mask (journal), 102
materialism, 17, 20, 21, 27, 28, 39, 56–7, 112, 121
Matthew (Apostle), 64–5
Matthews, Steven, Yeats as Precursor, 11
McCormack, W.J., 4, 10
McDonald, Peter, Serious Poetry: Form and Authority from Yeats to Hill, 1–2
McGuckian, Medbh, 174
mechanization, 105
mediumship, 7, 8, 17
metaphysical thought, 80, 110–14, 116–17, 118, 120, 123
Millevoye, Lucien, 140, 147
Milton, John, 31, 42
Modernism, 67, 73, 75, 80, 84, 88, 128, 163, 167, 168
   ancient sources/primitive rituals and, 9, 90, 105
   theories of language and, 101
modernity, 3, 7, 20, 27, 36
   distaste/hatred for, 15, 28–9, 81, 90, 91, 120, 121
Montague, John, 161, 167, 170–1
Moore, George, 95, 133, 138
Moore, Sturge, 154
Morris, William, 99, 118–19
Muldoon, Paul, 172–4
Müller, Max, 105
Murphy, William Martin, 62
music, 48–9, 96
Mussolini, Benito, 123
mysticism, 17, 33–4, 94–5, 100, 107
mythology, 20, 22
   Greek, 20, 37, 49, 54, 83
   Irish see Irish mythology

N

National Observer, 3
nationalism
   Abbey Theatre and, 96, 97, 98–9
   Anglo-Irish Ascendancy and, 4–5, 8, 23, 24–7, 78, 162, 163
   Catholicism and, 26, 122
   cultural see cultural nationalism
   democracy and, 10, 28
   fixed ideals and, 116
   Irish Ireland movement, 26
   language and, 22, 26

occultism and mysticism, 8, 33–4, 41
separatist, 23–4, 25, 26
Yeats as 'poet of national liberation', 8, 10
Yeats's drama and, 94, 95, 96, 97, 98–9
Yeats's early poetry and, 8–9, 76, 77, 88
Yeats's later poetry and, 5, 76–7, 78,
   82–3, 88, 90
Naturalist theatre, 100
Neoplatonism, 2, 111, 112, 113, 118, 131
Newton, Isaac, 112
Nietzsche, Friedrich, 17, 99, 114–15, 116,
   122
nihilism, 77
Nobel Prize for Literature, 160
Northern Ireland and Ulster, 2, 4, 23, 28,
   164, 171
Nutt, Alfred, 105

O

O'Casey, Seán, *The Silver Tassie*, 105–6
occultism and magic, 8–9, 16–18, 24, 29,
   35, 67–9, 71, 136
  Anglo-Irish Ascendancy and, 8, 25
  Easter Rising and, 28
  esotericism, 8, 23, 25, 26, 66–7, 104,
   105, 106, 107
  Hermeticism, 16, 33–4, 40
  mysticism, 17, 33–4, 94–5, 100, 107
  nationalism and, 8, 33–4, 41
  Order of the Golden Dawn and, 16–17,
   18, 67
  Rosicrucianism, 8, 16–17, 33–4
  sexuality and, 8, 9, 68
  spiritualism, 17–18, 67, 68
  Theosophy, 10, 16, 18, 67, 110
  Yeats's drama and, 94–5, 100, 103, 104,
   106
O'Connell, Daniel, 82
O'Connor, Ulick, 107
O'Curry, Eugene, 9
O'Donnell, Frank Hugh, 94
O'Grady, James Standish, 20, 86, 100
O'Leary, John, 23–4, 26, 86, 135, 145
O'Neill, Michael, 86, 88–9
Order of the Golden Dawn, 16–17, 18, 67
orientalism, 4, 9–10, 16, 18, 80, 84
Osgood and McIlvaine (publishers), 132
Oxford *New History of Ireland*, 4

P

Parnell, Charles Stewart, 62, 82–3, 122
partition, 4, 28
Pater, Walter, 89, 110, 131, 165
Patrick, St., 110

Pearse, Patrick, 90
Perloff, Marjorie, 1
Pethica, James, 128
philosophy and thought, 15–16, 18–19
  alienation, 113, 118
  the body and, 110, 112, 115
  empiricism, 39, 112
  individualism and, 118, 122
  integration and division, 110, 113, 118–20
  metaphysical, 80, 110–14, 116–17, 118,
   120, 123
  Platonism, 32–3, 34, 89, 110–15, 116, 117,
   118, 123
  rationalism, 15, 21
  temporality, 112–13, 115–16
  'Unity of Being', 109–10, 113–14,
   116–20, 121, 123
Picasso, Pablo, 105
Pilkington, Lionel, 97
Pirandello, Luigi, 100, 104, 106
Platonism, 32–3, 34, 89, 110–15, 116,
   117, 123
  the 'Good', 111, 112–13, 114, 118, 123
  ideal forms, 111–12, 114
  Nietzsche and, 114–15, 116
Plotinus, 110–11, 112, 113, 114
politics, 10–11
  eroticism and, 6
  fascist, 10, 28, 81–2, 89, 121
  Maud Gonne and, 7, 24, 78
  liberal, 10, 121, 123
  reactionary/authoritarian, 28–9, 89, 90,
   91, 118, 121, 123
  socialism, 164
  theatre/poetry and, 97–9, 171–2
  Unionist, 23
  'Unity of Being' and, 117–20, 121, 123
  women and, 7, 72–3, 78
  see also nationalism
Pollexfen, Susan (mother), 23, 137, 149
Porphyry, 111
post-colonial criticism, 4–5, 24–5, 26
Pound, Dorothy Shakespear, 128, 131, 134,
   151, 152–3
Pound, Ezra, 9, 29, 75, 84, 90, 136, 165,
   167, 168
  'Hugh Selwyn Mauberley', 71
  marriage to Dorothy Shakespear, 128,
   131, 134, 151, 152–3
  'Noh' or *Accomplishment* and, 102
  Olivia Shakespear and, 128, 150, 151–2
  treason charges, 134
  Yeats and, 48, 59, 128, 152–3
Pound, Omar, 153
Pre-Raphaelites, 131, 147
press, power of, 99

Protestantism, 3, 4, 6, 8, 22–3, 26, 28, 96,
  122, 162, 164
Purohit, Swami, 10
Purser, Louis, 141

Q

Quinn, John, 99

R

Raftery, Anthony, 79
Rapallo, 154
rationalism, 15, 21
Regan, Stephen, 10
reincarnation, doctrine of, 80
religion, 15–16, 17, 18–19, 25–6, 43, 44,
  58, 83
  Catholicism, 6, 8, 9, 26, 28, 115, 122
  mythology and, 22
  Platonism and, 110, 115
  Protestantism, 3, 4, 6, 8, 22–3, 26, 28,
    96, 122, 162, 164
  science and, 19, 29
  theatre and, 103, 104
Renan, Ernest, 5, 21
"reprobate traditions", 11
republicanism, 23–4, 25, 26
'revisionist' historians, 4
Rhymers Club, 59, 60–1, 64, 131, 133, 134
Richards, Shaun, Writing Ireland: Colonialism,
  Nationalism and Culture, 5, 25
Romanticism, 19, 80, 104, 121, 155, 164
  Yeats's early poetry and, 6, 31–6, 38–9,
    40–1, 43, 45–6, 75–6
Ronsard, Pierre de, 32, 56
Ronsley, Joseph, 14
Rosicrucianism, 8, 16–17, 33–4
Rousseau, Jean-Jacques, 109
Ruddock, Margot, 127
Russell, George (Æ), 10, 100

S

Saddlemyer, Ann, 6, 7–8
Said, Edward, 4, 9
Saussure, Ferdinand de, 101
the Savoy, 131, 137, 139, 141, 142, 144–5
science, 15, 17, 19, 20, 22, 29
the Scots Observer, 3
Shakespear, Henry Hope, 129, 130–1, 134,
  141, 152, 153
Shakespear, Olivia, 128–33, 134–7,
  138–40, 148–52, 153–6
  correspondence with Yeats, 129, 135–6,
    149, 150, 153, 154, 156

fiction writing, 129, 131–2, 135, 136–7,
  138, 145, 147–8, 149–50
influence on Yeats's writing, 129, 141–2,
  146, 147, 148, 151, 154, 155
post-1897 relationship with Yeats, 147–56
sexual relationship with Yeats, 128, 137,
  139–40, 141–4, 146–7, 148, 155
Yeats's obsession with Gonne and, 128,
  134–5, 145, 148
Shakespeare, William, 43, 84, 85, 87, 101
Shaw, George Bernard, 97
Shelley, Percy Bysshe, 31–3, 38, 39, 40, 84,
  98, 110
  Adonais, 31
  'Hymn to Intellectual Beauty', 34, 35
  'Ode to the West Wind', 34, 40, 45, 46
  Prometheus Unbound, 32
  The Triumph of Life, 32
Sheppard, Oliver, 90
Shields, George, 93
Sibelius, Jean, 22
'sky-woman' (speirbhean), 7
Sligo, 3–4, 23, 87, 107, 148, 151, 165
Smith, Stan, 9, 90
social class, 71, 88
  aristocracy, 5, 11, 54–5, 56, 70–1, 73,
    83, 88, 122
  inequalities and, 54–5
  merchant and clerical classes, 56, 57, 90
  middle class, 3, 49, 53, 56, 57, 90, 122
  peasantry, 26, 55, 71, 88, 94, 95, 121
socialism, 164
Somerville, Edith, 133
Soviet Union, 106
speirbhean ('sky-woman'), 7
Spencer, Herbert, 119, 120
Spender, Stephen, 166
Spengler, Oswald, The Decline of the West, 18,
  89, 104, 106
Spenser, Edmund, 35
spiritualism, 17–18, 67, 68
Stevens, Ashton, 151
Stone Cottage (Sussex), 152, 153
Surette, Leon, 9
Surrealist theatre, 100, 107
Swedenborg, Emmanuel, 95
Swift, Jonathan, 81, 82, 134
Symbolism, 16, 21–2, 24, 38, 42, 91,
  94–5, 110
  theatre and, 100, 102, 107
symbols and imagery, 5, 7, 8, 78, 80–1,
  161, 164, 169, 170–1
  angels, 56, 58
  'Big Houses'/Coole Park, 54–5, 78, 159,
    167, 168
  eagles, 54, 56, 61, 63

flying/the sky, 54, 56, 57, 61, 63, 79–80,
    168, 171
moon emblem, 7, 36, 63, 69, 73, 91
motif of heads, 49, 50, 51, 52, 55
occult, 16
peacocks, 57, 61, 168
Pegasus, 54, 80
Platonism and, 111
Romanticism and, 31, 32, 33–4, 35,
    40–1, 42, 45, 46
rose, 33–4, 35, 45–6, 76, 111, 159
Rosicrucianism/occultism, 8–9, 33–4, 35
swans, 79–80, 159, 160, 168, 170
towers, 159, 165, 167–8, 172, 173
Yeats's influence and, 159, 161, 163,
    165, 167–8, 169–71
Symons, Arthur, 39, 99, 131, 137, 143, 145
    lives at Fountain Court, 137, 139, 140, 142
Synge, John Millington, 24, 93, 94, 97, 99,
    107, 122, 127
    death of, 14, 27
    The Playboy of the Western World, 26–7, 57,
        62, 64, 97
    Riders to the Sea, 93
    In the Shadow of the Glen, 26, 94, 122
    The Tinker's Wedding, 99

T

Tagore, Gitanjali, 10
temporality, 112–13, 115–16
Tennyson, Alfred, 15, 94
Terry, Ellen, 93, 101
Thackeray, W.M., Henry Esmond, 150
theatre, 93–107
    commercialization of, 96, 98
    continental European, 93, 94, 95, 100,
        104–5, 106, 107
    Japanese Noh, 102–5, 107
    see also Abbey Theatre; Yeats, W.B., DRAMA
Theosophy, 10, 16, 18, 67, 110
Thomas Aquinas, St., 115
Thoor Ballylee, 154, 161, 167–8
Toller, Ernst, 106
Toomey, Deirdre, 148
Tremenheere, Caroline, 130
Tynan, Katharine, 136, 155
Tyndall, John, 15

U

Ulster and Northern Ireland, 2, 4, 23, 28,
    164, 171
Unionist politics, 23
United Ireland, 3
United Irishmen Rebellion (1798), 24, 26

Upanishads, 10
Utamaro, Kitagawa, 103

V

Vendler, Helen, 2, 78, 83, 89
Victorianism, high, 15
Villiers de l'Isle Adam, Phillipe Auguste, Axël,
    94, 100
Vlasopolos, Anca, 6

W

Wagner, Richard, 95, 100
War of Independence, Irish, 28, 71, 76
Waugh, Arthur, 132, 133
Wellesley, Dorothy, 127
'Western Wind' (English lyric), 89
Wilde, Oscar, 58, 94, 105, 137
will, power of, 106
Wittgenstein, Ludwig, 101
Woburn Buildings, 142–4
women and Yeats, 29, 127, 140
    Florence Farr, 93, 96, 127, 136
    Iseult Gonne, 141, 153
    Katharine Tynan, 136, 155
women in politics, 7, 72–3, 78
women in Yeats's writing, 6–7, 53, 63, 78,
    81, 86, 127–8, 129, 141–2, 146–7, 151,
    155
    Yeat's reshaping/renaming of women,
        128, 134
    see also Gonne, Maud; Gregory, Lady
    Augusta; Shakespear, Olivia; Yeats, George
    (née Hyde-Lees, wife)
Woolf, Virginia, A Room of One's Own, 54
Wordsworth, William, 41, 76–7
Wyndham Land Act (1903), 96

Y

Yeats, George (née Hyde-Lees, wife), 7–8,
    18, 128, 134, 135, 147, 151, 153, 155
    automatic writing and, 7, 18, 67, 71, 127
    first meeting with Yeats, 152
Yeats, Jack (brother), 4, 80, 137
Yeats, John Butler (father), 15, 16, 23, 86,
    119, 137, 143, 145, 148
Yeats, Lily (sister), 154
Yeats, Lolly (sister), 135
Yeats, Michael (son), 135
Yeats, Susan (mother, née Pollexfen), 23,
    137, 149
Yeats, W.B.
    1798 commemoration and, 24, 26
    Anglo-Irish Ascendancy and, 3, 4–5, 8,

22–3, 24–7, 28, 78, 162, 163
anti-democratic animus, 10, 11, 28, 81,
    89, 123
Celticism, 20–2, 26, 38, 100
childhood of, 15–16, 80, 87
co-editor/student of Blake, 17, 33, 45,
    46, 131, 137–8, 144, 164
Coole Park and, 54–5, 79, 84, 86, 129,
    145–6, 148, 154, 161, 167, 168
cyclical motion of history and, 18,
    19–20, 29, 69, 73, 83
death of, 155, 162
doctrine of conflict, 10, 66, 68, 69,
    121–2, 123
elitism, 28–9, 52, 122–3
epitaph, 4, 88
esoteric/mystical/occult beliefs *see*
occultism and magic
eugenics and, 28, 81, 87–8, 89
family background, 3–4, 15–16, 22–3
fascism and, 10, 28, 81–2, 89, 121
fondness for animals, 154–5
as Free State Senator, 10, 28
'Friends of My Youth' lecture, 14, 15
imperialism and, 3, 5–6, 10, 50, 51, 169
Leo Africanus and, 17, 19
'life experiment', 14–15, 29
life in London (from 1887), 16, 129, 135,
    137, 138, 139–40, 141, 142–4, 146
masks and, 68, 103, 163
Moore's *Evelyn Innes* and, 133
nationalism and, 4–5, 23–8, 76, 77,
    82–3, 122, 162, 163
    see also under nationalism
old age and, 69–70, 82, 86–7, 88–9, 112
John O'Leary and, 23–4, 26
orientalism, 9–10, 16, 18, 80, 84
philosophy and thought, 15–16, 18–19,
    32–3, 34, 80, 89, 109–23
    see also philosophy and thought
physical appearance, 132, 133
politics and, 10–11, 28–9, 73, 81–3,
    90–1, 98–9, 117–23
Ezra Pound and, 48, 59, 128, 152–3
prose and, 138
Protestant inheritance, 3, 4, 6, 8, 22–3,
    26, 122, 162
rejection of *The Silver Tassie*, 105–6
religion and, 15–16, 17, 18–19, 22,
    25–6, 43, 44, 58, 83, 104, 122
republicanism, 23–4, 25, 26
space and place, 137, 161, 169
views on violence/warfare, 10–11, 53,
    71, 73, 76, 81, 91, 169, 171, 172, 173
women and *see* Gonne, Maud; Gregory,
    Lady Augusta; Shakespear, Olivia;

women and Yeats; Yeats, George (née
    Hyde-Lees, wife)
Yeats, W.B., DRAMA, 93–107
co-authorship, 94, 95
continental European theatre, 93, 94, 95,
    100, 104–5, 106, 107
Edward Gordon Craig and, 98, 101–2,
    105, 107
early period, 75, 93–6
esoteric/mystic themes, 104, 105, 106,
    107
experimental, 96–7, 100, 101–2, 103–7
heroic ideal, 49–53, 56, 99
Irish mythology and, 49–53, 58, 99,
    100–1, 103, 104, 107
Japanese Noh theatre, 102–5, 107
joy/laughing theme, 49, 53, 55, 56, 57
late period, 105–7
leadership theme, 49, 50, 51–2, 53, 56,
    60
marionette acting style, 104–5
middle period, 49–53, 56, 58–9, 96–102
nationalism and, 94, 95, 96, 97, 98–9
occult/magic themes, 94–5, 100, 103,
    104, 106
poetic dialogue and drama, 94, 95, 96–7,
    100, 101, 107
psaltery experiment, 96–7, 100
spiritual themes, 97, 101, 102, 104, 105,
    106
    see also Abbey Theatre
Yeats, W.B., POETRY
ageing/old age theme, 69–70, 82, 86–7,
    88–9, 112
ancient sects/primitive rituals and, 9, 90,
    105
Auden on, 42–3
authority and power theme, 17
Big House theme, 54–5, 78, 159, 167,
    168
bitterness and anger theme, 61, 62, 63
Blakean contraries, 2, 33, 35, 36, 46
catastrophe and ruin theme, 67, 73, 83,
    84, 85
cold detachment and, 84, 85
Crazy Jane poems, 6, 81, 87, 115, 127,
    154, 162
death theme, 70–1, 80–1, 113
desire theme, 62–3
doctrine of conflict, 10, 66, 68, 69,
    121–2, 123
dream theme, 60, 61, 63, 64, 65
early, 5, 6, 8–9, 17, 31, 32–46, 48, 49,
    75–6, 111, 115–16, 118
elegiac, 77–9, 80, 85–6
Eliot on, 66

eroticism and, 6, 81, 82, 87
'ferocious humility' and, 87
gender and, 5–7
   see also gender and sexuality; women
   and Yeats
hatred/fanaticism theme, 76, 77, 90–1
the heart and, 33, 75–6, 77, 86, 88
heroic ideal, 36, 59–60, 73, 120
high Victorianism and, 15
humour and, 49, 53, 54
identity themes, 2, 87
imitators of, 48, 57, 63, 64
influence on modern poetry, 1, 2, 159–74
Irish mythology and, 35–6, 38–9, 40,
   41, 42, 44, 59–60, 127, 131
language, 2, 5, 6, 44–5
late period, 36–8, 75, 76–91, 114, 116,
   120
mediocrity/compromise themes, 49, 53,
   54, 55, 63, 90
middle period, 48–9, 53–7, 59–65
Modernism, 9, 67, 73, 75, 80, 84, 88,
   90, 128, 163, 167
opposite extremes in, 49, 53–5, 56–7
order and disintegration themes, 1–2,
   18, 123
outcast (fool/beggar/ghost) themes,
   56–7, 59, 60–1, 62, 63, 162
placing in journals, 2–3
'poet as hero', 36, 43–4
poet as legislator of the world, 40
poetic form, 1–2, 6, 32–3, 160, 165–7,
   173
poetic form (Shakespearean sonnet),
   84–5
poetic rhythm/metre, 32–3, 35–6, 37,
   44, 70, 80–1, 82
poetic rhythm/metre (hexameter lines),
   86
poetic rhythm/metre (*ottava rima*), 78, 79,
   83, 88, 89, 172
poetic rhythm/metre (trochaic tetrameter),
   77, 87
position of poems within
collection/book, 2, 66, 67, 69–70, 73
Ezra Pound on, 48, 59
primitive themes, 2, 9, 90, 105, 119–20
remorse theme, 76, 77
revisionary practice, 31, 36–8
Romanticism and, 6, 31–6, 38, 39, 40–1,
   43, 45–6, 75–6, 80, 121, 155, 164
Rosicrucian, 8
Shelley and, 31–3, 34–5, 38, 39, 40, 46
spiritual themes, 56, 57, 63
tragic joy theme, 75, 84, 85, 87, 164
Yeats as 'impeccable stylist', 77

see also symbols and imagery
Yeats, W.B., WORKS
Collections
   The Countess Kathleen and Various Legends and
   Lyrics, 34, 37, 93
   A Full Moon in March, 82
   The Green Helmet and Other Poems, 48, 49, 53,
      54, 56, 121
   Last Poems and Two Plays, 75, 87, 90
   Michael Robartes and the Dancer, 66, 67, 72–3,
      162
   New Poems, 82, 83–4, 87
   Parnell's Funeral and Other Poems, 84
   Responsibilities, 48, 53, 56–64, 121
   The Rose, 36, 45
   The Tower, 75, 76, 80, 106, 111, 123
   The Wild Swans at Coole, 66–72
   The Wind Among the Reeds, 31, 38, 39, 40,
      41, 91, 129, 146, 148, 151
   The Winding Stair and Other Poems, 43, 76,
      77–81, 82, 106
Essays and Non-Fiction
   'A General Introduction for My Work',
      84
   Autobiography, 146, 155
   'The Autumn of the Body' (essay), 39–40
   'The Celtic Element in Literature' (essay),
      21–2
   Dramatis Personae, 155
   'The Fool of Faery' (essay in the
   Kensington), 149
   'If I were Four and Twenty' (essays), 117
   Memoir, 146, 151
   On the Boiler (tract), 81
   Per Amica Silentia Lunae (essay), 67–8
   'The Philosophy of Shelley's Poetry'
      (essay), 31–2, 40
   'Poetry and Tradition' (essay), 27, 53
   'The Symbolism of Poetry' (essay), 34
   'The Theatre' (essay), 103
   A Vision, 7, 9, 18, 33, 67, 68, 69, 90,
      105, 109, 154
   A Vision (second version), 19–20, 67, 71
   'William Blake and His Illustrations to
   the *Divine Comedy*' (essay), 45
Novels and Stories
   'The Binding of the Hair' (story), 142
   John Sherman and Dhoya (novel), 138
   The Speckled Bird (novel), 148
   ' Where there is Nothing, there is God'
      (story), 113
Plays
   At the Hawk's Well , 102, 103–4
   Calvary, 104, 105
   Cathleen ni Houlihan (co-authored with
      Gregory), 94, 95, 96, 97

The Countess Cathleen, 26, 88, 94–5, 102, 128

The Death of Cuchulain, 87, 104

Deirdre, 94, 96–7, 100–1, 107

The Deliverer, 102

Diarmuid and Grania (co-authored with Moore), 95

The Dreaming of the Bones, 104–5

The Green Helmet: An Heroic Farce, 49–53, 56, 60, 63, 90, 99

The Herne's Egg, 106

The Hour-Glass , 58–9, 63, 102

The King of the Great Clock Tower, 105

The King's Threshold, 94, 98–9

The Land of Heart's Desire, 75, 93–4, 95, 134

Mosada, 9

On Baile's Strand, 88, 96, 99

The Only Jealousy of Emer, 104, 106

The Player Queen, 106

Purgatory, 87, 105, 106

The Shadowy Waters, 129, 148, 149, 150

Where There Is Nothing , 95, 99

The Words Upon the Window-pane , 105, 106

Poems

'A Coat', 49, 57, 63, 170

'A Dialogue of Self and Soul', 164

'A Memory of Youth', 63

'A Prayer for My Daughter', 73

'A Woman Young and Old', 5, 6, 81

'Adam's Curse', 63

'All Things Can Tempt Me', 54

'Among School Children', 172

'An Acre of Grass', 87

'An Image from a Past Life', 67

'An Irish Airman Foresees his Death', 67, 70, 71

'Aodh to Dectora' ('The Lover Mourns for the Loss of Love'), 103, 146, 147, 151

'At Algeciras - A Meditation upon Death', 80

'At Galway Races', 56

'At Parnell's Funeral', 82–3

'At the Abbey Theatre', 56

'Beautiful Lofty Things', 85–6

'Byzantium', 80–1, 155, 170

'Closing Rhyme', 57, 63

'Coole and Ballylee', 78, 79–80

'Coole Park, 1929', 5, 78–9

'Cuchulain's Fight with the Sea', 35–6

'Desert Geometry or the Gift of Harun Al-Raschid', 7, 9

'Dialogue of Self and Soul', 111, 168

'Easter 1916', 5, 7, 27–8, 67, 72–3, 76, 77, 80, 90, 116, 170

'Ego Dominus Tuus', 67–8, 72

'Fallen Majesty', 63

'Fergus and the Druid', 114

'Friends', 63

'He bids his Beloved be at Peace' ('The Shadowy Horses'), 141

'He gives his Beloved certain Rhymes', 142

'He mourns for the change that has come upon him and his Beloved...', 113

'He thinks of those who have Spoken Evil of his Beloved', 43–4

'He wishes his Beloved were dead', 113

'In Memory of Eva Gore-Booth and Con Markiewicz', 77–8

'In Memory of Major Robert Gregory', 5, 70, 77, 86

'Lapis Lazuli', 64, 84, 85, 86, 87, 164

'Leda and the Swan', 154, 170

'Man and the Echo', 89

'Meditations in Time of Civil War', 1–2, 76, 167, 172

'Meru', 84–5, 113

'Michael Robartes and the Dancer', 7, 72, 73

'Mohini Chatterjee', 80

'No Second Troy', 48, 53, 78, 128

'On Being Asked for a War Poem', 98

'O'Sullivan Rua to Mary Lavell', 144

'Pardon, old fathers', 59, 60

'Paudeen', 57

'Politics', 89, 98, 127

'Remorse For Intemperate Speech', 76, 77

'Reprisals', 71

'Running to Paradise', 61

'Sailing to Byzantium', 80, 105, 116, 155

'September 1913' ('Romance in Ireland'), 27, 57, 121

'Shepherd and Goatherd', 71

'Solomon and the Witch', 7, 67

'Solomon to Sheba', 71–2

'Song of Mongan', 103

'That the Night Come', 63

'The Cat and the Moon', 69

'The Circus Animals' Desertion', 77, 82, 87, 88–9, 160, 164, 172

'The Cold Heaven', 63

'The Desire of Man and of Woman', 103
'The Dolls', 63
'The Double Vision of Michael Robartes', 66, 69
'The Fascination of What's Difficult', 54
'The Grey Rock', 59–61
'The Gyres', 83–4, 85–6, 172
'The Hosting of the Sidhe', 38–9
'The Hour before Dawn', 62
'The Lake Isle of Innisfree', 32, 76
'The Lover tells of the Rose in His Heart', 33, 75
'The Magi', 57, 63
'The Municipal Gallery Revisited', 86
'The Phases of the Moon', 66, 69
'The Second Coming', 18, 67, 73, 83, 90
'The Secret Rose', 45–6
'The Song of Sad Shepherd', 46
'The Song of Wandering Aengus', 44–5
'The Sorrow of Love', 36–7
'The Spur', 82
'The Statues', 89–90, 91, 120, 172
'The Tables of the Law and The Adoration of the Magi', 148
'The Three Beggars', 62
'The Three Hermits', 61

'The Travail of Passion', 141
'The Valley of the Black Pig', 41–2
'The Wild Swans at Coole', 66, 69–70, 79, 159, 160, 171
'The Witch', 56
'Three Marching Songs', 82
'Three Movements', 43
'To a Friend whose Work has come to Nothing', 61
'To a Shade', 62
'To Ireland in the Coming Times', 8, 41, 76, 77, 88
'To the Rose upon the Rood of Time', 33–5, 111, 113, 114
'Under Ben Bulben', 81, 87–8
'Upon a House Shaken by the Land Agitation', 54–5, 79
'Vacillation', 75, 114
The Wanderings of Oisin, 3, 40, 44, 75, 88, 115–16
'When You are Old', 32
'Words For Music Perhaps', 81
Yeats, Reverend William Butler, 4
the Yellow Book, 131, 132
Young Ireland movement, 117, 121